BEASTS
OF
THE
FIELD

BEASTS
OF
THE
FIELD

The Revealing Natural History
of Animals in the Bible

Michael Bright

ROBSON
BOOKS

First published in the United Kingdom in 2006 by
Robson Books
151 Freston Road
London
W10 6TH

An imprint of Anova Books Company Ltd

The author has made every reasonable effort to contact all copright holders.
Any errors that may have occurred are inadvertent and anyone who for any
reason has not been contacted is invited to write to the publishers so that a
full acknowledgement may be made in subsequent editions of this work

ISBN 1 86105 831 4

British Library Cataloguing in Publication Data
A catalogue record for this book is available from the British Library.

Typeset by SX Composing DTP, Essex, Rayleigh
Printed by MPG Books Ltd, Bodmin, Cornwall

And out of the ground the Lord God formed every beast of the field, and every fowl of the air; and brought them unto Adam to see what he would call them: and whatsoever Adam called every living creature, that was the name thereof.

Genesis 2:19

CONTENTS

INTRODUCTION

Some of my wildlife filmmaking colleagues at the BBC's Natural History Unit once described to me an event they experienced while on location in the Holy Land. They had noticed rain beginning to fall in the distant hills after a long spell of hot, dry weather. The water rushed over concrete-hard soil, first as rivulets, then streams and finally as a raging torrent. In the space of a few minutes a flash flood rushed down towards the filmmakers. They headed for high ground and safety, but one thing lodged in their minds: not the fear of drowning in the rushing water, but the smell that enveloped them as the water soaked the dried stems, leaves and flower heads that had been scattered on the parched ground. The air was filled with the extraordinary perfume of myriad species of aromatic herbs and other flowering plants. It was an unforgettable moment, one that encapsulated for them the magic of a remarkable place.

Unfortunately, the beauty and tranquillity of this remarkable place are threatened almost daily. The Holy Land was much richer in wildlife in biblical times than it is today – more than three thousand years of war have taken their toll. It is true that buffalo have been introduced, as have the domestic cat and the wild rat, but bears and leopards – once widespread – are now scarce. Lions were once common here, but now they have disappeared altogether.

Yet remarkably, despite all this, the region is still awash with wonderful plants and animals. The Holy Land marks a crossroads between Europe, Asia and Africa – an intersection for animals migrating between the three continents. Here, birds more usually seen in the northern European countryside in summer – such as swallows, sand martins, yellow wagtails, blackcaps and garden warblers – can be found alongside sand partridge, spotted sand-grouse and lesser and pied kingfishers, birds more at home in Africa. Gazelles, hyrax and oryx came out of Africa too; deer, hares and foxes are European, while ibex and wild goats have their origins in Asia. There are even two species of northern European butterflies found on the mountains in Lebanon – the peak white (*Pontia callidice*) and the small tortoiseshell (*Aglais urticae*). They are refugees from the Ice Age, when the ice pushed creatures from Siberia and northern Europe far to the south. The famous cedars of Lebanon grow on the terminal moraine (debris) of what was once a giant glacier. But when the ice retreated these two butterflies were left behind and became isolated in the Lebanese mountains.

Today, the Holy Land has a variety of wildlife habitats, from snow-topped Mount Hermon in the north to the arid wilderness of the Negev Desert in the south. In the west the warm Mediterranean brushes a shore bordered by a fertile maritime plain, while in the east beyond Jordan are the vast hot deserts of Arabia. Sandwiched in between are not only the central mountains of Israel and the hills of the Eastern Range, but also a great tear in the earth's crust – part of the Great African Rift that has been splitting East Africa and the Middle East asunder for millennia. It contains a trough in which sits the Dead Sea – the lowest place on earth, at 411m (1,349ft) below sea level – and it extends into a relatively new arm (geologically speaking) of the Indian Ocean that we call the Red Sea.

Each area has its own assemblage of animals, of which birds are the most prominent. The northern mountains play host to Alpine choughs, members of the crow family more usually associated with the Matterhorn or Eiger in Europe, while the subtropical vegetation of the Jordan valley hides the Palestine sunbird, a small bird with African origins that occupies a similar niche to the hummingbirds of the New World. The Kentish plover searches through the flotsam and jetsam strewn along the high tide line of Mediterranean beaches, and common terns hover, ready to crash down onto shoals of small fish just below the surface of the sea. Sand grouse clamber over dry rocky areas and griffon vultures roost or nest in deep ravines, while the wetlands surrounding the Sea of Galilee are filled with pelicans and waterfowl that would not look out of place in the Danube delta.

Of course, many animals that live in the Holy Land are described or mentioned in the Bible, but often as not their true identities are far from clear. Today, we have comprehensive and detailed field guides with which to name each species we see, but those ancient Bible writers and the seventeenth-century translators who made their words accessible in a version still familiar to us today were virtually in the dark. Many writers, from ancient to modern times – including Pliny, Strabo, Theophrastus, Galen, Herodotus, Frederick Hasselquist, Henry Tristram, Peter France and Yehuda Feliks – have examined the Bible and attempted to decipher which animals those ancient writers encountered. The problem is that the Bible is not a natural history document, and commentators have tried desperately to find exactness where none was ever intended. Some passages do include remarkably accurate field observations; others present us with animals that could only be figments of a writer's imagination. We also must bear in mind, of course, that the writers of the Bible were not naturalists: they were priests, prophets and in some cases kings. They would have been exposed to travellers' tales and folk legends as well as the careful observations of the ancient scholars.

Their approach to animals was often more symbolic than scientific: they used them in metaphors and parables to add drama, jeopardy or colour to a story.

It may be stating the obvious, but we must remember also that the Bible was written over a long period and in many different parts of the region. The same animals might well have had a whole host of different names, depending on where the writer was based. The same holds true today. Take the lowly woodlouse (*Oniscus asellus*), for example: there are about 150 common English names for this creature recorded throughout the British Isles, including coffin-cutter, scabby sow bug, chizzler, footballer, granny picker, loafer, parson's pig, pollydishwasher and tank. There are 34 names devoted to it in the English county of Devon alone.

There are also grounds for confusion when words become transposed, thereby referring to quite distinct and unrelated animals. In English there are many examples, such as goose barnacle and barnacle goose, spider crab and crab spider, and mouse deer and deer mouse. Then there are the words that hint at something they are not: cuttlefish and crayfish are not fish, and glow-worms, woodworms, mealworms, slowworms and army worms are not worms. Maybe these are eccentricities of the English language, but they illustrate how confusing the common names of animals can be. It was not until the eighteenth-century Swedish botanist Carolus Linnaeus provided the scientific world with the basis of a universal taxonomic system that observers speaking different languages were able to discuss a particular animal and know precisely which one they were all talking about. Even this has been fraught with difficulties, for an animal's scientific name can change frequently as more is discovered about it and its relatives.

Moreover, there is not just one Bible, but many – even in English. In this book I have chosen to quote passages mostly from the King James translation of 1611, known more widely as the Authorised Version (referred to as AV from here on), an edition that, though nearly four hundred years old, has probably had more influence on the English-speaking world than any other. It is not without its problems, however. The King James version was translated from Hebrew, Greek and Latin, so all manner of zoological errors have crept in during the translation process. The Vulgate, the Latin Bible of the Church of Rome, was started in the fourth century and prepared mostly by the monastic scholar Jerome. There was also the Septuagint Bible, an ancient Greek translation from the Hebrew of the Jewish scriptures (including the Apocrypha, fourteen books that were included as an appendix to the Old Testament in the Septuagint and the Vulgate but not included in the Hebrew canon) that ran to many revisions from many different scholars after it was first prepared during the first three centuries CE.

These and many other learned works would have been available to the AV's seventeenth-century translators. They would also have been influenced by the natural historians of the day, whose bestiaries and all-encompassing tomes often drew on the supernatural to interpret natural events – natural historians such as Bartholomew of England (Bartholomeus Anglican), who wrote *Bartholomeus De Proprietatibus Rerum*, published in 1535, and Edward Topsell, with his classic tome *The History of Four-Footed Beasts and Serpents and the Theatre of Insects*, completed in 1607. The translators would also have had access to the *Physiologus*, a Greek work written in the fourth century with 49 chapters concerning biology and geology that were gleaned from Indian, Hebrew and Egyptian animal lore, as well as the works of philosophers, such as Aristotle and Pliny.

With such a diversity and varied quality of sources, the Bible translators may have included the occasional crypto-beast. This might explain why unlikely creatures such as satyrs, dragons and unicorns make appearances in the Holy Book. Are they simply images that help the writer or translator spice up his tale, or are they rather misinterpretations of known animals?

Moreover, what about those big events, such as the Flood or the Plagues of Egypt? Did they really occur or are they simply flights of fantasy? Modern science is beginning to give us clues. Take the Flood, for example. Archaeologists have revealed that almost every culture on earth has a flood legend. The Babylonian epic Gilgamesh tells of Utnapishtim, who built a boat and saved his family, friends and animals from the deluge. The ancient Greeks and Romans had Deucalion and Pyrrha, who saved their children by building a boat. The Irish Queen Cessair sailed for seven years after the sea overwhelmed Ireland, and indigenous peoples throughout the Americas have stories about catastrophic floods. In the Black Sea, however, there's good evidence of a real flood of biblical proportions.

This tantalising discovery was made by Robert Ballard, who had famously explored the wreck of the *Titanic* in 1985 with remotely operated submersibles. Ballard explored the depths of the Black Sea over the course of a series of dives in the late twentieth century and early twenty-first century. His remarkable discoveries included the remains of man-made structures, such as planks, wattle-and-daub buildings, rubbish heaps and ceramic jars, beside an ancient coastline about 170m (550ft) below the present low-tide mark. Ballard's discovery supports the notion put forward by Columbia University geologists William Ryan and Walter Pitman, who suggested that about 7,500 years ago a postglacial rise in sea level as the ice sheets melted caused the waters of the Mediterranean to burst through a natural dam at the Bosphorus and to swamp lakeside communities around what is now the Black Sea. Whether this was in fact the biblical flood is difficult to say, but it was certainly a disaster for the people who lived there, and stories related to it would have been passed on orally or in written folk tales.

In the following pages we will try to sift out fact from fiction, and – with the help of the many eminent scholars who have written about creatures great and small down the centuries – attempt to present a meaningful account of biblical animals and some of the events relating to them that are mentioned in the Bible.

One of the main ways that animals are classified in the Bible is according to whether they were 'clean' or 'unclean'. Cattle, sheep and goats are considered clean and therefore it is permitted to eat them, while pigs are unclean and so eating them is forbidden. Moses is credited with introducing this categorisation, and most animals mentioned in the Bible are classified as such. They are listed in Leviticus and there is an echo of the list in Deuteronomy, but why they should be there at all is not really known. Several reasons have been given.

One possibility involves totemism. Some tribes worshipped animals that can either be a symbol of the tribe's identity or act as its protector. By making a particular animal somehow 'dirty', a tribe was in effect being aggressive towards a rival tribe that was identified with that animal. The unclean list might then have been a way to avoid paying any homage whatsoever to an animal worshipped by an aggressive neighbour. For example, the main sacrificial animal of the Canaanites was the pig, which might well explain why Mosaic law placed pigs on the unclean list. Another reason for classifying an animal as unclean might be that the animal in question has unpleasant eating habits of its own. Carrion-eaters fall into this category. They feast on dead and decaying flesh that might well be contaminated. Still other animals may have been regarded as unclean because they inspired superstitious fear, like the bat, or deep loathing, like the rat.

Whatever the reason (and it might well have been a combination of those listed above), Moses drew up a 'hit list'. Of the mammals, his laws restrict people to eat or sacrifice only ruminants: the animals must have divided hooves and chew the cud, though camels have both attributes but are still considered unclean. Pigs, hares (and rabbits), rock hyrax, moles, rats, mice and bats are also considered unclean, as are most other quadrupeds.

Fishes with fins and scales are permissible, but anything without them is not – the lobsters, crabs and prawns so beloved of northern and eastern gastronomes are on the restricted list, for instance. All amphibians and reptiles are unclean, as are most insects and other invertebrates. The exceptions are locusts, grasshoppers and crickets.

Birds are a problem, because the Bible translators had difficulty with their true identity. The general feeling seems to be that birds of prey – such as eagles, owls, hawks, falcons, buzzards and vultures, together with members of the corvid family, such as crows and ravens, all of which take carrion from time to time – are unclean. Seagulls, storks, herons, pelicans and cormorants are all unclean, too, as is the hoopoe (called the lapwing in the AV). The swan is included in the unclean list, although swans were not often seen in the Middle East, so the AV translators might have got the species, or even the family, wrong.

One would have thought that such strict regulations (and the Hebrews were not the only folk in the region to have such constraints) would have been to the advantage of at least some of the Middle East's wildlife, but think again. Down the centuries, anything that could be hunted has been hunted, so the surviving fauna of the Holy Lands is a shadow of its former self.

To know what it was really like and which animals were present before the slaughter of modern times, we must turn to people like the Swedish naturalist Frederick Hasselquist, a pupil of Linnaeus, who travelled for four years in the Middle East noting the plants and animal life he discovered along the way. He died aged 31 on his way home in 1752, and Linnaeus later published his extensive notes posthumously in a work entitled *Iter Palaestinum*. Hasselquist saw birds of prey trained by Arabs for hunting, green woodpeckers in Galilee's oak woodlands and nightingales among the willows of Jordan. Larks were everywhere in the eighteenth century, but near Jerusalem Hasselquist encountered an Egyptian vulture. While noting its ugliness, he recognised its value in clearing the piles of dead asses and camels that were a distinct danger to human health.

A hundred years later, the Reverend Henry B Tristram – an English naturalist vicar and traveller, and author of *The Natural History of the Bible, Flora and Fauna of Palestine* and *The Survey of Western Palestine* – journeyed extensively through the Holy Land from 1858 to 1881. Botanical and zoological collectors accompanied him and together they gathered the information that enabled him to publish his comprehensive works. Both Hasselquist and Tristram saw Palestine and its neighbouring countries in a state that might have been not very different from when the Bible was written. So, with Tristram and other naturalists to help guide us, let us embark on an armchair journey of discovery.

MYSTERIOUS CREATURES

The Authorised Version of the Bible (AV) mentions several animals that do not exist. Today, we would probably label them 'crypto-beasts', but to the seventeenth-century translators of the AV they were to all intents and purposes real. The problem was that the naturalists of the day also considered them real, so the science on which the learned scribes could call was fundamentally flawed. Nevertheless, in most cases there is a hint of truth behind the myth. In this chapter we separate fact from fiction and try to identify the living animal hidden behind the mythical beast.

UNICORN

One creature that seems quite out of place in the Bible is the unicorn. In *Through the Looking-Glass* Lewis Carroll summed up the enigma: '"Well, now that we have seen each other," said the Unicorn, "If you'll believe in me, I'll believe in you."'

The unicorn is clearly a mythical beast – a horse-like or kidlike creature with a single horn on its forehead. It appears in mythological stories from all parts of the world, and in Europe at least it has always been associated with virtue and purity. As a biblical animal it was interpreted symbolically in the early

Christian Church, and medieval writers likened it to Christ, who raised up a 'horn of deliverance' for mankind.

In the ancient Greek bestiary *Physiologus*, the animal is considered to be strong and fierce and can only be caught by a maiden. If the maiden is left alone in a place where the unicorn is known to exist, it will come to her. It will approach her gently and rest its head on the virgin's lap, whereupon hunters can leap out and catch it. The French naturalist Philip de Thaun spiced up the story somewhat in his *Le Livre des Creatures*, telling how the unicorn was attracted to the virgin's exposed breast, which it kissed before going to sleep. The events of a unicorn hunt are captured in a series of seven sixteenth-century Belgian tapestries. Today, they are exhibited in the Cloisters, the Metropolitan Museum of Art's building dedicated to medieval art, at Fort Tryon Park, New York.

One of the unicorn's first known appearances is on Assyrian bas-reliefs from Nimrud, but the first descriptions come in Greek literature. In the third century BCE Herodotus wrote of the 'horned ass of Africa', but the first description of an animal with a single horn was by Ctesias, the Greek physician and historian, who was travelling in Persia in about 400 BCE. He had heard from Indian merchants of a creature about the size of a horse with a white body, purple head, blue eyes and on its forehead a cubit-long (the distance from the point of the elbow to the tip of the middle finger) black-coloured horn with a red tip and white base. It was said that anyone who drank from the horn was protected from stomach upsets, epilepsy and various poisons. Ctesias reported that the unicorn was fast moving and difficult to capture, and that in powdered form its horn protected against deadly poisons. He was clearly describing the Indian rhinoceros (*Rhinoceros unicornis*) however, and not a unicorn. Both the Indian rhino and its cousin the Javan rhino (*R. sondaicus*) have a single horn, unlike the two horns of other species. Marco Polo must have met the rhinoceros during his journeys in the East during the thirteenth century. He was on the lookout for a unicorn but was unimpressed that this fearsome and (in his opinion) 'ugly' beast should be considered its true identity: 'They delight much to abide in mire and mud. 'Tis a passing ugly beast to look upon, and is not in the least like that which our stories tell us as being caught in the lap of a virgin.'

Marco Polo's experience of the animal was in Java the Less, where rhinos were then numerous, but his reference to the unicorn and the virgin in this context throws up a puzzle. The island is now known as Sumatra, and, confusingly, the Sumatran rhino has two horns.

The Greek philosopher Aristotle considered the unicorn to be a 'real' animal, but was uncertain about the magical properties attributed to its horn. Likewise, the Roman naturalist Pliny the Elder described the unicorn in Book Eight of his *Historia Naturalis*, believing it to be real and living in India. Pliny's unicorn was a formidable beast called a *monoceros* that was hunted by the Orsean Indians – it 'has a stag's head, elephant's feet, and a boar's tail, the rest of its body being like that of a horse. It makes a deep, lowing noise, and one black horn, two cubits long about 1.2m (4ft), projects from the middle of its forehead. This animal, they say, cannot be taken alive.'

Again, the description indicates a creature remarkably similar to the Indian rhinoceros, although two cubits long for its single horn might have been a bit of an exaggeration. The Roman scholar Gaius Julius Solinus, who is thought to have lived in the third century CE, described an identical creature, adding that the unicorn had a reputation as a 'monster of terror' and that the horn was so sharp that it could spear something, or somebody, with considerable ease.

So-called 'unicorn' horns of this size once changed hands for considerable sums of money. Queen Elizabeth I and King Charles I of England, Ivan the Terrible of Russia, and the Vatican all possessed horns literally worth their weight in gold. At the marriage of Catherine de Medici to the French Dauphin on 28 October 1533, the bride's uncle – Pope Clement VII – gave a piece of 'genuine' unicorn horn to Francis I of France. Of course, none of them actually possessed a unicorn horn; in fact, they had acquired the elongated tusk (tooth) of the male narwhal (*Monodon monoceros*), one of the small Arctic whales. Queen Elizabeth's horn, which was about eight spans and a half (1.94m or 76.5in) in length and valued at £10,000 in 1598, was found in 1577 on an island near Frobisher Bay, Canada. James I inherited a cup made of 'unicorn horn' from Elizabeth I, which he gave to his new queen, Anne of Denmark. In 1641 a 'unicorn's horn' covered in silver plate that was spotted in the Tower of London by the Marquis de la Ferte Imbaut, the Marshal of France, was estimated to be worth £40,000 – the equivalent today of more than a million pounds sterling.

In days gone by, powder ground from the tusk, known as 'alicorn', was believed to have medicinal qualities. James I gave a 'unicorn horn' potion to his ailing son but it didn't cure him, though he did not die on this occasion. After the 'treatment', he still complained that he had a headache and the physicians applied the flesh of freshly killed cocks and pigeons instead; such was the sorry state of medicine at the time!

Alicorn was also said to neutralise poisons and was much in demand at a time when assassins and traitors were rampant. Noblemen would pay 40,000 gold pieces or more for a piece of alicorn. So great was the supposed power of unicorn potions that the animal became the symbol of the apothecary.

The unicorn itself is mentioned in the AV about nine times, but in most cases it is given characteristics that do not square with most people's vision of a unicorn. It is given qualities of immense strength, for example: 'God brought them out of Egypt; he hath as it were the strength of a unicorn' (Numbers 23:22).

The creature is mentioned in the company of bulls and bullocks. 'And the unicorns shall come down with [the lambs and goats], and the bullocks with the bulls' (Isaiah 34:7); 'His glory is like the firstling of his bullock, and his horns are like the horns of unicorns: with them he shall push people together to the ends of the earth' (Deuteronomy 33:17). In Job 39:9–10 a distinctly agricultural theme emerges: 'Will the unicorn be willing to serve thee, or abide by thy crib? Canst thou bind the unicorn with his band in the furrow? or will he harrow the valleys after thee?'

Could the unicorn of the Bible be something more familiar, perhaps? Those ancient Assyrian bas-reliefs give us a clue. One of them depicts King Ashurnasirapal II, the Hunting King, running down a beast that looks remarkably like a large bull except that it has one horn, not two. In reality, the beast has two symmetrical horns – as the Assyrian artists produced the creature in strict profile, they have depicted only the horn nearer the viewer. The beast he was hunting was known as the *rimu* or *rumu*, thought to be the same as the Hebrew word *re'em*, meaning wild ox.

The confusion that led to the unicorn appearing in the Bible came in 250 BCE or thereabouts, when the first Greek translators of the Septuagint, who were unfamiliar with the wild ox (it was already rare in the wild in Greece and the Near East), used the translation *monokeros*, meaning one-horn, probably on the basis of the bas-reliefs. When this was translated into Latin as *unicornis*, it became 'unicorn' in English.

The mix-up was made worse by a bit of fudging on the part of the English translators. The Hebrew word is in fact singular, yet in the verse from Deuteronomy – 'horns of unicorns' – the translators have opted for the plural. In Hebrew it should read 'horns of the unicorn', indicating that the *re'em* had more than one horn. In order to retain the unicorn without any contradiction, the word was pluralised, so the translators ended up making two errors. The same error occurs in Psalm 22:21: 'Save me from the lion's mouth: for thou hast heard me from the horns of unicorns.'

Interestingly, in the Latin Vulgate, which was the standard biblical text for roughly a thousand years from about CE 400 to CE 1400, this section of the psalm in Latin reads as *'libera me abore leonis et a cornibus unicornium humilitatem meant'*, which translated into English means 'Save me from the wrath of the lion and the horns of the unicorn.' The 'horns' are plural; the 'unicorn' is singular.

The translators were undoubtedly torn between several identities for the *re'em*, despite the fact that the Hebrew word for unicorn is something quite different. It is the *had-keren*, from *keren* (or *qeren*) meaning 'horn' and *had* (or *'echad*) meaning 'one'. A margin note in the AV next to Isaiah 34:7 indicates that the translators did consider the rhinoceros as an identity for the unicorn; after all, the Vulgate includes *rhinoceros* as translation of the Greek *monokeros* instead of *unicornis*. The pressure on them to include the unicorn, though, must have been enormous.

For many people in medieval and Renaissance times, the unicorn was very real. In Topsell's *Four-Footed Beasts* (1607), the author takes the subject seriously:

> We are come to the history of a beast whereof divers people in every age of the worlde have made great question, because of the rare vertues thereof; therefore it behooveth us to use some diligence in comparing together the several testimonies that are spoken of this beast, for the better satisfaction of such as are now alive, and clearing of the point for them that shall be borne hereafter, whether there bee a Unicorne; for that is the maine question to be resolved.

Much was written about the unicorn, probably more than any other mythical beast. The Italian naturalist Ulisse Aldrovandi (1522–1605) dedicated more than sixty pages of his *Historia Monstrorum*, published posthumously in 1642, to the subject. Although published some years after the AV, it illustrates the interest in unicorns at the time, so maybe it was this kind of obsession that influenced King James's seventeenth-century translators and caused the unicorn to enter the Good Book. In 1625, several years after the publication of the AV, Samuel Purchas's *Purchas his Pilgrimes* reported: 'Of the unicorn, none hath been seen these hundred years past.' That said, in 1646 the English physician and author Sir Thomas Browne wrote in his *Enquiries into Very many received Tenets, and commonly presumed truths* that he thought unicorns might exist:

> Although we concede there be many Unicorns, yet are we still to seek; for whereunto to affix this Horn in question, or to determine from which thereof we receive this magnified Medicine, we have no assurance, or any satisfactory decision. For although we single out one, and eminently thereto assign the name of the Unicorn; yet can we not be secure what creature is meant thereby; what constant shape it holdeth, or in what number to be receive.

Modern translators have now substituted the words 'wild ox' for 'unicorn'. Some commentators have considered the wild bison or buffalo as a candidate, but the true identity of the mysterious unicorn is probably the aurochs (*Bos primigenius*), the original wild cattle that gave rise to all modern cattle, and which feature in European Stone Age cave paintings, including those at Lascaux in southwestern France. The aurochs was an immense beast that would have made even our largest domestic bulls seem puny. A bull aurochs stood more than 1.57m (5ft) at the shoulder and was all muscle, most of it concentrated in the forequarters. Each horn of a full-sized bull would have been about 80cm (31in) long.

After the last ice age ended, the aurochs was widely distributed across Eurasia, from the Atlantic to the Pacific and from the tundra in the north to India and into North Africa in the south. Gaius Julius Caesar, one of the later emperors of Rome, knew the aurochs as the *urus*, an inhabitant of the Hercynian forest in Germany. In his *Bellum Gallicum* (*The Gallic Wars*) of 50 BCE he wrote: 'There is a third kind, consisting of those animals which are called uri. These are a little below the elephant in size, and of the appearance, colour and shape of a bull. Their strength and speed are extraordinary; they spare neither man nor wild beast which they have espied.'

The aurochs eventually became extinct. The last individual died in 1627 in a Polish hunting reserve – it had been carefully protected there, but had succumbed to disease from neighbouring domestic cattle.

Some idea of how the aurochs – albeit in a smaller version – behaved can be gained by observing the Chillingham cattle in Northumberland, England. Here the Tankerville family, and more recently the Chillingham Wild Cattle Association, have kept safe a large herd of a relic medieval stock of domestic cattle that were probably brought together in 1225 in a baronial hunting park. Today, they are more or less wild – that is, they are not culled and are left to fend for themselves for most of the year but receive a hay supplement in winter. They must not be touched, however. The rest of the herd will kill any animal that comes into direct contact with humans – so the story goes.

The Chillingham cattle breed all year round. Unlike buffalo and other wild cattle, Chillingham cows tend to move away from the herd and give birth alone. They also stand when giving birth, and eat the afterbirth. The newborn calf is licked to prevent fly infestation and to reinforce the bond between mother and calf. It also stimulates the calf to defecate for the first time. When the calf has stood and fed from the udder, both mother and calf return to the herd, where the newborn creature provokes much interest from the other cows, though not the bulls. With no seasonal rut, the bulls are constantly busy updating who is dominant to whom. They gather into groups of two to three bulls, each group occupying a home range that overlaps with the home ranges of other groups. Groups try to ignore each other, but bulls within a group indulge in fencing and sparring matches.

Bulls are dominant to cows, but both have dominance hierarchies. It's not all about sex, though, and it doesn't mean that the most dominant get all the food. Bulls share their winter hay with other bulls as long as they receive a submissive gesture, but cows are intolerant of other cows and calves.

It is easy to distinguish the bulls from the cows: the former have stout, curved horns while the latter sport less robust, lyre-shaped horns. Curiously, though, every individual has a white coat tinted beige with dust, foxy-red ears and a dark muzzle, a far cry from the dark-coloured coat of the ancient aurochs. One explanation might be that the druids selectively bred for white-coated cattle, as white was preferential in sacrificial ceremonies. All in all, the Chillingham herd is a living experiment that has been running for hundreds of years, and the closest you'll come to seeing a living *re'em* or aurochs.

Interestingly, there is a mythical beast in Hebrew legend that also answers to the name *re'em*. It is a giant among giants and so only one pair is allowed to exist at any one time. In order that they do not destroy every living thing, they must spend most of their life at opposite ends of the earth. They are permitted to meet every seventy years, when they mate and the male dies. The female *re'em* is pregnant for twelve years and then always gives birth to twins. Like a mother octopus, she dies immediately. The babies turn away from each other the moment they are born, one travelling east and the other west, to meet again in another seventy years.

With such formidable real and unreal beasts from which to choose, what is the source of the unicorn? In Hebrew legend the unicorn was the first animal to be named by Adam. Its horn was created before its hooves, so as the beast came up from the primordial mud its head emerged first, complete with horn. When the Lord heard Adam speak its name, He reached down and touched the unicorn's horn, elevating it above all other beasts. Another Hebrew folk story tells that when Adam saw the setting sun for the first time he was worried that it would not return again. As far as he was concerned, the end of the world had come almost before it had begun. So, in an effort to avoid this catastrophe, he sacrificed something special to God, and the special creature was a unicorn.

This may explain why the unicorn was not on the Ark. There is another explanation, though. According to yet another Jewish folk story, a pair of unicorns was included but the two 'special beasts' insisted on taking up so much space that Noah sent them off. They either drowned or still survive in some remote corner of the world (and can be seen only by people of true virtue) – or, of course, they could have turned into narwhals!

It is just possible, therefore, that in looking for a mythical beast that answered the description of the *re'em*, the translators plumped for the closest thing with which they were familiar – the unicorn. The existence of the beast may have gained further credibility after a report that the German monk Felix Fabri made in 1483 after travelling in the Sinai Desert. In the account of his journey, he claimed to have seen a unicorn. Fabri had probably seen an oryx, however – a desert-living, horse-like antelope with long, nearly straight horns that look, from the side at least, like a unicorn's horn. There are several species living in arid regions in Africa, but the one that inhabited the Holy Land was the Arabian or white oryx (*Oryx leucoryx*), the only species to be found in the wild outside the African continent. The Arabian oryx has a white body, like that of a unicorn, and black markings on the face. It was common in Palestine until not so long ago. Until the middle of the eighteenth century, oryxes were common in most of the deserts of the Middle East, including the Negev and the Sinai. C S Jarvis, governor of Sinai in the 1930s, wrote that they were still plentiful there in the early nineteenth century, and T E Lawrence (of Arabia) reported seeing them being shot in Trans-Jordan during the First World War.

Before the Second World War, Bedu tribesmen hunted the oryx on foot or from camels. Its meat was a delicacy, and the horns were sold in city markets. After 1945, however, four-wheel-drive vehicles and automatic weapons caused oryx populations to shrink rapidly and the animal became extinct in the wild in 1972. A small group that had managed to survive in the sandy deserts in the southeast of the Arabian Peninsula were taken into private collections in Arabia and a few were kept in the 'World Herd' in the USA. They were reared in captivity for later release in the stony deserts of Oman.

The Arabian oryx is a remarkable animal, capable of tolerating daytime temperatures that reach 48–50°C (118–122°F) in the shade and freezing desert nights when the temperature plummets to 6–7°C (43–45°F). On cold mornings when the hairs on its body stand erect to absorb the sun's warmth, its coat is like suede.

The animal's hooves are splayed, an adaptation to walking on sand. It is not a fast mover, but can trek for hours, covering up to 30km (19 miles) at night. Over large parts of its home range rain may not have fallen for many years, so food can be in widely scattered clumps. The Arabian oryx travels in mixed-sex groups of up to twenty individuals, a subdominant male in the lead and the dominant male bringing up the rear. It is smaller than other oryxes, so it can shelter under small desert trees during the hottest parts of the day. The Arabian oryx's main natural predators would have been the Arabian wolf and the striped hyena, but humans have had the biggest impact on numbers.

This creature might well have been the inspiration for the Arabian version of the unicorn, the *karkadann*, another beast that was believed to have had magical qualities. As this suggests, the unicorn is not an exclusively Judaeo-Christian phenomenon. Elsewhere in the world it appears in religion, literature and art.

The unicorn or *ch'i-lin* (kilin) has been a feature of Chinese mythology for thousands of years. Like Adam's unicorn, it sprang from the primordial mud, though it differs slightly in having the body of a deer, the tail of an ox, the hooves of a horse and a single short horn on its forehead. Its belly is yellow but its back is multicoloured, with red, yellow, blue, white and black hair representing the five sacred colours. Although this is its most common form, it can take on different shapes and sizes, and can even appear covered in green lizard-like scales. It is supposed to live for a thousand years, and while it is alive it never walks on or eats any living thing.

The unicorn was considered a harbinger of good, and in Chinese mythology stands alongside three other animals of good omen – the dragon, phoenix and tortoise. It appears infrequently, and the fact that a unicorn has not been seen in a long while indicates that we are going through a period of 'darkness'. Many of its appearances have coincided with significant events during the reigns of great Chinese rulers, such as the time of the origin of writing in the garden of the 'Yellow' Emperor Huang Di during the reign of Emperor Fu His in the 27th century BCE.

According to Chinese legend, the unicorn became the protector of saints and sages, and it is the bearer of news of babies. In 551 BCE the pregnant mother of Confucius was said to have met a unicorn in the forest. It presented her with a piece of jade bearing an inscription that signified that her son would possess great wisdom.

The Japanese unicorn is another kind of beast altogether: it has an immense shaggy mane and is built more like a bull (perhaps this is a curious throwback to the aurochs). This creature was considered to be a fearsome beast, and was used by judges to determine the guilt of prisoners. The unicorn fixed the defendant with an icy stare and if he or she were guilty it would spear them through the heart with its horn.

In India the unicorn is credited with saving the nation from Genghis Khan and his Mongolian hordes. As they approached the Indian border, a unicorn is said to have knelt before Khan; believing it to be a sign from heaven, he withdrew his army. This was the last 'sighting' of a unicorn.

In Europe the image of the unicorn appears regularly, for it became an important symbol in heraldry. The royal arms of Great

Britain and Northern Ireland features a silver unicorn with gold horn, hooves, mane and tufts and a gold coronet collar and chain (representing Scotland) standing opposite a royally crowned gold lion guardant (representing England). The unicorn became part of Scotland's coat of arms in the late fourteenth century, when Robert III called on the virtue and strength of the creature as an inspiration for rebuilding the nation. In 1603, when James VI of Scotland became James I of England and Scotland, he ordered a new coat of arms to be drawn up that included the lion of England and the unicorn of Scotland. The two characters also appear on the Canadian coat of arms.

It's worth mentioning one more sighting of a unicorn in the Bible; mentioned in Daniel 8:5, it took place in the third year of the reign of Belshazzar. Daniel relates that in one of his visions he found himself standing by the River Ulai at Susa in the province of Elam watching a strange sheep: 'And as I was considering, behold, an he goat came from the west on the face of the whole earth, and touched not the ground: and the goat had a notable horn between his eyes.'

Bizarrely, during the twentieth century, several attempts were made to create 'unicorns' artificially. In the 1930s the veterinarian Dr W Franklin Dove from Maine operated on the horn buds of an Ayrshire calf so that a single horn grew out of the middle of its head, and in 1980 two California naturalists – Morning Glory and her husband Otter G'Zell – used the same tissue-grafting technique on a white goat to create 'Lancelot', a living 'unicorn' attraction that was exhibited by the Ringling Brothers and Barnum and Bailey Circus.

So, was the animal in Daniel's dream based on a creature he had actually seen, maybe some mutant goat whose image stuck in his mind? It is plausible, but it still fails to make a case for a living, breathing unicorn. The unicorn, at least for the time being, must remain in the fantasy world.

SATYR

Isaiah, a prophet who lived in Jerusalem in the late eighth century BCE, makes two references to the mythical satyr in the AV: 'But wild beasts of the desert shall lie there; and their houses shall be full of doleful creatures; and owls shall dwell there, and satyrs shall dance there'; 'The wild beasts of the desert shall also meet with the wild beasts of the island, and the satyr shall cry to his fellow' (Isaiah 13:21 and 34:14).

In Hebrew the word is *sa'ir*, meaning 'hairy one', and indeed these celebrated satyrs were seriously hairy. The satyr is a forest god whose forepart is human and the hindquarters goat (though the Anatolian satyr is part man and part horse). He stands on two legs rather than four, and is blessed with pointed goat ears and horns and a short goat tail. According to Pliny, satyrs had a predilection for sexual activity and were said to pursue nymphs all over the countryside. They also enjoyed playing practical jokes.

How such a creature came to be in Isaiah's writings is a mystery, though another mistranslation comes immediately to mind. The creatures to which Isaiah refers are probably the wild or feral goats that clambered over ruins in ancient Babylon and Edom. In fact, the word *sa'ir* appears in the Bible more than fifty times in total. In many cases in the AV it is translated as 'devil': 'And they shall no more offer their sacrifices unto devils, after whom they have gone a whoring' (Leviticus 17:7); 'And he ordained him priests for the high places, and for the devils, and for the calves which he had made' (2 Chronicles 11:15).

More recent interpretations suggest that the *sa'ir* is a goat idol. In the passage in 2 Chronicles a 'devil' stands by golden calf idols. Most modern translators have opted for a pagan god represented by a goat, i.e. 'goat-demons' and 'demons', but let's look again at what other wildlife might explain Isaiah's satyrs.

One animal with a superficial resemblance to a hairy human that readily comes to mind when demons and mischief are mentioned is the baboon (*Papio* spp.). Bartholomew and Topsell both mention it, Bartholomew distinguishing several kinds of satyr including those with heads like hounds, called *Cynocephali*. Topsell wrote:

> As the Cynecephall or Baboun-Apes have given occasion to some to imagine there were such men, so the Satyres, a most rare and seldome seene beast, hath others to think it was a Devil . . . it also being probable that the Devils take not any daenomination or shape from Satyres, but rather the Apes themselves from Devils whome they resemble, for there are many things common to the Satyre-apes and devilish Satyres, as their human shape, their abode in solitary places, their rough hayre, and lust to women, wherewithal other Apes are naturally infected; but especially Satyres.

The baboon was known in the Holy Land in ancient times, though it was not a resident there. The Egyptians worshipped it and images of baboons decorate many ancient monuments. The species depicted would have been the hamadryas or sacred baboon (*Papio cynocepalus hamadryas*). This creature was sacred as it was thought to be one of the embodiments of Thoth or Djhowtey (the other was the ibis), the god of reckoning and learning, scholars and scribes; Thoth was credited with inventing writing and creating languages. Mummified baboons' bodies have been found around the cult's centre near Hermopolis and Thebes. The baboon was also domesticated for everyday tasks, such as collecting figs. Today, the species is found in the rocky deserts and semi-deserts of Ethiopia and the southwestern corner of Saudi Arabia.

It's easy to see how they would fit the bill as satyrs. Adult male hamadryas baboons look extremely hairy, with a cape of long, grey hair on their shoulders, and even bear a resemblance to humans with their pink-skinned faces and rumps. Each has a harem of several females that lives within a larger troop, and in each group the male is king. Male baboons are seen to herd their charges, threatening them and occasionally biting them on the neck. In fact, they run about rather like satyrs chasing nymphs.

COCKATRICE

The cockatrice is another mythical beast, yet there are four references to it in the Old Testament – three in Isaiah and one in Jeremiah. Isaiah makes it quite clear that this is one very unpleasant animal indeed: 'for out of the serpent's root shall come forth a cockatrice, and his fruit shall be a fiery flying serpent'; 'They hatch cockatrice' eggs, and weave the spider's web: he that eateth of the eggs dieth, and that which is crushed breaketh out into a viper' (Isaiah 14:29 and 59:5). Isaiah mentions the creature again in the context of that magical kingdom where lions, leopards and lambs sit down together: 'the weaned child shall put his hand on the cockatrice' den' (Isaiah 11:8).

The prophet Jeremiah, who lived in the latter part of the seventh century and the early part of the sixth century BCE, also includes it: 'For, behold, I will send serpents, cockatrices, among you, which will not be charmed, and they shall bite you, saith the Lord' (Jeremiah 8:17).

Modern translators plump for 'poisonous snake' as an identity for the cockatrice, citing the adder or viper – *tsepha* or *tsiphon* in Hebrew – or the Egyptian cobra (*Naja haje*), also known as the *basilisko*, meaning 'kinglet'. But the cockatrice itself has quite an ancestry. It has its origins in Greek and Roman mythology, when it was simply a serpent, but it has been glamorised somewhat by later European chroniclers. At first it was referred to as the basilisk (king of the serpents):

> What availed,
> Murrus, the lance by which thou didst transfix
> A Basilisk? Swift through the weapon ran
> The poison to his hand: he draws his sword

And severs arm and shoulder at a blow:
Then gazed secure upon his severed hand
Which perished as he looked. So had'st thou died,
And such had been thy fate!

It became known as the cockatrice in the thirteenth century CE. The word 'cockatrice' might well have come from the Greek *krokodeilos* or *cocodrillus* in Low Latin, which in turn gave rise to the French word *caucatrice*, meaning 'crocodile'. As the language of the English court at the time was French, the word entered the English language first as 'crocatrix' to denote the crocodile, and later as cockatrice, a quite different serpent. It was considered to be related to the wyvern, a heraldic dragon feared for its wickedness.

The cockatrice has a scaly dragon's body with clawed, membranous wings, an eagle's legs and talons, a cock's head and bright red comb, red or black eyes and a barbed tail. It is created during the early 'dog days' of summer – between July and early September, when the dog star Sirius is in the ascendancy. A seven-year-old cock (not a hen) lays an egg covered with a tough, thick skin rather than a shell, which can withstand the hardest of blows. The egg is round rather than elliptical, has a muddy yellow colour and is deposited in a dung heap.

Modern science explains the conception of the cockatrice by reference to the commonplace change that occurs in the endocrine balance of the domestic hen and which induces transsexuality, allowing the afflicted creature to crow and to grow a comb and wattles while continuing to lay eggs. Medieval man attributed this to the work of the devil, and thus the cockatrice came to represent evil incarnate. It gave rise to some unusual reports. In 1471 a cockerel that laid an egg in Basle, Switzerland, was tried for 'unnatural practices' and sentenced to death by burning. In July 1834 the *Edinburgh Evening Courant* reports that a turkey cock in East Lothian hatched a brood of chickens. The word 'cockney', incidentally, is thought to have come from 'cock's egg': at one time country folk thought that city dwellers were malnourished and fed on cocks' eggs, the small white lump found inside cockerels that resembled an egg.

The egg was said to have been incubated by a snake or a toad, after which a cockatrice about 15cm (6in) long would emerge. Pliny described the way in which it moved: 'He moveth his body forward not only by multiplied windings like other serpents, but he goeth with half his body upright and aloft from the ground.' This could refer to the way the Egyptian cobra raises the front part of its 2m (6.6ft) long body about 30cm (12in) off the ground, expands its 15cm (6in) wide hood and moves in this upright fashion towards an adversary or potential predator. This species is particularly bold and aggressive, and it would have been common in the Middle East in ancient times.

The cockatrice is sometimes described as gigantic, but tradition-ally a fully grown specimen is no more than 30cm (12in) high. It may be small but it has formidable weaponry: its breath can pound rock and kill any living thing; it can rot fruit off trees and poison any stand of water from which it drinks. The creature's most formidable weapon, however, is its ability to kill with just a stare.

This part of the legend could well have come from the way in which cobras 'spit' poison. The snake rears up with its hood expanded, looking as large and as fearsome as possible, and then shoots out a stream of venom from the specially adapted fangs in the front of its upper jaw. This enters the eyes, nose or mouth of the victim, which usually dies. To the ancient observer, the snake had stared at its assailant and killed it. Whatever the origin, the fourteenth-century English poet Geoffrey Chaucer was impressed. He wrote in *The Parson's Tale* (one of *The Canterbury Tales*) that the cockatrice (which he called 'basilicoc') 'sleeth folk by the venim of his sighte'.

William Shakespeare attributed the same powers to the creature: 'they will kill one another by the look, like cockatrices' (*Twelfth Night*, III.iv). By Shakespeare's time the terms 'cockatrice' and 'basilisk' were interchangeable. When Lady Anne was complimented on the beauty of her eyes by the Duke of Gloucester (the future King Richard III), the creature is mentioned again: 'Would they were basilisks, to strike thee dead!' (*Richard III*, I.ii).

It was a theme picked up by the nineteenth-century poet Percy Bysshe Shelley in his 'Ode to Naples':

> Be thou like the imperial Basilisk
> Killing thy foe with unapparent wounds!
> Gaze on Oppression, till at that dread risk
> Aghast she pass from the Earth's disk:
> Fear not, but gaze—for freemen mightier grow,
> And slaves more feeble, gazing on their foe . . .

The cockatrice, or basilisk, also possessed such a powerful poison that, according to Pliny, if it were speared from horseback, both the rider and horse would be killed as the venom rose up through the shaft. Likewise, the first-century Spanish poet Marcus Annaeus Lucanus noted:

> What though the Moor the basilisk hath slain,
> And pinned him lifeless to the sandy plain.
> Up through the spear the subtle venom flies,
> The hand imbibes it, and the victor dies.

Its Achilles heels, however, are crowing cocks and weasels. If a cockatrice should hear a cock crowing, it dies shortly afterwards, while the weasel was reputedly immune to the cockatrice's poison. If bitten, the weasel is said to eat rue (*Ruta graveolens*), a strongly smelling shrub common to the Mediterranean and the only one that fails to shrivel under the cockatrice's breath. Thus fortified, the weasel kills the cockatrice using its own deadly venom. Consequently, travellers such as the Crusaders who journeyed through cockatrice country used to carry weasels with them as protection.

Again, we can find a genuine precedent in natural history for this. The mongoose, which has a similar shape to the weasel but is much bigger, will fight with a cobra and appears to be immune to its poison; it steers clear of the snake's fangs by making lightning attacks at its rear. (This characteristic piece of behaviour was made famous by Rudyard Kipling in the tale of Riki-tiki-tavi and his duel with the cobra.) The species present in the Holy Land is the Egyptian mongoose (*Herpestes ichneumon*). It was sacred to the ancient Egyptians, who carved mongoose figures on the walls of their tombs and temples. Today, the mongoose is still found throughout the region, including Israel, where some well-studied mongoose families have taken to fishing in artificial fishponds.

The cockatrice has appeared several times in folklore. At the time of Pope Leo IV (847–55), a cockatrice was said to have been discovered in the vault of a chapel dedicated to Saint Lucia (or Lucea). Reputedly, its breath poisoned the air and many people in Rome died.

In 1538 a so-called cockatrice hatched in the cellars of Wherwell Priory, Hampshire, England. It killed several people, and a reward of a hundred acres of land was offered to anybody who could rid the village of the devilish beast. Many sword-swinging knights died in the attempt, but a local labourer named Green solved the problem by using his brain instead of brawn. He lowered a mirror into the cockatrice's den, which reflected back the creature's fatal stare; the cockatrice was killed by its own weapon. To this day there is a plot of land in Harewood Forest called Green's Acres, and in the museum at Andover there is a weathervane in the shape of a cockatrice that once adorned the spire of St Peter and the Holy Cross in Wherwell village. It was placed there to warn away the devil.

Another 'cockatrice' was released from a wall in the Cumbrian village of Renwick in 1733. Builders were taking down the old village church in order to build a new one when a creature flew out of the walls and attacked them. One John Tallantire armed himself with the branch of a rowan tree and fought the creature. The choice of rowan, or 'witch tree', was significant as its berries and wood are considered to prevent bad luck. The druids used the berries in their magical rituals, though today the tree is better known for the jelly made from its berries that accompanies wild game. Although the cockatrice was the favoured identity of the creature at the time, by the nineteenth century local folk opted for something more plausible and settled that it was a bat, and to this day the village people are known as 'Renwick Bats'.

DRAGON

Another, somewhat larger beast with reptilian connections is the dragon, and it, too, turns up in the Good Book – not in the AV but, curiously, in more modern translations. In the Book of Isaiah in the Good News Bible, the great prophet describes how the people of Judah (the southern kingdom) were under threat from Assyria and seeking refuge in Egypt: 'The ambassadors travel through dangerous country, where lions live and where there are poisonous snakes and flying dragons . . . The help that Egypt gives is useless. So I have nicknamed Egypt, "The Harmless Dragon"' (Isaiah 30: 6–7). Here the translators appear to have plumped for the traditional mythical western dragon, a powerful but malevolent creature that (against all the laws of physics) flies. The AV, however, refers not to dragons but to flying serpents: 'The burden of beasts of the south: into the land of trouble and anguish, from whence come the young and old lion, the viper and fiery flying serpent' (Isaiah 30:6).

The discrepancy between dragons and serpents here may be due to some confusion in the translation from the Greek. In Greek a *drakon* is not the mythical dragon but a large snake. So when Pliny writes about a 'dragon' in his *Natural History*, he is referring probably to a snake such as a python:

In Aethyopia there be as great dragons bred as in India namely twenty cubits long . . . It is reported that upon their coast they are in wrapped foure or five of them one with another, like to a hurdle or latisse-worke, and thus pass the seas to find out better pasturage in Arabia, cutting the waves and bearing their heads aloft, which serve them instead of sailes.

The Greek cubit was about 46cm (18in) and the Roman cubit about 44cm (17in), so a 20–cubit snake would be about 9m (30ft) long – a respectable size for a python.

The confusion continued into European translations of Greek mythology, and it is now believed that all Homer's dragons are actually serpents. Proteus turned himself into the shape of a dragon that was a serpent. The dragons of Diodorus Siculus that defeated elephants were serpents, and the dragons of Lucretius that contributed to the tail of the chimera were serpents. The uncertainty continued into the Middle Ages, when the dragon had a more snake-like image and was often called a 'worm' or 'wurm', such as the Lambton Worm. At the time of the Crusades, the Lambton Worm was a dragon that terrorised an area around Lambton Hall, a fortified manor house at Bournmoor, County Durham. The house was demolished in 1787.

Most chroniclers acknowledged that the dragon was not real, but there were a few exceptions. One of these was Athanasius Kircher. In 1665 he took disbelievers to task in his *Mundus Subterraneus*:

No one can or should doubt, unless perchance he dares contradict the Holy Scripture, for it would be impious to say as much when Daniel mentions the worship accorded to the dragon Bel by the Babylonians, and after the mention of the dragon in other parts of the Scriptures.

Ulisse Aldrovandi was another believer. His *Serpentum et Draconum Historiae* includes a woodcut dated 1551 of a true Ethiopian dragon. The beast is described as having large wings, two ears, scales over the entire body, five protuberances along the back, a flexible tail and two feet armed with sharp claws. The body is coloured dark green, which fades to yellow along the tail. As evidence for the existence of such a beast, he quotes the sighting of a great dragon the size of a bear with huge, wide wings that frequented Cotone, a region of Pistoria in Italy.

Like most of the strange beasts that featured in the encyclopaedic bestiaries of the Middle Ages, the dragon has medicinal value. Topsell noted a number of handy dragon preparations:

> The fat of a dragon, dryed in the sunne, is good against creeping ulcers; the same mingled with Honey and Oyl helpeth the dimnesse of the eyes. The eyes being kept till they be stale, and afterwards beat into an Oyl with Honey and made into ointment keep any one that useth it from the terrour of night visions and apparitions.

This, however, was nothing compared to the concoction whose ingredients included a whole host of body parts of ravaging beasts. Topsell was sceptical:

> There is no folly comparable to the composition which the Magitians draw out of a dragon to make one invincible, and that is this: they take the head and tail of a Dragon with the hairs out of the forehead of a lyon and the marrow of a lyon; the spume or white mouth of a conquering horse, bound up in a Harts skin, together with the claw of a dog, and fastened with the crosse nerves or sinew of a hart or of a roe; they say that this hath much power to make one invincible as hath any medicine or remedy whatsoever.

To say that the dragon has had a bad press in the western world would be an understatement (Puff the Magic Dragon apart), but this view is not universal. The dragon's character differs according to where you encounter it. It is acknowledged all over the world that the dragon is a symbol of immense strength, but in the Far East it is considered both all-powerful and benevolent, whereas in Europe it is the epitome of evil.

BEHEMOTH

Two monsters that appear in the Bible were even more powerful than dragons. They were Behemoth and Leviathan and according to the apocryphal Book of Enoch, written between 150 and 80 BCE, were made by God not long after the start of His Creation:

> And that day will two monsters be parted, one monster, a female named Leviathan in order to dwell in the abyss of the ocean over fountains of water; and [the other], a male called Behemoth, which holds his chest in an invisible desert whose name is Dundayin [Dendain], east of the garden of Eden.

> 1 Enoch 60:7–8

In the Book of Edras the monsters' creation and their domains are more precisely delineated. They were given life on the fifth day, after God had commanded the water to create living creatures:

> Then you kept in existence two living creatures; the name of one you called Behemoth and the name of the other Leviathan. And you separated one from the other, for the seventh part where the water had been gathered together could not hold them both. And you gave Behemoth one of the parts which had been dried up on the third day, to live in, where there are a thousand mountains; but to Leviathan you have the seventh part,

the watery part; and you have kept them to be eaten by whom you wish, and when you wish.

4 Edras 6:47–52

In some legends the two beasts are thought to be deadly enemies who battle at the beginning of time and must be destroyed before they destroy God's Creation. In Hebrew legend Behemoth was a mythical animal that was the greatest creature on land, just as Leviathan was the greatest in the sea. Unfortunately for Behemoth, it was created both male and female and so was unable to procreate. If it had done so, it could have taken over the world. Nevertheless, while it lived it had a hearty appetite. The legend tells how it required the food from a thousand mountains a day to satisfy its hunger: 'Surely the mountains bring him forth food, where all the beasts of the field play' (Job 40:20).

Its ability to consume vast quantities of water has a parallel in the ancient legend. The Bible tells us: 'Behold, he drinketh up a river, and hasteth not: he trusteth that he can draw up Jordan into his mouth' (Job 40:23). The legend tells how all the water flowing through the River Jordan for an entire year was sufficient for only one of Behemoth's gulps. Such was its thirst, the giant was given the sole right to drink from the stream called Yubal, which flowed from Paradise.

In the Bible itself Behemoth appears first in the concluding part of Job, when God is showing the wretched citizen of the land of Uz the extent of his power. Might Behemoth, like other monsters, be an imaginary beast with supernatural powers? After all, God was drawing attention to mankind's insignificance and lack of control over nature compared with Heaven's, so maybe there is no animal on earth that could fit the bill. Perhaps Behemoth is not a real animal, but a mythical beast – maybe one that is based partly or wholly on a real creature. Many commentators have tried to identify it, so let us speculate, too.

Behemoth's description in the Bible varies slightly from translation to translation, and its true identity is difficult to decipher, despite the zoological detail in each account, but let us start at the beginning: 'Behold now Behemoth, which I made with thee; he eateth grass as an ox' (Job 40:15). Here the mystery beast is identified immediately not only as a herbivore or plant-eater, but also specifically as a grazer rather than a browser. The animal probably fed on grasses and sedges, rather than browsing on bushes or small trees.

The description continues: 'Lo now, his strength is in his loins, and his force is in the navel of his belly' (Job 40:16). This seems to suggest a large and powerful animal, but different translations differ in emphasis. The AV states that 'his force is in the navel of his belly', though it is difficult to say exactly what this means.

We continue: 'He moveth his tail like a cedar: the sinews of his stones are wrapped together' (Job 40:17). This is the most interesting passage. The Revised Version of the Bible, which was published in the 1880s, states: 'He makes his tail stiff like a cedar.' It all seems to hang on how we view the cedar.

The cedar (*Cedrus* spp.) was a very important tree in biblical times. Of the four living species, it is probably the Cedar of Lebanon (*Cedrus libani*), a dome-shaped tree found naturally in Lebanon and the Taurus Mountains of Syria, with which the people of the Middle East would have been most familiar. Its wood was used in the construction of temples. It is a massive tree, growing up to 40m (130ft) tall and having tiers of fan-shaped branches that push upwards towards the top of the tree but hang horizontally towards its base. This is one of the most majestic of conifers and one of the largest trees that people in biblical times would have encountered. It is this size that also seems to have impressed modern translators of the Bible.

Two biblical translations suggest that Behemoth's tail was very large and supported itself. In fact, some of the more outrageous accounts consider Behemoth to have been a giant plant-eating reptile, such as a sauropod dinosaur. These creatures grew to extraordinary sizes, the length of several buses and the weight of many elephants. They had long necks, huge bodies and massive tails. In some illustrations these gigantic dinosaurs, such as *Brachiosaurus*, are shown with the tail held above the ground, a counterbalance to the long neck at the front end and a prop when reaching up into trees. The image certainly fits with the more modern translations, but there is a fundamental flaw: dinosaurs died out 65 million years ago. Not only that, it is unlikely they ate grass 'Like an ox', for grasses evolved at the time the dinosaurs died out, and the wear on their teeth shows that they browsed on tough leaves in the treetops, as giraffes do.

Today, dinosaurs are only found as fossils (unless you consider birds to be living dinosaurs), and there is no large living herbivore with a tail like a dinosaur. The nearest living animal to have a tail that is 'stiff like a cedar' is the crocodile. It would have been known and feared in biblical times, and it is the choice of the New English Bible for 'Behemoth', but it does not fit here. The crocodile does not eat grass or any other vegetation, unless it has already been converted into good, firm protein by an antelope or gazelle: it is exclusively a meat-eater.

Perhaps the size and self-supporting nature of Behemoth's tail are the wrong route to follow when comparing it to a cedar. Maybe the more relevant piece of evidence is not the *size* of the tree but the *shape* of its branches. Each branch is like a brush, and there are two large herbivores living today that have brush-like tails – the elephant (family: Elephantidae) and the hippopotamus (*Hippopotamus amphibius*). The elephant's tail has a long 'stalk' with a brush-like end that can be used like a fly swat, while the hippopotamus has a stumpy *brush-shaped* tail that can be 'wagged' like a rotary muck-spreader. Indeed, the hippo uses its tail exactly like a muck-spreader to 'scent mark' its territory with dung.

These two familiar animals are also recognisable in the next verse: 'His bones are as strong pieces of brass; his bones are like bars of iron' (Job 40:18). Maybe the elephant better fits this description, with its pillar-like legs. The thirteenth-century theologian Thomas Aquinas plumped for the elephant, even though elephants do not appear in the Bible – only their ivory is mentioned. It's a curiosity, for the Asian elephant (*Elephas maximas*) once ranged from Syria and Iraq right across Asia to the Far East. You'd think it would get a mention.

However, an elephant tends to browse rather than graze, using its trunk like a hand to gather bunches of vegetation. The trunk is such an obvious feature that its absence in the description of Behemoth would seem to eliminate the elephant from the list of candidates.

The next couple of verses seem to clinch it: 'He lieth under the shady trees, in the covert of the reed, and fens. The shady trees cover him with their shadow; the willows of the brook compass him about' (Job 40:21–22). Mention of the river, fens and marshland, and of reed, willows and thorn-bushes, seems to point to the hippopotamus – the 'water-horse'. Hippos are found in or close to rivers and lakes, spending much of the day actually in the water but coming out to feed at night on land. They eat grass, like an ox. When the sun comes up, they must find shelter, a mud wallow or submerge in water, for they lose water through the skin much faster than other large animals. Under similar atmospheric conditions, and weight for weight, a hippo loses up to five times more fluids through sweat than a human. Hippos spend the day in water; from time to time males open their mouths in a wide 'yawn', a warning to other males to keep their distance. At such times it certainly looks as if the beast could swallow the entire river in one gulp.

While the hippo is a temptingly close match, it may have been only an inspiration for some ancient legend rather than the true source of Behemoth. The word 'Behemoth' comes from the Hebrew word *behemah*, meaning 'beast', and could be translated variously as 'great beast', 'domestic cattle' or 'wild beast' depending on the context.

So, rather than giving Behemoth an identity, maybe the hippo was the inspiration for both Hebrew legend and Bible story. There is one drawback, however. Both tales mention Behemoth spending time in the River Jordan, and hippos today are found only south of the Sahara. Could hippos ever have been seen in the Bible lands? The answer is yes, though not specifically in the Jordan. They lived in the swamps to the north of the Sea of Galilee. In fact, hippos were once found in rivers and lakes right across Africa and the Middle East at places where the water temperature remained between 18°C and 36°C (64°F and 97°F) throughout the year. Before the eighteenth century, they inhabited the full length of the Nile, and mosaics show how the ancient Egyptians would spear them from boats. The Talmud (the code of Jewish civil and religious law) indicates one occasion when the Pharaoh could not get to sleep because of the noise the hippos were making in the Nile. When he finally dropped off, he dreamed of fat and thin cows and asked Joseph to interpret his dream. Unfortunately, the last of this northern population of hippos disappeared from Egypt in 1816.

These animals would also have been familiar with the inundation of the Nile, which could well have given rise to the reference to Behemoth being 'unafraid of a rushing river'.

There is also a semantic link between hippos and Bible monsters. The Hebrew word 'Behemoth' and the Egyptian word for hippopotamus – *p-ehe-mou*, meaning 'water ox' – have an uncanny similarity. Weighing in at 4,500kg (9,920lb), the hippo would have been one of the largest and most powerful indigenous animals that anybody in the region would have encountered – a reasonable prototype for the ultimate mythical beast.

LEVIATHAN

Leviathan appears to have its origins in prebiblical Mesopotamian myth dating from the early second millennium

BCE. Stories mentioning this colossal beast were discovered on clay tablets at Ugarit – an ancient Canaanite city whose ruins were found in 1929 at Ras Shamra on the coast of northern Syria – and are known as the Ugaritic myths. One myth tells how at the beginning of time, Yamm – a deity who ruled the oceans, rivers and lakes – was awarded the divine kingship by El, or 'god', the head of the pantheon. Yamm summoned Baal – the god of storms – to serve him but Baal refused. He fought Yamm and won, thus becoming the divine king. The defeated Yamm is thought by some scholars to be the same deity as Lotan, for there are references in the stories to Baal's defeat of Lotan. And Lotan is known in Hebrew lore as Livyatan or Leviathan – the primeval and twisted serpent with seven heads.

According to Hebrew legend, Leviathan was produced on the fifth day of Creation as the monstrous ruler over all aquatic and marine animals. There were originally two such creatures – a male and female – but their combined strength would have wreaked havoc in God's Creation, so He removed one, the female. The surviving male was so large that it took the River Jordan to quench his thirst (a characteristic shared with Behemoth), and when he was hungry his hot breath made the sea boil. His fins were so brilliant that the sun's rays were put in the shade and his eyes shone so brightly that they lit up the sea.

Leviathan was one of God's pets. It was written that each day God read the Torah for three hours, judged the world for a further three hours, attended to the needs of all living creatures for three hours and then, for the last three hours, played with Leviathan. According to the myth, God will slay Leviathan during the last days of the world. Tents will be made out of his skin to shelter the pious while they feast on his flesh. What remains of the skin will be stretched over Jerusalem and its brilliance will illuminate the entire world.

Similar accounts are found in other myths: the Babylonians told of combat between their god Marduk and the gigantic monster Tiamat; the Hittites had a weather god who killed the dragon Illuyankas; and in the Old Testament of the Bible, Yahweh (who shares the title 'cloud rider' with Baal) was the dragon slayer and Leviathan represented Israel's enemies who were to be slain by God. The Bible version is foretold in Isaiah: 'In that day the Lord with his sore and great and strong sword shall punish Leviathan the piercing serpent, even Leviathan that crooked serpent; and he shall slay the dragon that is in the sea' (Isaiah 27:1).

There are several references to Leviathan in the Bible. Asaph – who lived at the time of David and Solomon (1040–940 BCE) – wrote a psalm in which Leviathan appears as the seven-headed sea serpent killed by God; its flesh is distributed to the Hebrews in the wilderness: 'Thou brakest the heads of Leviathan in pieces, and gavest him to be meat to the people inhabiting the wilderness' (Psalm 74:14). In the Book of Job, Leviathan is depicted as a sea monster that symbolises God's power.

With such a varied literary history, there is no doubt that Leviathan, like Behemoth, is a mythological creature, a fantasy animal that could be a fusion of known living creatures. The Book of Job offers a more detailed description:

> Canst thou draw out Leviathan with an hook? or his tongue with a cord which thou lettest down? Canst thou put an hook into his nose? or bore his jaw through with a thorn? . . . Shall the companions make a banquet of him? shall they part him among the merchants? Canst thou fill his skin with barbed irons? or his head with fish spears? . . . None is so fierce that dare stir him up.

> Job 41:1–2, 6–7 and 10

These first few lines suggest a large sea creature. In *Paradise Lost* John Milton opted for a whale – after all, whales are the biggest and most powerful creatures to have lived on the earth, and the fin whale (*Balaenoptera physalus*), the second-largest living whale, is an inhabitant of the Mediterranean Sea:

> There Leviathan,
> Hugest of living creatures, on the deep
> Stretched like a promontory, sleeps or swims,
> And seems a moving land, and at his gills
> Draws in, and at his trunk spouts out, a sea.

Paradise Lost, VII 411–416

Milton erred slightly with his reference to gills, for whales are mammals and do not possess gills. Also, the habit of fishing with 'hooks' is usually associated with fish rather than whales. There is, however, a fish of sufficient size and power to fit the bill and that is the whale shark (*Rhincodon typus*) – the largest fish in the sea. Whale sharks are truly gigantic. Specimens over 17m (56ft) in length have been claimed, though today a good-sized specimen would be about 10m (33ft) – still a sizeable giant.

The whale shark is a filter feeder, so is unlikely to be caught on a fishhook, and it has the toughest skin imaginable. On its back there is a 14cm (5.5in) layer of gristly connective tissue covered by skin with a pattern of dermal denticles or 'skin teeth', each about 0.75mm (0.023 in) long, giving it the texture and strength of steel. The muscles below can be tightened to make it as impenetrable as a steel-braced truck tyre. Harpoons, buckshot and rifle bullets tend to bounce off, making the shark invulnerable to just about anything except a large ship.

Some years ago, when scientists were not as enlightened as most are today, the famous underwater explorer William Beebe came across a 12.8m (42ft) long whale shark. He tracked the fish for several hours and then, knowing the skin to be very tough, ordered two of his crew to jump on the creature's back and ram home harpoons with line and oil drum attached. The two men, according to Beebe, 'made a beautiful pole-vaulting dive, with the harpoon between them. They struck hard and leaped into the air and let their whole weight bear down, driving the harpoon home.'

Understandably, the gentle giant crash-dived into the abyss, but resurfaced about fifteen minutes later, the line and drum still attached. The fish had clearly descended to great depths, as the drum had been crushed by immense pressure into the shape of an hourglass. When the crew came to shoot more harpoons into its back, they simply bounced off.

Whale sharks are found in tropical and subtropical waters worldwide, including the Red Sea and Persian Gulf. Ultimately the whale shark cannot be the inspiration for Leviathan, though – according to the Good News Bible, Leviathan has legs:

> Let me tell you about Leviathan's legs and describe how great and strong he is. No one can tear off his outer coat or pierce the armour he wears. Who can open his jaws ringed with those terrifying teeth? His back is made of rows of shields, fastened together and hard as stone. Each one is joined so tight to the next, not even a breath can come between. They all are fastened so firmly together that nothing can ever pull them apart.
>
> Job 41:12

In the AV the passage differs slightly:

> I will not conceal his parts, nor his power, nor his comely proportion. Who can discover the face of his garments? or who can come to him with his double bridle? Who can open the doors of his face? His teeth are terrible round about. His scales are his pride, shut up together as with a close seal. One is so near to another, that no air can come between them. They are joined one to another, they stick together, that they cannot be sundered.
>
> Job 41:12–17

Mention of scales and legs knocks out the whale as a contender for the real-life Leviathan, too. The description indicates not a fish at all, but a reptile – and one that fits the bill is the crocodile. In biblical times crocodiles were common in the River Nile. Indeed, Africa's most numerous species is named after the river – the Nile crocodile (*Crocodylus niloticus*). At one time it was found along the length of the Nile, including the delta region, and in other rivers in biblical lands. Herodotus, writing in the fifth century BCE, echoes the Bible text with his description of a crocodile: 'Its claws are strong, the scaly skin on its back cannot be sundered. In Egypt it is called *champsa*, but the Ionians call it *krokodil*.' He also wrote about the creature's biology, drawing attention to the way 'It inhabits the land and the water, lays and hatches its eggs on the former and spends much of its days there, but passes the night in the water.'

The Nile crocodile was (and still is in Africa south of the Sahara) a formidable and powerful beast, with individuals growing up to 6m (20ft) long. One specimen shot in Uganda in 1953 was 5.94m (19.5ft) long and had a belly girth of 2.24m (7ft 4in), while another killed in 1948 in Lake Victoria was alleged to be 6.4m (21ft) long. Imagine a beast like that rising up from the water. Its size and propensity to attack using surprise as a means of bringing down its prey must have impressed the ancients.

Some were so amazed that they worshipped the creature. The crocodile was sacred to the ancient Egyptians. It appeared in large numbers at the time of the annual September flooding of the Nile valley, and so was thought to be in some way linked to the way in which the farms on either side of the river were revitalised each year by the precious silt washed down and deposited on the land. There was even a crocodile-god known as Sobek or Souchos, the son of Neith, the oldest goddess. Sobek was an important god who would 'endure forever', while the fortunes of other gods fluctuated according to changing circumstances. He was usually seen as a crocodile head on a human body. Depictions of the god found in tombs show him bearing a symbol of eternity, the ankh, in his right hand while in his left he holds a staff. His headdress includes a sun disc, for by the time of the New Kingdom in about 1400 BCE, Sobek was worshipped as a manifestation of the sun god Ra, and known as Sobek-Ra.

The crocodile god's most important temples are to be found at Kon-Ombo in Upper Egypt and Crocodilopolis in the Fayoum. Crocodiles were kept in pens and adorned with gold and precious stones. Bracelets were placed on their front feet. When they died they were embalmed, and crocodile mummies over 5m (16ft) long have been found in the Maabdah Caves in Central Egypt, where they are piled in stacks up to 9m (30ft) high.

The crocodile cult was widespread throughout Egypt – and indeed, wherever there were crocodiles in the wild. The cult of Sobek, for example, also flourished in the Nile delta region. Here crocodiles were adopted as 'pets', and when they died they were carefully preserved; there was a large temple at Tebtunis dedicated to Sobek.

If Egyptians considered the crocodile to be so powerful, why couldn't the inspiration for Leviathan of Hebrew lore be a crocodile? The Greek geographer Strabo, who lived in the first century BCE, visited another city with the name Crocodilopolis, located south of the Mt Carmel range in what was then southern Phoenicia. It was on the coast and surrounded by swamps, and crocodiles were captured there as late as the early twentieth century. It was here that Pliny, and later the European Crusaders, drew attention to crocodiles in the Nahal ha-Taninim, which flows into the Mediterranean from the hills of Samaria. The river runs close to Caesarea, where it is still known locally as the 'Crocodile River'. In the nineteenth century crocodiles were also reported living in the Qishon and Yarqon rivers in northern Israel. The Reverend Henry B Tristram was presented with the carcase of a crocodile estimated to be about 3.5m (11.5ft) long. It had been caught in one of the nearby rivers. Jacob Schumacher, the American vice-consul in Haifa, took part in a crocodile hunt in

1878 near the site of the Zikhron Ya'aqov railway station. He noted that crocodiles were common in the Nahal ha-Taninim area and the surrounding swamps. Another hunt was said to have taken place in 1905, and crocodile skins were offered for sale in Haifa during the First World War. The whole area has since been drained.

It is not known whether a crocodile cult existed here in ancient times, but the close proximity to Palestine has prompted some scholars to suggest that the crocodile is indeed one of the inspirations for Leviathan. However, as we read on, doubt sets in: 'By his neesings a light doth shine, and his eyes are like the eyelids of the morning' (Job 41:18). The word 'neesings' is open to many interpretations, though the most obvious and commonest translation into modern English is 'sneezing'. Crocodiles, though, tend not to sneeze (except in children's stories). They snort occasionally, but technically they do not sneeze, that is, clear the respiratory tract by the explosive expulsion of air. Water is kept out of the lungs and windpipe by nasal valves that close when submerging, so there is no need to eject water when resurfacing. The nostrils also sit on top of the upper jaw so there is no 'blowhole' that collects water. Therefore the crocodile does not 'blow' a fountain of spray like a whale or dolphin. There is, however, another reptile that comes close to what one might call sneezing. In the Galapagos Islands, off the coast of Ecuador in the eastern Pacific Ocean, the marine iguana (*Amblyrhynchus cristatus*) sneezes salt. It is one way for this marine reptile to rid its body of excess salt, the result of living in the sea. It is just possible that crocodiles living in salty conditions at the mouth of the Nile may have adopted a similar behaviour. Saltwater crocodiles (*C. porosus*), which live in the sea and in estuaries in southern Asia and the northern parts of Australia, regulate salts with the help of glands at the base of the tongue. The mainly freshwater Nile crocodile appears to have the glandular openings but it is not comfortable in salt water, becoming lethargic and even dying after a while. So, should a Nile croc find itself in the Nile delta, as some inevitably did, what better way to rid itself of salts than to sneeze like the marine iguana? Maybe this is fanciful, but a sneezing croc backlit by the sun would account for the observation 'By his neesings a light doth shine'.

The reference to glowing eyes is more easily explained. Crocodiles have a reflective tapetum (layer of membrane) at the back of the eye, as cats and dogs do. This causes the familiar 'eye shine', when light is reflected from the animal's eyes like twin battery torches. An ancient hunter or fisherman out at night might well have seen the light of his flaming torch reflected back from a crocodile's eyes. Reading on, however, we find ourselves getting into the real fantasy stuff: 'Out of his mouth go burning lamps, and sparks of fire leap out. Out of his nostrils goeth smoke, as out of a seething pot or cauldron. His breath kindleth coals, and a flame goeth out of his mouth' (Job 41:19–21).

If we think of this as real fire and smoke, then we're into the mythical world of dragons, but if we consider things that *resemble* fire and smoke, other identities for Leviathan suggest themselves. These take us away from crocodiles and into the world of creatures such as the Nile monitor lizard (*Varanus niloticus*), which preys on crocodile eggs. Like many other lizards, the Nile monitor has a tongue that constantly flashes in and out, like a flickering flame. When hunting or foraging, the animal 'tastes' the air with its tongue, and can follow the odour of prey from some distance away or find eggs buried under the sand.

The description of smoke is a bit more difficult to place, though 'smoke' could be condensed water vapour or 'steam' from the nostrils on a cold morning; after all, it can be very cold in the desert first thing in the day. The next verse also presents us with a problem if crocodile is the favoured identity for Leviathan: 'In his neck remaineth strength . . . The flakes of his flesh are joined together: they are firm in themselves; they cannot be moved. His heart is as firm as a stone; yea, as hard as a piece of the nether millstone. When he raiseth up himself, the mighty are afraid' (Job 41:22–25).

Crocodiles don't really have necks as such and they don't tend to rise up. The exception is the saltwater crocodile in Australia. Large specimens have been seen to rise out of the water to a bait hanging from a tourist boat and almost 'tail walk' like trained dolphins. Otherwise crocs tend to remain close to the ground, walking firmly on all fours.

Monitor lizards, however, do rise up. Monitors have long necks, and when two male monitors contest the right to mate with females, combat often involves the two standing on their hind legs and wrestling each other to the ground. The most imposing monitor lizard is the Komodo dragon (*V. komodoensis*), a gigantic beast that grows to 3m (10ft) long and is the largest lizard in the world. Today, it feeds on carrion – dead goats and buffalo – but it once fed on pygmy elephants. It lives on the Indonesian island of Komodo and its neighbouring islands, so it is unlikely that people of the Middle East would have seen such a giant, but tales from the Far East could well have reached here in biblical times.

Living 'dragons' aside, perhaps we should consider even bigger and more powerful reptiles. Again, the dinosaur proponents would have us believe that Leviathan, like Behemoth, was a dinosaur. Predatory dinosaurs, such as *Tyrannosaurus rex*, certainly had powerful necks and when they rose up they must have been terrifying, but, as we know, they died out millions of years before human beings evolved, so I'm afraid we must rule them out. By verse 30, though, we have a new problem – an anatomical one: 'Sharp stones are under him: he spreadeth sharp pointed things upon the mire' (Job 41:30).

Here the writer has taken us into the realms of fantasy again. Most scaly vertebrates – sharks, fish and reptiles – have relatively smooth undersides. The scales here tend to be softer and less spiky. This is a must for animals that live for at least part of their life on land, such as lizards and crocodiles, for they need to be able to slither their bodies over the ground without snagging on rocks and vegetation. As a result, this is the most vulnerable part of their body, and not at all what would be expected of an impregnable Leviathan. This seems to pose a problem, but then we come to an aspect of the creature's behaviour when in water: 'He maketh the deep to boil like a pot: he maketh the sea like a pot of ointment' (Job 41:31). This brings us back once again to the crocodile. When male crocodiles are advertising for a partner, they produce a low-frequency sound that makes the surface of the water all around them 'dance'. It is an amazing sight, just like 'boiling water' or a bubbling 'pot of oil'.

There is a plausible explanation for the next verse, too: 'He maketh a path to shine after him; one would think the deep to be hoary' (Job 41:32). In tropical and semi-tropical seas and estuaries there are bioluminescent, single-celled algae that 'shine' only when they are disturbed. If a large animal, such as a dolphin, whale or even a crocodile, is swimming through the water containing these organisms, it will leave behind a brilliant, luminous wake that continues to glow for several minutes after it has passed by.

Crocodiles and hippopotamuses were the largest and most powerful creatures encountered by the ancient human inhabitants of the Bible lands. It is therefore entirely possible that these two creatures were the earthly models for the monstrous mythical beasts Leviathan and Behemoth.

2

PLAGUES OF EGYPT

About 3,300 years ago, not long after the construction of the pyramids in Egypt, a series of catastrophic events hit the country. They have come to be known as the ten plagues and were so devastating that they were recorded in several written accounts. An Israelite's perspective on the events is given in the Torah and the Old Testament of the Bible (dated to about 1447 BCE). The disasters are also documented in the Ipuwer Papyrus, a manuscript written around 1780–1600 BCE (a tumultuous time of the Middle Kingdom during which five dynasties – three Egyptian and two foreign – vied for power) that gives an Egyptian's take on events, and which now resides in the Leiden Museum in Holland.

There has been much debate about whether the plagues were real or simply an ethical guide aimed at teaching people that if they misbehaved, disasters would follow them. Scientists have studied evidence that the events did actually happen and sought rational explanations for the occurrence of all the plagues described. However, it is only in the past few decades that sufficient scientific knowledge has been available to attempt such research. This has involved considerable debate about how each plague could have developed, but the 'why' – at least in biblical terms – is generally agreed. The ancient Egyptians had 39 principal gods, and it is thought that the plagues represented a confrontation between these Egyptian gods and the one true God, Yahweh. Each plague, therefore, targeted a key Egyptian deity; taken as a whole, the plagues were a demonstration to Pharaoh that his gods were ineffective.

In order to make the greatest impact, God first chose to strike at the very heart of Egyptian life. Ancient Egypt's most valuable resource was the River Nile, and it was protected by the Nile goddess, Hapi. She ensured that the river not only provided water and fish, but also regularly submerged agricultural land in the flood plain on either side. The deposit of silt each year boosted the fertility of the region, and so the Nile was really the lifeblood of Egypt and a prime target for Yahweh, ably assisted on earth by the two Israelite leaders Moses and Aaron. The first plague saw the river run with blood, making the water undrinkable and killing the fish:

> and he lifted up the rod, and smote the waters that were in the river, in the sight of Pharaoh, and in the sight of his servants; and all the waters that were in the river were turned to blood. And the fish that was in the river died; and the river stank, and the Egyptians could not drink of the water of the river.

> Exodus 7:20–21

The observation is echoed in the Ipuwer Papyrus: 'Plague is throughout the land. Blood is everywhere . . . the river is blood.' Was this blood real blood or a metaphor? After all, there are several similar references in the Bible to the colour of the moon that are clearly meant to be taken metaphorically: 'The sun shall be turned into darkness, and the moon into blood' (Joel 2:31); 'and the sun became black as sackcloth of hair, and the moon became as blood' (Revelations 6:12).

More prosaically, the red colour could have been due to red-coloured pigment suspended in the water. Unusually heavy rain in the Ethiopian Highlands could well have flushed down red earth. An alternative source might have been dust from the Sahara falling as 'red rain'. This even happened over southern Britain in February 1903, and was recorded in the scientific journal *Nature:*

> Dust or 'red rain' fell over an area of 20,000 square miles [51,800 sq km] in the southern half of England and Wales as well as in many countries of the Continent. It is estimated that in England and Wales alone the total quantity of dust was not less than 10 million tonnes. It was traced back to the Sahara, south of Morocco, where it was raised by a strong north-east wind; it travelled on the western side of an anticyclone over south-west Europe for a distance of at least 2,000 miles [3,200km] in a wide sweep around Spain and Portugal . . . in Europe the fall was associated with oppressive heat, and visibility was limited to short distances.

Both events are intriguing, and would certainly have coloured the river red. Neither would have made the water undrinkable, however, and they also fail to account for the mass mortality of fish. There are ancient records, though, describing how the River Nile has a red colour when it is at its lowest, some time in May, and at this time fish have also been known to die.

Another suggestion is that the first plague was caused by the disease schistosomiasis, especially the condition caused by the parasitic flatworm or blood fluke (*Schistosoma haematobium*), which has the water snail (*Bulinus*) as its intermediate host. It can cause, among other things, hematuria, which results in the urine becoming bloody because the fluke's eggs puncture the bladder wall. The disease is common on the Nile and on many other African rivers, where the symptoms are sometimes referred to as 'male menstruation', since boys aged between twelve and fifteen years of age begin to urinate blood. Mummies in Egyptian tombs have been found with blood fluke eggs in their remains, so it is not a far cry to imagine an epidemic of this disease and the water tainted with blood. However, hematuria usually occurs quite a while after the first exposure, so it would have taken years rather than months for an infected population to turn the water red with blood; moreover, compared to the volume of water that flows down the River Nile, the amount of urine produced would be negligible.

For a more plausible explanation we must turn to another natural phenomenon. The red coloration could well have been due to a 'red tide', or HAB as it is known today, meaning 'harmful algal bloom'. During such an event the water surface can have a brownish-red or a greenish-yellow sheen. It is caused by a 'bloom' of tiny, single-celled red algae that live in the water, and it often occurs after a long spell of hot, dry, still weather when the water column is not stirred up. The algae are dinoflagellates (Dynophyta), often of the genera *Karenia* (formerly *Gymnodinium*) and *Gonyaulax*. They manufacture nerve toxins that are among the most potent known to science, so when these tiny organisms are ingested by fish, the latter usually die. For some unknown reason, some animals such as shellfish and certain fish species survive but the poisons become concentrated in their flesh; if people eat contaminated fish or shellfish they can become seriously ill. Ciguatera results from eating contaminated fish, while paralytic shellfish poisoning follows eating contaminated oysters, mussels and clams. This danger has led the French to bring in a 'red tide' warning system to ensure that such shellfish do not reach market.

One of the most infamous red tides occurred at Venice, Florida, in 1947. The local people woke up one autumn morning to find millions of dead fish piled up on the beaches and what was described as a 'choking' gas in the air. The bloom began in the Gulf of Mexico and was blown by the wind towards the shore. By the time it hit Venice it was several kilometres across, though some red tides have been known to cover several *hundred* square kilometres. Locals complained of a burning sensation in the eyes and nose and a choking cough.

Not all fish are killed in such an event, and the survivors can be easy food for dolphins – though as the poison produced by the algae builds up in their bodies, the dolphins, too, succumb. It is thought that this is what happened to seven hundred dolphins that died on the Florida coast in 1987.

Generally, however, a red tide is mainly a marine phenomenon. It is something that usually happens out at sea, along coasts or in estuaries. The Red Sea was depicted on the famous Mappa Mundi – kept at Hereford Cathedral and dated to about 1300 – as a body of red water (other seas and rivers are shown in blue and green), probably because at certain times of the year it had extensive red algae blooms. An ancient Babylonian map describes the Persian Gulf as a 'bitter river', probably for the same reason. There are instances of red tides in rivers and lakes, too. In Australia blooms have occurred in slow-flowing rivers, such as the Swan and Canning rivers at Perth, Western Australia. Between April and June 2003, for instance, a bloom of the algae *Karlodinium micrum* caused a fish kill that did for more than 300,000 black bream. Rainfall in April followed by calm, sunny weather over the next couple of months is thought to have triggered the event. The heavy rain washed nutrients from farms and towns into the rivers so that a high level of soluble oxidised nitrogen – the kind that plants like – built up in the water and caused the algae to grow and multiply. It is quite conceivable that a similar catastrophic bloom could also have developed on the Nile during conditions of low flow, high levels of nutrients and little mixing of water.

It is also possible that the first plague was brought about by a species of diatom. For many years, scientists believed that these organisms, found in the phytoplankton (plant plankton), were harmless. In 1987, however, three people died and more than a hundred became ill after eating blue mussels that had been gathered at Prince Edward Island, Canada. When the mussels were analysed it was discovered that they were laced with domoic acid, a toxin produced by a diatom that causes Amnesic Shellfish

Poisoning (ASP) in humans. Since then, there have been several other recorded incidents involving these organisms. In 1991, for instance, many pelicans and cormorants on the California coast were killed after eating anchovies containing toxin from the diatoms. Today, these poisonous diatoms turn up all over the world.

There is, however, one particularly nasty alga that can occasionally be found in slow-flowing river systems, including brackish waters. It is known popularly as the 'cell from hell', and its scientific name is *Pfiesteria piscicida*. It was discovered in 1989 by JoAnn Burkholder and Howard Glasgow from Carolina State University. They revealed that it has a strange nineteen-stage life cycle, and at one point the organism becomes an extremely dangerous flesh-eater that leaves fish with large, open, bleeding sores. It made headline news when it attacked fish in rivers in North Carolina during the 1980s and 1990s, leaving the fish as bloody carcasses floating on the surface. A second species, *P. shumwaye*, was discovered in 2000 and behaves in a similar fashion. Both organisms produce a cocktail of toxins, with at least one chemical killing the fish and another that opens up the fish's skin, enabling the algae to feed on the flesh inside. The blood plague in these incidents was real blood, not red algae.

John Marr, once director of the Bureau of Preventable Diseases in the USA, and his colleague Curtis Malloy, an epidemiologist with the Exponent Health Group in Washington DC, believe that *Pfiesteria* is a rational explanation for the first biblical plague. And that's not all. They also observed that the organism would have killed the fish that usually eat frogspawn, and that the mass of jelly on the outside of the frogspawn eggs might well have protected them from the cause of this plague. With its natural population control removed, the frog population could have increased exponentially, in such huge numbers that many would have been forced to move far from rivers and wetland areas in order to find food. This would have given rise to the second plague: 'And

Aaron stretched out his hand over the waters of Egypt; and the frogs came up, and covered the land of Egypt' (Exodus 8:6).

This second plague involved a creature Egyptians associated closely with the Nile – the frog. It was worshipped in the form of Heqt or Heka, a statue with a frog's head. Frogs and toads were held in high esteem in ancient Egypt and the act of killing one was punishable by death. The frog also represented a healthy harvest, for when the Nile was about to overflow its banks there would be many frogs about. The plague of frogs demonstrated that Heqt had lost control.

The Hebrew word for frog in the Bible is *tzepharde'a* or *tsephardea*, meaning 'marsh-leaper', which could well have referred to the mascarene rocket frog (*Ptychadena* [*Rana*] *mascariensis*), the most common of Egypt's water frogs. The edible frog (*Rana esculenta*) is also found in Egypt, as well as Israel, Syria and Palestine. It is larger, greener and noisier than Europe's common frog (*R. temporaria*); huge congregations of this frog gathered in wetland areas at night can be deafening. Whether these frogs could ever congregate in such large numbers as to constitute a plague is a moot point, however. Tristram points out that the plague probably occurred in spring, when the current generation of frogs would have been tadpoles and not adults. His conclusion is that the event must have been 'supernatural'. If, however, the plague had occurred later, after the Nile had reached its highest level and the waters were beginning to recede, then the spawn in the mud would have given rise to myriads of tiny frogs. Normally, they remain in the marshes, but on this occasion they were everywhere:

> And the river shall bring forth frogs abundantly, which shall go up and come into thine house, and into thy bedchamber, and upon thy bed, and into the house of thy servants, and upon thy people, and into thine ovens, and into thy kneadingtroughs.
>
> Exodus 8:3

Perhaps significantly, the Egyptian hieroglyph for 'myriads' is a frog. Another explanation is that the plague was not of frogs but of toads, the most common in Egypt being the leopard toad (*Bufo regularis*), though Degen's toad (*B. vittatus*) and the green toad (*B. viridis*) are also present. At breeding time – which tends to be later in the spring than that of frogs – toads migrate back to their breeding ponds, sometimes from some distance away and in huge numbers. It is quite possible that Moses and Aaron were able to predict when such a migration would be underway. The toads, of course, would get everywhere, particularly in buildings constructed on land reclaimed from wetland sites where the toads had previously spawned. This occurs on a small scale in places where a pond has been filled in and toads turn up on the porch each spring looking for their birthplace, much to the householder's annoyance.

Eventually, the plague of frogs was brought to an end: 'And the Lord did according to the word of Moses; and the frogs died out of the houses, out of the villages, and out of the fields. And they gathered them together upon heaps: and the land stank' (Exodus 8:13–14).

Insufficient food could have been an explanation for the frogs' (or toads') demise, but they might also have been contaminated with *Pfiesteria* and, like the fish, eventually died.

Without frogs to keep small insects under control they, too, proliferated. The targets for the next couple of plagues were Kheper, the scarab deity represented by beetles and other insects, and Geb, the 'great cackler' responsible for earth and vegetation. When the insect population exploded and the third plague hit the country, Kheper was proved powerless: 'Aaron stretched out his hand with his rod, and smote the dust of the earth, and it became lice in man, and in beast; all the dust of the land became lice throughout all the land of Egypt' (Exodus 8:17).

The Hebrew word here is *kinnim*, meaning either 'lice' or 'gnats' depending on which authority you read, though any one of a hundred species of insects that bite humans could be implicated. If recent archaeological reports are anything to go by, however, a plague of lice would have had minimal impact, for at the time people were quite literally 'lousy' anyway. Plague or no plague, human head lice were a common occurrence in ancient times. Research in 1990 at archaeological sites at Qumran, close to where the Dead Sea scrolls were discovered in 1947, has shown that these ancient people were clearly heavily infested with head lice. Itchy scalps must have been a widespread irritation. The lice were discovered on wooden hair combs about two thousand years old; along with their eggs, they had been combed from the locks of Jewish guerrillas who had fought the Roman legions in the Negev Desert. They were perfectly preserved, for the area is very dry with an average annual rainfall of no more than 8cm (3in). Debris between the teeth of the first comb to be found included the remains of ten lice in various stages of development and 27 eggs, ten of which were still to hatch and the embryos still visible inside. Egyptian nobility, however, were probably less infested than the rest of the population, so a plague of lice would have had a more lasting impression on them.

Other identities for *kinnim* include fleas, which are a global pest and potential carriers of bubonic plague; mosquitoes, known for carrying such terrible diseases as malaria and yellow fever; and sand flies (*Phlebotomus papatasii*). Sand flies are common in the Levant. They are much smaller than mosquitoes and have an almost silent flight, which means that their victims do not know they are there. When they bite they give a sharp sting that becomes an unpleasant itch, and they can carry pappataci fever, a virus disease of brief (often three days') duration, which causes fever, headaches, pain in the eyes and general malaise.

An alternative insect suggested by Marr is *Culicoides*, a biting midge (or punkie) that creates a louse-like irritation when it bites and is active at twilight when the air is calm. The males are nectar feeders but the females need a blood meal for their eggs to develop and mature. This is when they become a problem, for they carry viruses of the family Reoviridae, one of which causes African horse sickness and another of which is the agent of blue tongue in cattle and sheep, a fact that is very relevant to the fifth of the ten plagues.

In the meantime, along came the fourth plague: 'and there came a grievous swarm of flies into the house of Pharaoh, and into his servants' houses, and into all the land of Egypt: the land was corrupted by reason of the swarm of flies' (Exodus 8:24). According to Tristram, who travelled in the Holy Land in the 1860s, flies plagued people in the region at the best of times, and they still do so today. They remain the worst disease-carrying insects on the planet. There are two Hebrew words that translate as 'flies'. The relevant word in this context is *arob*, meaning 'swarms of flies'. It is mentioned only in the passage above, in a poem by Asaph and in another about God and His people: 'He sent divers sorts of flies among them, which devoured them'; 'He spake, and there came divers sorts of flies' (Psalms 78:45 and 105:31).

Both passages suggest that a range of flies were involved in the plague and the first indicates that they were probably 'biting' or 'blood-sucking' flies. Flies present in the region vary from the common housefly (*Musca domestica*) to blood-sucking horseflies and gadflies, and biting midges, gnats and mosquitoes. Tristram recorded the torment of houseflies and horseflies in these parts, but he recognised the greater medical importance of mosquitoes that not only suck blood but also spread dangerous diseases. At the time of the fourth plague, mosquitoes and flies could well have found ideal breeding conditions in the brackish water ponds that were left behind when the flood waters of the Nile receded.

Modern commentators favour the stable fly (*Stomoxys calcitrans*) as the species of the fourth plague. It resembles a housefly in size, shape and colour, but it has a stout, black proboscis with which it can pierce the skin of its hosts. Both sexes feed on blood, and victims are typically bitten on the legs, belly or ears. The stable fly is a prolific breeder, especially when large quantities of animal dung and other detritus have accumulated in the soil. It lives for two to three weeks, deposits up to 120 eggs at one sitting, and development from eggs to adults takes about 28 days, so it could form large swarms and reach plague proportions quite rapidly. Its bites are painful, and it leaves large puncture wounds that could leave its host open to infection. German researchers have implicated it in the spread of the HIV virus from chimpanzees to humans.

It is also quite possible that the huge swarms of flies – especially *Culicoides* midges and stable flies mentioned above – carried deadly viruses or bacteria, and it is these that triggered the fifth plague, an outbreak of a disease – *debher* in Hebrew, meaning 'destruction' – that wiped out the country's domestic livestock.

> Behold, the hand of the Lord is upon thy cattle which is in the field, upon the horses, upon the asses, upon the oxen, and upon the sheep: there shall be a very grievous murrain. And the Lord shall sever between the cattle of Israel and the cattle of Egypt: and there shall nothing die of all that is the children's of Israel. . . And the Lord did that thing on the morrow, and all the cattle of Egypt died: but of the cattle of the children of Israel died not one.
>
> Exodus 9:3–6

It is also recorded in the Ipuwer Papyrus: 'All animals, their hearts weep. Cattle moan.'

Egyptian cattle were protected by Apis, the bull god, and Hathor, the cow-like mother goddess, so it is likely that it was these two gods that Moses and Aaron were denouncing. The disease they had conjured up could have been one of several. Marr and Malloy have suggested epizootic infections – diseases that affect animals but not people – such as African horse sickness, which causes death in equines within hours of being infected, and blue tongue, which has a similar effect on cattle and sheep; both diseases are spread by *Culicoides*. This would have accounted for horses, mules, donkeys, cattle, sheep and goats (though not camels). Anthrax and foot-and-mouth disease have also been proposed, but these are diseases that can also affect humans, so do not fit the biblical description. Then there is rinderpest, one of the morbilliviruses that provokes epidemics and pandemics in domestic livestock and wildlife, such as the terrible outbreak that wiped out 90 per cent of domesticated cattle and bovine wildlife in Africa south of the Sahara between 1887 and 1891.

An outside candidate is *Pfiesteria* or one of its bacterial or algal relatives. In 1984 a small herd of cows in Montana collapsed and died just ten minutes after drinking from a pond coated with what was described as a 'pea-green film'. The culprits were in fact cyanobacteria, but this case does reveal how these micro-organisms can turn up in unexpectedly large numbers in unexpected places. At one stage in its life cycle, *Pfiesteria* steals the green pigment chlorophyll from green algae and masquerades as a harmless organism. Conceivably, it could have an adverse effect on mammals as well as fish. In her Carolina State University laboratory, the scientist Jo Ann Burkholder saw two dinoflagellates fight over a cluster of human blood cells, noting: 'The first organism attached to the blood cell and began to suck it up, then another approached and began a tug-of-war for it.' In Burkholder's original laboratory, her exposure to the organism resulted in memory loss, disorientation, mood swings, nausea and impaired immune systems. Today, the research is exploring the effects of *Pfiesteria* on mammals as well as fish.

By now, the plagues were coming thick and fast. The next – the sixth plague – was particularly revolting: 'they took ashes of the furnace, and stood before Pharaoh; and Moses sprinkled it up toward heaven; and it became a boil breaking forth with blains upon man, and upon beast' (Exodus 9:10).

This was a swipe at Thoth, the god of magic and healing, and the legendary Egyptian physician Imhotep, who was also worshipped as a god. What the Egyptian magicians had failed to recognise, perhaps, were the symptoms of a rare but highly contagious airborne bacterial infection known as 'glanders'. At the turn of the twentieth century, it was an important cause of death in horses, and there were fatal infections in humans. One of its symptoms is pustular skin lesions. It was also called the 'forgotten disease', a disease that was prevalent in the past but one that could be summoned at any time as an agent of biological warfare. It was used, allegedly, by the Germans in the Second World War, when secret agents planted in the USA inoculated horses and mules destined for the British lines. Glanders was first described by Aristotle in 330 BCE, and is still found in the Middle East and Africa. It is caused by the bacterium *Pseudomonas mallei*, which can be spread in the air or carried by insects. In the biblical plague – *shechin* in Hebrew, meaning 'boils' – the stable fly could have been the carrier.

With their livestock destroyed, the Egyptians were completely dependent on a good harvest for survival. It should not come as a great surprise, then, that the seventh and eighth plagues targeted Egypt's crops. Two gods were under attack here – Seth, the harvest god, and Nut, the sky goddess. It was now time for the weather to take a turn for the worse:

> And Moses stretched forth his rod toward heaven: and the Lord sent thunder and hail, and the fire ran along upon the ground; and the Lord rained hail upon the land of Egypt. So there was hail, very grievous, such as there was none like it in all the land of Egypt since it became a nation. And the hail smote throughout all the land of Egypt all that was in the field, both man and beast; and the hail smote every herb of the field, and brake every tree of the field.
>
> Exodus 9:23–25

Hail can be a particularly devastating phenomenon. Hailstones as large as 13cm (5in) across have been known, which are potentially dangerous to man and beast, and violent storms in the recent past have deposited up to 1m (3.3ft) of ice on the ground, more than enough to smother crops. An extraordinarily heavy hail fall occurred in the Northern Transvaal of South Africa and was reported in the scientific journal *Nature* in 1936. The event occurred on 1 February, and resulted in the deaths of nineteen local people:

> About 3in [7.5cm] of rain fell in a few minutes and then came the hail, which consisted of jagged lumps of ice. In 30 minutes the hail was lying everywhere to a depth of 3ft [90cm], and in some cases the dead natives had to be dug out of it. There were many cattle killed, which the natives afterwards dragged away on sleighs. Whole crops were obliterated, and there are said to be over 1,000 native families afflicted in the area.

In the early afternoon of 7 April 1961, hailstones of 12.5cm (5in) diameter were observed by Captain D Calvert and his crew in the SS *Afghanistan* when anchored off Umm Said in Qatar on the Persian Gulf. The events were recorded in the *Marine Observer* (32:112–13,1962):

> within a few minutes the hail was very dense and of a size larger than tennis balls, some hailstones being estimated to be 5in [12.5cm] in diameter . . . the size of the hail may be judged from the fact that the sea was a mass of white foam caused by the splashes from the hail, the splashes being 2 to 3 ft [60–90cm] high; the damage done to the brass binnacle covers for both gyro and magnetic compasses, which were dented to a depth of 3/4in [2cm] is another indication. Over 80 holes were found in the boat covers the following morning.

Meteorological events such as these are not uncommon. Unusually violent hailstorms hit Guildford County, North Carolina, on 9 June 1856, Clermont-Ferrand, France, on 13 November 1928 and Baghdad, Iraq, on 24 April 1930, while there was an extraordinary fall of 'explosive hail' in the USA in 1912. On all occasions considerable damage was done to property and crops. In the Bible plague, however, it seems that not everything was ruined: 'And the flax and the barley was smitten: for the barley was in the ear, and the flax was boiled. But the wheat and the rie were not smitten: for they were not grown up' (Exodus 9:31–32).

This seems to date the season in which the plague occurred, about nine months after the first plague when the new crop was beginning to mature in January and February. The word 'rie', incidentally, refers to a species of hard, rough-grained wheat, known today as 'spelt', *Triticum spelta*, an ancient cereal crop that was cultivated 9,000 years ago and was the stable grain crop of the Egyptians and Assyrians. The surviving crops were not to survive for long, however:

> Moses stretched forth his rod over the land of Egypt, and the Lord brought an east wind upon the land all that day, and all that night; and when it was morning, the east wind brought the locusts. And the locusts went up over all the land of Egypt, and rested in all the coasts of Egypt: very grievous were they; before them there were no such locusts as they, neither after them shall be such. For they covered the face of the whole earth, so that the land was darkened; and they did eat every herb of the land, and all the fruit of the trees which the hail had left: and there remained not any green thing in the trees, or in the herbs of the field, through all the land of Egypt.
>
> Exodus 9:31–32

Locusts are the scourge of farmers in many parts of the Middle East. The species most likely to swarm in such numbers as to 'cover the face of the earth' is the desert locust (*Schistocerca gregaria*). These insects swarm in huge numbers and consume every living plant in their path. A single swarm covering an area of 2.6 sq km (1 sq mile) might contain up to 200 million locusts. Nothing survives.

The desert locust lives in the dry, semi-arid regions of Africa and the Middle East, and is found as far east as Bangladesh and as far west as the middle of the Atlantic Ocean; it has even appeared in Spain. Its appetite is awesome: each adult locust eats its own weight in grain or vegetation each day, a large swarm consuming in excess of 20,000 tonnes daily. In 1889, a locust swarm containing an estimated 250 thousand million insects, and weighing 500,000 tonnes, was seen to cross the Red Sea. In 1978 in Ethiopia a swarm that covered an area of 415 sq km (160 sq miles) and travelled at 16km/h (10mph) for up to twenty hours a day chomped its way through enough grain in six weeks to feed a million people for a year. But the largest known swarm was seen in South Africa in 1784. Estimates suggest that it covered some 5,000 sq km (1,930 sq miles). It was blown out to sea, but when the dead locusts were washed back on shore a bank of the dead insects 1.2m (4ft) high piled up on beaches along an 80km (50 mile) stretch of coastline.

On the occasion of the eighth plague, the swarm came up from the eastern desert between the Nile and the Red Sea. In Bible times such an event would have caused people to take stock of the situation. Pharaoh summoned Moses and Aaron and said he had sinned against the Lord their God, and asked for forgiveness. He was almost at the point of letting the children of Israel go. Pharaoh relented for a moment, so the insects were swept away: 'And the Lord turned a mighty strong west wind, which took away the locusts, and cast them into the Red sea; there remained not one locust in all the coasts of Egypt' (Exodus 10:19).

But not for long – Pharaoh changed his mind again, so drastic action was called for. With the ninth plague, Moses and Aaron took on the mightiest of Egypt's gods – Ra, the chief god, who was represented by the sun. It was Ra who brought heat and light to the world and was the source of all life.

> And the Lord said unto Moses, Stretch out thine hand towards heaven, that there may be darkness over the land of Egypt, even darkness which may be felt. And Moses stretched forth his hand towards heaven; and there was a thick darkness in all the land of Egypt three days.

> Exodus 10:21–22

According to the Ipuwer Papyrus, 'The land is without light.'

Here a sandstorm is the most obvious cause, one with the same magnitude as the storm – known as the *hamsin*, *khamsin* or *cashimh* – that hit Cairo for three days in 1997. It is carried on a hot south or southwest wind that blows at the time of the spring equinox, and is known to produce darkness that would have rivalled the worst of the London smogs. The sandstorms may last for two to three days, blocking out the sun in a dark, dusty haze. Such a storm paralysed the US military during the recent war in Iraq in 2003.

There is, however, an alternative explanation, and here we return once again to epidemiology and disease. The darkness, according to Marr and Malloy, could well have been an outbreak of Rift Valley Fever, discovered in 1900 in Kenya. This is an acute, fever-inducing viral disease that affects livestock, such as cattle, buffalo, sheep, goats and camels, and also humans. It is caused by a virus of the genus *Phlebovirus* and is carried by *Aedes* mosquitoes and other biting insects. One of its symptoms is temporary blindness, for a common complication is inflammation of the retina, the layer of light-sensitive nerve cells at the back of the eye.

Most people recover after a few days, but up to 10 per cent of victims are left with permanent sight loss. Outbreaks occur in most countries south of the Sahara, but it was discovered in Egypt in 1977.

By the time of the ninth plague, the Egyptians would have been reeling with the onslaught of epidemics, denied healthy foods and seriously vulnerable to diseases of any kind. They probably rushed out to the fields to save what little food they could recover and stockpile it without thought for the conditions in the warehouses. The crops were damaged, moist from hail and rain, and contaminated by the droppings of locusts. This led to the tenth and last plague, which was an attack on Pharaoh himself. The Pharaoh of Egypt supposedly descended from Ra, who had been so thoroughly humiliated by plague nine. Now, even the offspring of Egypt's man-god was to be killed, and as Pharaoh's son was considered a god, his death also meant the death of one of Egypt's gods:

> And it came to pass, that at midnight the Lord smote all the firstborn in the land of Egypt, from the firstborn of Pharaoh that sat on his throne unto the firstborn of the captive that was in the dungeon; and all the firstborn of cattle.
>
> Exodus 12:29

This tenth plague is a little more difficult to explain than the rest. Martin Blaser of Vanderbilt University suggested that the same organism that caused the Black Death in Europe in the fourteenth century – a bacterium called Yersina pestis spread by the fleas on rats – was to blame. Marr and Malloy, however, had a more ingenious explanation. This time they focused on poisonous moulds. They reasoned that the ancient Egyptians had harvested and stored the grain when it was wet and covered with locust droppings. The grain storage pits were hot and humid and therefore an ideal breeding ground for bacteria and moulds. A likely culprit was found by Edwardo Montagnia, from the Atlanta Center for Disease Control, when investigating eight child deaths in Cleveland in April 1996. He discovered a black mould, *Stachybotrys atra*, which grows rapidly on the top layers of a grain store, breaking down cellulose and producing toxins on its spores. These cause bleeding in the lungs and eventually death.

The rest of the story relies on a cultural link. Only the top layers of grain would have been contaminated, and this would have been served first to important people in a family or the most important of the family's livestock. The first-born was considered the most important thing a family possessed, so he or she would have received the first helpings – and often as not an additional helping. In this way, the first-born in each family received a lethal dose of mycotoxins.

Whatever its cause, this tenth plague did the trick. The Pharaoh relented and the children of Israel were allowed to leave Egypt. Mysteriously, throughout this time the Israelites themselves were spared any suffering – their water was drinkable, they did not suffer boils, their livestock was unaffected, and the first-born in each family was safe. One explanation is that the Israeli community was housed in 'the land of Goshen', thought to have been located on the eastern side of the Nile delta and some distance from the main Egyptian conurbations. The main urban centre would have been at Memphis, to the south of present-day Cairo, about 128km (80 miles) southwest of Goshen, and this geographical separation might well have protected its inhabitants from many of the horrors inflicted on the rest of the kingdom. The *Culicoides* midge that Marr and Malloy suggest carried the agent of the fifth plague, for example, is not a strong flyer. Its wings are no more than 2mm (0.08in) in length and it can fly no more than 100m (330ft) at a time. Isolation in the delta could well have protected the children of Israel from the fly and its harmful passengers.

There have been many theories that seek to find a comprehensive explanation for all these plagues, from the epidemiology of diseases by Marr and Malloy described above to the argument that they were simply a succession of natural events. One of the most famous hypotheses is the English literature scholar Greta Hort's 'ecological domino' theory, proposed in 1957, which has anthrax at its core. Hort argued that an unusually severe Nile flood in July brought down red mud from upriver together with red algae and anthrax bacteria that contaminated the water. This set off a deadly chain of events. The algae killed the fish. The frogs became sick and climbed ashore, and then died. This contaminated the soil, which in turn infected livestock with anthrax. Biting flies, such as *Stomoxys calcitrans*, carried the anthrax to other animals and humans, causing boils. The exceptionally severe weather that caused the floods also brought hail and triggered locust plagues. The huge quantity of mud brought down by the flood dried out and a dust storm created the darkness. And it was the first fruits of crops, rather than first-born children or cattle, which were lost in the tenth plague. The problem with this theory is that anthrax is a soil-based bug, not an aquatic one, and it is specific to mammals, not frogs and fishes.

Immanuel Velikovsky provided an extraterrestrial theory. He proposed that many biblical events were the result of a cosmic catastrophe. According to Velikovsky, at the time of the great plagues of Egypt the Earth was passing through the tail of a comet, now known as the planet Venus, before it went into its present orbit around the sun. Red dust turned the waters (including those of the Nile) red, and made them unfit for drinking. A rise in temperature caused by the close proximity of the new planet caused frogs, flies and locusts to propagate more rapidly. The plague of hail was not actually hail but a shower of meteorite debris. Thunderous noise accompanied the event, the 'fire' was naptha, a bitumen-like substance, which ignited in the Earth's atmosphere, and the 'ashes of the furnace' (Exodus 9:8) were fallout from the comet's tail that caused the 'blains upon man and beast'. Curiously, legends from many parts of the world, from the Inuit to the Incas, seem to give credibility to Velikovsky's ideas. The Peruvians, for example, have stories that tell of blood raining from the sky and the Tatars of the Altai in Central Asia speak of blood turning the entire world red.

Another, more down-to-earth theory, from Dorothy Vitaliano of Indiana University, involves the eruption of a volcano on the Greek island of Santorini in the Mediterranean in the sixteenth century BCE. According to this hypothesis, after the major eruption – the equivalent of thirty or forty Mt St Helen's eruptions – an enormous ash cloud drifted towards Egypt. It's certainly true that volcanic shards subsequently found in Egypt could have come from the explosion. Climate modelling has revealed that the cloud could have plunged the area into darkness by blotting out the sun and could have brought about a reduction in rainfall, causing a drought. The ash might also have been deposited in the Nile delta area, causing the river to back up and stagnate. The acidic dust could have settled in the river itself, the contamination triggering a series of catastrophic events: the frogs are driven on to land; the dying frogs attract flies; the flies transmit disease to cattle and to humans, giving rise to boils and ultimately fatalities.

There is, however, some debate over the chronology at play here. The Thera-Santorini event has been dated using ice core samples, tree ring dating and Carbon 14 dating of relevant volcanic rocks, and is generally agreed to have struck in 1628 BCE. Some scholars, however, have opted for a date some time between 1520 BCE and 1450 BCE, based on the dating of pottery fragments, and still others for a much later date as late as 1380 BCE to 1370 BCE, placing it in what is known as the Amarna period. The plagues followed by the Exodus are thought to have taken place during this period.

Plagues, of course, are not confined to the period of the exodus from Egypt. The Hebrew word for plague – *negha* – occurs more than a hundred times in the Bible. It is used, for example, in a description of leprosy.

> When a man shall have in the skin of his flesh a rising, a scab, or bright spot, and it be in the skin of his flesh like the plague of leprosy; then he shall be brought unto Aaron the priest, or unto one of his sons the priests: And the priest shall look on the plague in the skin of the flesh: and when the hair in the plague is turned white, and the plague in sight be deeper than the skin of his flesh, it is a plague of leprosy: and the priest shall look on him, and pronounce him unclean.
>
> Leviticus 13:2–3

Tough times indeed. Leviticus 13 and 14 have a total of sixty references to the plague of leprosy. The disease we know today as 'the plague' (bubonic plague), however, has occurred frequently in the Holy Land. In fact, records of outbreaks in the southeast between Gaza and Bubastis have been so frequent as to classify the disease as endemic. The relatively short incubation period and the rapidity of full symptoms have meant that people have considered it a manifestation of divine anger. It is not unusual for 60 per cent of people stricken with plague to succumb within three or four days, sometimes within ten hours of contracting the disease. There are reports of epidemics in villages in which three hundred out of five hundred inhabitants died within 21 days.

The next major plague recorded in the Bible hit the children of Israel themselves. It accompanied a fall of quails, and may have been a salmonella outbreak or an early appearance of 'bird flu'. It is also possible that birds were carrying some kind of 'plague' from the disease-stricken region of Serbonian . . . but there was more: 'Even those men that did bring up the evil report upon the land, died by the plague before the Lord' (Numbers 14:37).

And more:

> And Aaron took as Moses commanded, and ran into the midst of the congregation; and, behold, the plague was begun among the people . . . And he stood between the dead and the living; and the plague was stayed. Now they that died in the plague were fourteen thousand and seven hundred, beside them that died about the matter of Korah. And Aaron returned unto Moses unto the door of the tabernacle of the congregation: and the plague was stayed.

> Numbers 16:47–50

And still more: 'And those that died in the plague were twenty and four thousand'; 'Behold, these caused the children of Israel, through the counsel of Balaam, to commit trespass against the Lord in the matter of Peor, and there was a plague among the congregation of the Lord' (Numbers 25:9 and 31:16).

Plagues were evidently rife in ancient times. There had been another outbreak at the time the Ark was captured: 'But the land of the Lord was heavy upon them of Ashdod, and he destroyed them, and smote them with emerods, even Ashdod and the coasts thereof' (1 Samuel 5:6). 'Emerods' has been translated in more recent versions of the Bible as 'tumours', though these could have been the glandular enlargements associated with bubonic plague. Further evidence pointing to the disease is found later: 'Wherefore ye shall make images of your emerods, and images of your mice that mar the land' (1 Samuel 6:5). The mice mentioned here could well have been field mice that, when conditions are right, undergo population explosions that can only be described as taking on 'plague' proportions. Huge tracts of crops have been destroyed by such plagues.

On the other hand, the correct translation for 'mice' could be 'rats'. When rat populations rise alarmingly, their increase is sometimes accompanied by the rapid spread of bubonic plague. Fleas that live on rats carry the disease, and they also bite humans. When the offending organism enters the human body, it quickly invades the lymph glands, such as those in the groin, and these enlarge enormously; death is painful. In the mid-fourteenth century a pandemic of bubonic plague was thought to have wiped out half the human population of Europe. It was called the Black Death.

3

JONAH AND THE WHALE

The story of Jonah and the Whale appears – unsurprisingly – in the Book of Jonah. It tells of Jonah, son of Amittai of Gath-hepher and one of the Minor Prophets from Galilee, who was believed to have lived about 800–780 BCE. At the time, Assyria was all-powerful and an enemy of Israel. Its forces committed atrocities against the Israelites, so God asked Jonah to go to its capital, Nineveh, to persuade the Ninevites to repent or suffer the consequences. Instead of going east to Assyria, however, Jonah panicked. Whether he was too scared to go to Nineveh or whether he wanted retribution to fall on the heads of the Ninevites by not warning them, is not revealed. Whatever the reason, he tried to escape his duty, boarding a ship in Joppa (known as Jaffa or Yafo, and a suburb of Tel Aviv today) that was heading for Tarshish (probably Cadiz in Spain).

One night early in the journey, a huge storm hit the ship. The crew prayed to their own gods while Jonah slept below decks. The captain thought that something was amiss and he pulled Jonah from his bed. Jonah was interrogated and confessed that he was running away from God. He suggested that the crew should throw him into the sea; they did so and the storm abated. But God was not going to let him drown – as Jonah was sinking, a huge sea creature described in some Bible translations as a 'whale' and in others as a 'great fish' or 'sea monster' swallowed him up. He was confined inside its belly for three days and three nights, during which time he prayed and composed a psalm. When God was assured that Jonah was repentant, the creature spewed him up on to the nearby shore and he was saved. It was at a place identified as the 'Gate of Jonah' not far from Alexandretta or Iskenderen in southern Turkey, close to the Syrian border.

Religious scholars have long debated whether Jonah's story is an historical account or a dream or vision. They seem equally divided. The story is, after all, a kind of *katabasis* (literally 'going down' in Greek), a journey of descent into darkness and the world of the unconscious. A katabatic story has been described as 'a journey of the Dead made by a living person . . . who returns to our world to tell the tale'. In Jonah's case, a sea creature of some kind gobbled up our hero. Its jaws represented the gates of Hell, and while Jonah was inside he was lost 'deep in the world of the dead . . . into the land whose gates lock shut for ever', according to the Good News Bible. He was then regurgitated, just as Jason was swallowed alive by a dragon-like sea monster and spewed up again during his quest for the Golden Fleece. Having come to terms with the powers of darkness, Jonah was then reborn into the light.

In a similar vein, Gilgamesh travelled to the Netherworld and Odysseus into the Pit of Souls. The most famous example of katabasis, however, is that of Christ visiting Hell during the three days and nights after he died on the cross. Indeed, Jesus quoted Jonah's adventure as a symbol of his resurrection when the law teachers and Pharisees demanded that he perform a miracle in front of them. The only miracle he gave them was that of the prophet Jonah: 'For as Jonah was three days and three nights in the whale's belly; so shall the Son of man be three days and three nights in the heart of the earth' (Matthew 12:40).

These accounts also suggest rites of passage in which the hero withdraws from the world, reaches some higher religious state through suffering, fear or solitude, and returns to the world reborn. In Jonah's case, the whale might also represent the womb, symbolising the wish that we all have, according to psychoanalysts, to revert to a foetal state. Whatever the interpretation, the Jonah story appears in other religions, folklore and mythologies as well.

In Greek legend the *Heracleid* recounts how Heracles (the legendary hero, who was also thought to have been based on a real man, a chieftain of the kingdom of Argos) was swallowed by a whale and remained in its belly for three days. Coincidentally, the story takes place near Joppa, thought to be one of the oldest cities in Israel and probably the oldest port in the Levant. It was founded by Japheth, son of Noah, forty years after the flood. Greek authors trace the city's foundations to Jopes, another name for Cassiopeia.

In Persian folklore another hero – Jamshyd – was swallowed by a sea monster and later spewed up onto the shore. In India, Samadeva Bhatta was swallowed by a fish and later emerged unharmed when it was cut open. And the hero Saktideva was swallowed by a giant fish and disgorged on his quest for the Golden City. Also, Vishnu the Avatar is shown in illustrations rising out unharmed from the mouth of a giant fish.

It is a story that has been told since time immemorial. Whales and their propensity to swallow and regurgitate people has been a popular topic for tall tales down the centuries. In 1785 Rudolf Erich Raspe introduced us to *Baron Munchhausen's Narrative of His Marvellous Travels and Campaigns in Russia*. The book tells of the boastful exploits of the boastful Baron who one day was on a ship that was confronted by an enormous whale. It was so big that he and the crew could not see the end of it, even with a telescope. The whale swallowed the ship in one enormous gulp. A second gulp of water floated the ship into the whale's stomach. Eventually, the crew decided to jam the monster's mouth open with two masts strapped together to prevent its jaws from closing. When the whale yawned, the masts were planted and the ship sailed out, together with a fleet of 35 ships that had also been trapped inside.

Even children's literature has explored the theme. In Carlo Collodi's *The Adventures of Pinocchio*, which appeared in book form in 1883, the wooden boy is confronted with a 'gigantic Dog-fish . . . more than a kilometre long, not counting its tail'. It sucks Pinocchio into its mouth and down into its stomach. After a conversation with a philosophical tuna that feels it is 'more dignified to die in the water rather than oil', the boy spots a light in the distance and finds it is a candle held by his father Geppetto. He had been living inside the creature for two years, surviving on the provisions it had swallowed when it engulfed the ship on which he was travelling. In the story Pinocchio is given the chance to rescue his father and help gain him the right to become a real boy. He struggles to the monster's tongue, the size of 'a lane in a large park', and hauls his father past its three rows of teeth and out through its mouth. Its mouth is open while it sleeps because it suffers from asthma. The only conclusion can be that Collodi's giant 'Dog-fish' is, in fact, an air-breathing mammal – a whale.

Is Jonah's story no more than a fable, a parable or an allegory? Maybe it is best we leave it to the theologians to debate an answer, but for the time being, let us explore the question of whether a whale or any other giant sea creature would, or even could, swallow a person and the latter survive the experience.

As might be expected, a number of tales of 'Jonah and the Whale' have been handed down over the years. One early example was reported in the *Massachussetts Gazette Boston Post Boy and Advertiser*, dated Monday, 14 October 1771. The report described how a whaling ship arrived at Edgartown carrying Marshal Jenkins, a whaler who had been in a boat that was bitten in two by a whale. Jenkins had been thrown into the water and was then caught in the whale's mouth. The whale had pulled him below, but later rose to the surface and discarded him. Much battered and bruised, he was taken on board the mother ship, and after a couple of weeks he had fully recovered.

In 1947 Edgerton Y Davis, a surgeon with the harp seal fleet out of Newfoundland, told of a young sealer who fell from an ice floe off St Johns, Newfoundland, in 1893 (*Man in Whales*, *Natural History*, 1947). An enormous bull sperm whale, which was apparently lost and in Arctic waters out of season, swallowed him. When the whale's stomach was opened up, the man was found inside. He was badly crushed 'in the region of his chest', according to Davis, and partially digested. The gastric mucosa (the lining) in the whale's stomach had encased his body like a snail's foot, yet curiously some lice on the sailor's head were still alive. It is another entertaining story, though strangely Davis waited for more than a half-century to tell it. Victor Scheffer, award-winning author of *The Year of the Whale* – an imaginative book on sperm whale biology – is sceptical. He quotes the story but 'ventures to doubt it'.

One tale in particular has been cited over the years as proof that the story of Jonah and the whale is factually credible. Indeed, some devout Christians and creationists often quote it as evidence that all events in the Bible are true. The story was reported in such august organs as the *New York Times* and *Princeton Theology Review* and featured in the books *Can a Young Man Trust His Bible?*, by Arthur Gook, a missionary to Iceland, and Sir Francis Fox's autobiography *Sixty-Three Years of Engineering*, published in 1924. It involved a sperm whale (*Physeter macrocephalus*) – probably a large bull sperm whale, because only males frequent the South Atlantic where the following events unfolded.

In February 1891 the whaling ship *Star of the East* was a few hundred kilometres to the east of the Falkland Islands when the lookout spotted a sperm whale about 3km (2 miles) away on the starboard quarter. Long boats were launched and they pursued the whale. The first boat to get close speared the whale with a harpoon. It sounded, pulling the boat some 5km (3 miles) on a hair-raising excursion that was to become known in later years by

Yankee whalers as a 'Nantucket sleigh ride'. It then turned and headed back to where it was first harpooned. As soon as its back broke the surface, the crew of the second boat let loose another harpoon. Understandably, the whale thrashed about and then struck off on another jaunt for 2km (1.2 miles) and sounded again. The lines went slack. As the crews were pulling them in, the whale surfaced again but it struck one boat with its nose and capsized it, tossing its occupants into the water. The other long boat picked up survivors, but two of the crew were missing, presumed drowned.

Some time later, the whale died from its harpoon wounds. Working through the day and part of the night, the ship's crew brought it alongside and, using axes and spades, hacked away the valuable blubber. The following morning, they hoisted the whale's stomach on to the deck, but were startled to find that there was something moving inside. They cut it open, and there before their eyes was one of the missing sailors. He was doubled up and unconscious, but still alive.

The unfortunate young man was hauled out, laid on the deck and bathed in seawater. This brought him round, but his speech was incoherent and for some time he behaved like a raving lunatic. He was taken to the captain's cabin where, with care and attention from the captain and his officers, he recovered and was back to work after three weeks. His skin, though, bore the scars of his curious adventure. Where the whale's gastric juices had started to work, his face and hands were bleached white and his skin wrinkled.

Later, he described how he remembered being lifted up by the whale, caught up in the whale's thrashing at the surface, and then slipping down a smooth passage. His hands came into contact with a slime that shrunk from his touch. He could breathe but was overcome by the heat and fainted. The next thing he recalled was waking up in the captain's cabin. When the ship returned eventually to England, the young man was treated for his skin condition at a London hospital.

His name was John Bartley. It is said that he survived to a ripe old age, but his skin was always yellow and like parchment. Bartley became a whaling legend but eventually left the sea and set up a cobbler's shop in Gloucester; his gravestone there bears the epitaph 'James Bartley, 1870–1909, a modern Jonah'. His story is a terrific yarn, but there is a fundamental flaw: little, if any, of it appears to be true.

The story went into the history books and has been copied from book to book, and nowadays from one website to the next, without its authenticity being verified. Until Professor Edward B Davis of Messiah College, Grantham, Pennsylvania, came along, that is. Davis looked at the evidence and found it wanting. He felt that the story of John Bartley, the supposed modern Jonah, should be consigned to maritime mythology, not history.

According to *Lloyd's Register of British and Foreign Shipping*, the *Star of the East* was certainly a real ship – a barque made of iron. It was 183ft (56m) long and 734 tonnes (1.47 million lb) net, and was built in Glasgow by C Connell & Co. The ship was owned by Sir Roderick Cameron and registered in London. When, commissioned, its captain was Captain W Esson, but at the time of Bartley's supposed adventure, Captain J B Killam had taken over. According to Lloyd's, the *Star of the East* left Auckland, New Zealand, on 27 December 1890, bound for New York, where she arrived on 17 April 1891. She could have been off the Falklands in February 1891, but at this point two awkward facts can be ignored no longer – she was a merchantman not a whaler; and John Bartley was not registered as one of the crew. To confound the story further, some time later, in 1907, the wife of the ship's captain stated quite categorically in a letter published in *The Expository Times* that 'There is not one word of truth to the whale story. I was with my husband all the years he was in the *Star of the East*. There was never a man lost overboard while my husband was in her. The sailor has told a great sea yarn.'

What is more, commercial whaling did not start in the

Falklands area of the South Atlantic until 1909 and, according to whaling historians, in those days it is unlikely that the stomach of a whale would have been hoisted on to the deck – it would simply have been discarded. It was only in later years, when whales were hauled aboard factory ships, that scientists became interested in the bits less interesting to whalers – such as the stomach, where they might find pieces of giant squid.

Dr Ray Gambell, the retiring Director of the International Whaling Commission in Cambridge, who was interviewed along with Professor Davis for a BBC Radio 4 *Making History* programme (25 August 2000), also pointed out that there would be no air inside a whale's stomach for a person to breathe and that the animal's digestive juices get to work the moment something edible enters the stomach.

In 1942 George Macloskie put forward a rather fanciful notion that attempted to explain the mystery in his article 'How to Test the Story of Jonah' in *Bibliotheca Sacra*. He wrote that when the whale expelled superfluous water from its mouth after eating, a person trapped in the mouth might reach the laryngeal pouch below the larynx. In a large whale the pouch would be large enough to hold a human. The victim would be able to breathe the whale's own air supply and not be attacked by its digestive juice. The more likely explanation, though, is that the entire episode was made up. So how did the story arise?

It is thought the story of Bartley and the whale first appeared in an edition of the *Yarmouth Mercury* dated 22 August 1891. The *New York Times* picked it up some years later and published it on Sunday, 22 November 1896 (though it credited the *South Yarmouth Mercury* as the source). The lie, though, probably had its origins in another event, for Davis points out that there was a whale story in Great Yarmouth that appeared in the *Yarmouth Independent* in June 1891. This account told of a 9m-long (30ft) rorqual (baleen whale) that came close to shore. It was chased by several boats and hit the pier at Gorleston, just to the south of Great Yarmouth, where it ran aground and died. The whale was stuffed by a taxidermist and transported around the country on a horse-drawn trailer accompanied by the East Anglian naturalist Arthur Patterson. It was eventually exhibited at the London Westminster Aquarium under the name 'The Gorleston Whale'. Newspaper reports at the time mentioned that the whale had inspired several exaggerated stories. Davis suggests that the John Bartley story was simply one of them.

There is, however, a curious postscript. Captain J B Killam was born in Yarmouth – not Yarmouth, England, but Yarmouth, Nova Scotia. Maybe there is more to the story than meets the eye, after all.

Certain curious details from ancient history suggest that there may have been some factual basis for the tale of Jonah. At the time in which the biblical events were set – the reign of Jeroboam, King of Israel (787–747 BCE) – the Phoenicians seem to have controlled Joppa, and it was probably a Phoenician boat that would have carried Jonah. Joppa was also a whaling port and a well-publicised skeleton of a 12m (40ft) long whale was on display in one of its temples. Could it have inspired the Jonah story? Some time later, in 58 BCE, Marcus Scaurus seized the skeleton and transported it to Rome, an incident recorded by Pliny the Elder (CE 23–79). In present-day Jaffa a whale sculpture can be seen in the south of the old city commemorating the event.

Could a sperm whale swallow a person whole? Scientists assigned to whaling factory ships have found great chunks of prey, such as giant squid, inside sperm whales' stomachs. Squid biologist Malcolm R Clarke, for example, writes about a 10.49m (34.5ft) long giant squid – measured from the end of its body to the tip of its longest tentacles – almost intact in the stomach of a 14m (47ft) long bull sperm whale caught off the Azores in 1959.

In *The Animals of the Bible* (1964) Roy Pinney mentions the director of a natural history museum who was often asked if the story of Jonah was true and whether a man could be swallowed by a whale. He responded by trying to push his body down the throat of an obligingly dead, stranded 18m (60ft) long sperm whale and reported that although he could just about squeeze through, a fat man could not have made it. The only conclusion we can glean from that experiment is that Jonah was of modest build. However, in the *Daily Mail* of 14 December 1928, G H Henn, from Birmingham, England, recalls how at the turn of the century the carcase of a large whale was displayed for a week on some wasteland in Navigation Street, outside New Street Station. Henn and eleven other men entered its mouth, passed down its throat and moved about in a chamber that was 'equivalent of a fair-sized room'. He noted that, 'Its throat was large enough to serve as a door.' And Frank Bullen records in his *The Cruise of the Cachelot* (1899) that a whale was once seen to regurgitate 'a massive fragment of cuttlefish – tentacle or arm – as thick as a stout man's body'.

Whales under stress often regurgitate their stomach contents. Whalers have noticed that a whale in its death throes will bring up its last meal, sometimes vomiting up huge chunks of giant squid and whole shark. The whale might also have become stranded. Sperm whales are mid-ocean animals and when close to shore they sometimes get into difficulties. Most probably their echo-location system is switched off when cruising and they are operating on 'automatic pilot'. When they hit a sandbank in shallow water, they are rudely awakened and their sensory systems are overwhelmed. As a result, they strand themselves, and a person trapped in a stranded sperm whale would have the opportunity to leave.

What of sperm whale distribution? Could a large whale have passed Jonah's boat in the eastern Mediterranean? It seems a person is less likely to be gobbled up in these parts, for this species is not common here. However, they *do* occur in these waters. The Israeli Marine Mammals Research and Assistance Centre (IMMRAC) reports that single individuals and small pods of up to five whales are seen in the eastern Mediterranean. At 6am on 7 April 1996, for example, Yoram and Suzette Greenberg, owners of the yacht *Amonte*, observed a larger pod of eight to ten sperm whales about 5 nautical miles to the east of Rhodes in the Greek islands. They were able to compare the length of the whales with that of their 14m-long (47ft) yacht, and estimated two of them to be 15m (49ft) long.

From time to time, dead or dying sperm whales have been washed ashore on the Israeli coast, though these are thought to be whales that have strayed from their normal haunts or carcases that have drifted long distances across the Mediterranean.

The dwarf sperm whale *Kogia simus* has been found now and again in the Mediterranean. A dead specimen was washed ashore on the coast of Tuscany in 1988, and a living whale was stranded at Eraclea Minoa, near Agrigento on the Sicilian coast, on 8 September 2002. The Sicilian animal was just 2m (6.5ft) long, but they can grow to 3m (10ft) – not a likely candidate, though, for Jonah's abductor.

Joppa's temple skeleton is more likely to have been that of a fin whale (*Balaenoptera physalus*), the largest whale species to be found in these waters. Unlike the sperm whale, it is a filter feeder; its teeth have been modified as comb-like bristles or 'baleen' (whalebone) that enable it to sieve krill and small fish from the seawater. In this group of whales – which includes the blue whale (B. *musculus*), the largest animal ever to have lived on earth – the throat is narrow, far too narrow to swallow an adult human. There are records of large whales choking to death on nothing more than a seabird. In 1829, for instance, a humpback whale (*Megaptera novaeangliae*) that had washed ashore at Berwick in the British Isles had six cormorants in its stomach and another stuck in its throat. According to observer G M Allen, it is thought the seventh bird caused the whale to choke.

None other than Rudyard Kipling explained 'How the Whale Got His Throat' in one of his *Just So Stories*, published in 1902. This was also a Jonah-like tale, involving a 'mariner of infinite-resource-and-sagacity'. Kipling's whale ate all the fishes in the sea except one, a small 'Stute fish, that swam just behind the whale's right ear so it was out of harm's way. One day, the whale stood on his tail and announced that he was hungry, so the 'Stute fish asked if he had tasted man. The whale promptly swallowed a man, named Fitch, who was adrift on a raft, but this was no ordinary man, for when inside the whale's stomach 'he stumped and he jumped and he thumped and he bumped, and he pranced and he danced', etc., etc., until the whale could stand it no more. The whale asked the 'Stute fish what he should do. 'Tell him to come out,' said the tiny fish. At that moment, Fitch the Mariner walked out of the whale's mouth, but while he was inside he had 'cut up the raft into a little square grating', which he jammed into the whale's throat. From that day hence, according to Kipling, 'The whale could neither cough nor swallow, nor could he eat anything except very, very small fish; and that is the reason why whales nowadays never eat men or boys or little girls.'

If Jonah's rescuer was not a giant whale, what was it? It could be that the monster was a one-off. After all, according to the scriptures, God had 'prepared' it to swallow Jonah. Also, the Bible was written in Hebrew, Aramaic and Greek, so translators from those languages could have opted for the word 'whale' to describe the creature simply because it was the largest animal known at the time.

Were any other sea creatures in the Mediterranean of the eighth century BCE capable of swallowing a person whole? The great white shark (*Carcharodon carcharias*) is an obvious contender. It is the largest predatory fish in the sea and is the shark that has clocked up the greatest number of recorded attacks on people. Large specimens have been reported reliably to grow up to 6m (20ft) and there have been unsubstantiated claims for even bigger ones. Bite marks on whale carcases off southern Australia indicate great whites up to 8m (26ft) long in those waters. On 1 April 1987

Peter Riseley claimed a 7m (23ft) shark in a gill net at Kangaroo Island, Australia. (Scientists who have studied the photographs, however, are questioning the length claimed by the fisherman and believe it is about a metre shorter.) In 1894 Captain E S Elkington chanced upon a great white that was estimated to be 1.2m (4ft) longer than his 10.5m (35ft) launch. He watched the beast for about half an hour just outside Townsville, Queensland, Australia. An even larger shark was claimed in June 1931, when an 11m (37ft) specimen was trapped in a herring weir in New Brunswick, Canada. In his book *South African Beachcomber,* the South African writer Lawrence Green mentioned an even bigger fish. Green's shark was reputed to be 13m (43ft) long. It was found at False Bay, Cape Province, at the end of the nineteenth century.

Record-breaking great white sharks have been reported in temperate seas off South Africa, Australia, the Maldives, Japan and the Pacific and Atlantic coasts of North and South America, but they also frequent the Mediterranean; the channel between Sicily and Tunisia is full of them (relative to the rest of the Mediterranean). Since 1862 there have been more than a hundred sightings of great white sharks in the Sicilian Channel. In fact, about 40 per cent of great white sightings in the Mediterranean and northeastern Atlantic have been there. But they are found elsewhere, too.

In 1891 a giant great white was caught during naval man-oeuvres in the Adriatic Sea. It was estimated to be 10.06m (33ft) long and weighed 4 tonnes. In April 1987 what was claimed to be a 7m (23ft) long specimen was displayed on the quayside at Marsaxlokk, on Malta, but more recent estimates based on photographs taken at the time indicate that the shark was no more than 5m (16ft) long. Nevertheless, the shark (a female) had a blue shark, a large swordfish and a dolphin in her stomach. Later the same year, two white sharks became entangled in nets off the Egadi Islands, on the west coast of Sicily, one a female 5m long.

In the eastern half of the Mediterranean, great white sharks more usually appear among the islands off the Croatian coast, between Pula and Split. Here they feed on bluefin tuna (*Thunnus thynnus*), a known prey item of Mediterranean great whites. Sometimes they go for people, too. In September 1971 a large shark, probably a great white, fatally attacked a Polish tourist, Stanislaw Klepka, who was swimming off the coast of Ika, near Opatija, Croatia. In August 1974 a German swimmer called Ralph Schneider was bitten by a great white at Omis, near Split, Croatia. He also died as a result of the attack.

During the summer of 1989, a large great white nicknamed 'Willie' (actually a female) was sighted several times in the Adriatic. She was estimated to be more than 5m (16ft) long. In September that year she surprised sports anglers off Pesaro, Italy, where she circled boats and broke fishing lines. In December 1991 a 2.1m (7ft) long youngster was caught by commercial fishermen off Ancona, and in March 1992 a 2.3m (7.5ft) long specimen was caught in nets off Termoli; both places are on Italy's Adriatic coast. In July 1993 a large great white was spotted near Losinj Island, in the Kvarner Gulf, and a month later, fishermen caught a 5m long specimen off Sibenik. Both sites are on the Croatian side of the Adriatic, but great whites do appear on the Italian side, too.

On 27 August 1998 a large female great white, estimated from video footage to be about 5.5m (18ft) long, approached a fishing boat approximately 35km (22 miles) off the coast at Senigallia, between Ancona and Rimini in the Adriatic. A sports angler on board was fishing for sharks in about 70m (230ft) of water, and had caught a thresher shark (*Alopias vulpinus*) that was tied up alongside. Some time later, a very large great white appeared. It circled the boat and grabbed the burlap sac hanging from the stern and then took a half-metre-wide chunk out of the thresher. It also managed to take some glass fibre and teak pieces from the boat's hull. According to my colleague Ian Fergusson, a British expert with a special interest in great white sharks in the Mediterranean and northeastern Atlantic, it was one of the largest great whites ever captured on video, and it was a female. From the pictures, he estimated that she weighed about 2,000kg (4,400lb) and her largest teeth were 5cm (2in) long from root to tip. Great whites are less common further east, though not unknown. Fergusson suggests that the scarcity of great white shark sightings in the Levantine Basin in the southeastern Mediterranean is due in part to higher temperatures and salinities. Nevertheless, from time to time there are sightings. In March 2005, for instance, three sharks were caught in nets off the coast of Ashdod, between Tel Aviv and Gaza. One was 5m (16ft) long, and when its belly was cut open at Ashdod marina a small dolphin was found inside. It was cut up and distributed before it could be identified properly, but the size and prey indicate it was probably a great white shark.

Many of the identified sharks have been females, and there is some evidence to suggest that the eastern Mediterranean, particularly the archipelago off the Croatian coast of the Adriatic, could be a pupping and nursery site for great white sharks, though in 1934 a gravid (pregnant) female was caught at Agamy Beach, near Alexandria, indicating perhaps that nursery sites could be or could have been close to the Holy Land. It took Egyptian fishermen in three boats to haul her ashore. She was estimated to be about 4.3m (14ft) long and weighed 2,540 kg (5,600 lb). When she was cut open, nine 60cm (2ft) long embryos were found inside. This puts the great white shark firmly in the right area to be a stand-in for Jonah's whale. And there have been sightings of great whites off the coasts of Cyprus, Lebanon and Israel, as well as shark attacks by species unknown off Egypt (three), Greece (six) and Lebanon (three).

Humans are not the primary targets of great white sharks, though. In the Mediterranean they hunt or scavenge a variety of foods – bottlenose, striped and common dolphins, tuna, bonito, swordfish, blue and shortfin mako sharks, rays, sea turtles, dead whale and dolphin carcases and dead domestic mammals that have drowned or have been washed into the sea. Should one accidentally or deliberately swallow a person, however, what are the chances of them being vomited up again?

Sharks *do* regurgitate food items, such as human arms and legs, which they bring up when under stress – but an entire human? To date there are no records of a shark doing so, though an historical account of one incident comes close. According to E B Pusey's *The Minor Prophets* (1886), in 1758 a sailor fell overboard from a frigate that was sailing in the Mediterranean in stormy weather. A monster great white shark, which was known as a sea-dog in those days, took the unfortunate seaman into his wide throat. His fellow crewmen leaped into the ship's sloop and tried to help their comrade. The captain of the ship ordered a small cannon to be fired at the giant fish, which must have been thrashing around at the surface. It was struck by the cannonball and promptly vomited up the sailor, who was still alive . . . or so the story goes – nobody has checked this one either. The sloop picked him up and the shark was harpooned. It was estimated to be about 6m (20ft) long, quite a size for a great white. It was dried and presented by the captain to the sailor. He subsequently went around Europe – Franconia, Erlangen, Nurnherg – exhibiting both the shark and himself.

More usually, bodies are found inside sharks, and by the time they are examined, both victim and shark are usually dead. On 2 October 1954, for example, a 0.9 tonne (2,000lb) great white caught off Nagasaki, Japan, was found to have a thirteen-year-old boy in its stomach, and it is not unusual for these giants to contain even bigger corpses.

There are a couple of historical accounts of giant sharks taking whole human prey. In 1776 the Welsh naturalist Thomas Pennant described how a great white shark was caught with 'a whole human corpse . . . in the stomach'. In 1909 three partially clothed human cadavers – an adult male, adult female and a young girl – were found in the stomach of a 4.5m (15ft) long female great white shark that was caught in fishing nets off Capo San Croce, a peninsula that separates the Golfo di Augusti from the Golfi di Catania between Syracuse and Catania, Sicily. They were thought to be earthquake victims that the shark had scavenged after a tidal wave (tsunami), triggered by the tragic Messina earthquake of 1908, had washed them out to sea.

Ian Fergusson thinks that it is not stretching the imagination too much to think of a great white shark being caught, hauled ashore, eviscerated and a whole human corpse falling out on to the fish market floor; and that would certainly have caused a stir. It is not hard to imagine, then, a local folk tale emerging that became ever more surreal every time it was told. Could this have been the origin of Jonah's story?

Ancient Greek writers such as Aristotle and Herodotus knew the great white shark. They referred to it as the 'Lamia' monster and even today Greek and French Provencal fishermen know the shark as 'lamie'. Herodotus tells how thousands of soldiers and seamen were 'seized and devoured by monsters' when the Persian battle fleet was destroyed in a storm near Mt Athos (or Ayos Oros) in the northern Aegean Sea in 492 BCE.

One of the earliest shark attacks on pictorial record was discovered in the Mediterranean. It was found on the sides of a vase dated about 725 BCE. Fragments of the vase that was excavated at Lacco Amenal in Ischia, Italy, depicts a shipwrecked sailor being devoured by a shark.

Pliny the Elder mentions sponge divers in the Mediterranean caught up in 'frantic combats with sea-dogs which attack the back, the heels, and all the pale parts of the body'. And the Greek poet Leonidas of Tarentum describes how a sailor was bitten in two by a sea monster. The man's companions interred what remained after the attack – thus he was buried, according to the poet, 'both on land and in the sea'. Records show that in medieval times, great whites were caught occasionally between Sète and Nice, France.

In 1566 the French naturalist Guillaume Rondelet first put forward the notion that a great white shark and not a whale swallowed Jonah. He risked the condemnation of the Vatican by suggesting that a whale's throat is too narrow and that the great white shark had the capability to swallow Jonah whole. His proposition was based on reports of a shark containing 'two tunny and a fully clothed sailor'. The tunny were probably the enormous bluefin tuna, which grow up to 3m (10ft) long. In the mid-eighteenth century Linnaeus put forward a similar proposition. Rondelet, though, went one better. He wrote about whole men, complete with armour, found inside large great white sharks. They were caught close to Nice and Marseilles, though today his tales are maybe a touch too much for *us* to swallow . . .

In fact, wearing armour might be the only way to survive passage in and out of a white shark's mouth, for squirming past the shark's extremely sharp, triangular teeth would be a greater miracle than being swallowed and spewed up by a whale. Up to 28 full-size teeth in the top jaw and another 25 in the lower are backed up by rows of smaller, slowly growing teeth that move forward to replace the front set when they drop out. Although whole seals, porpoises and other sharks have been found in the stomachs of great white sharks, the manner in which the shark feeds would mean the bodies would be severely lacerated.

On contact with the prey, the lower jaw moves forwards and upwards, impaling the prey on the slightly narrower bottom teeth. Then the upper jaw drops as the mouth closes. If the prey is very large, such as a whale carcase, the top teeth are used to carve through blubber or flesh, the shark shaking its head from side to side to help the slicing. If the prey can be swallowed whole, the movement between the top and bottom jaws gradually draws the victim into the mouth, the shark's teeth keeping it from escaping. Each tooth is serrated, like a saw, and together an entire mouthful can slice through skin, flesh, bone and even turtle shells.

The chance of Jonah entering or leaving unscathed through the jaws of a great white shark is highly unlikely, then. But there was once a creature that could have swallowed a half-dozen Jonahs in a single gulp without them touching the sides. It is a giant shark, known popularly as megalodon but more scientifically as *Carcharodon megalodon*. This shark is known only from its fossil remains, in particular its teeth. A single front tooth is 15cm (6in) long, and it is serrated like the teeth of the great white shark, though megalodon was not an immediate ancestor of today's giant, but a close relative. What is to follow may seem fanciful, but again, let's speculate.

Megalodon had its heyday in the Miocene about ten million years ago, but there are a few stories that indicate (albeit rather contentiously) that it could have lived into more recent times. Between 1873 and 1876, when the British research ship *Challenger* was sailing the world's oceans on the first global oceanographic expedition, the crew dredged up two fossil megalodon teeth from the floor of the southern part of the South Pacific Ocean at Station 281 in 4,360m (14,300ft) of water. When they examined them, however, they found that they were 'fresh' – that is, fresh geologically speaking. One was dated at approximately 24,000 years old and the other at 11,000 years. This meant that the owner of the younger tooth was swimming the oceans at the same time that people were crossing the Bering land bridge from Asia into North America – in other words, the shark was contemporaneous with humans.

Since these dramatic revelations were made, the teeth have been re-examined and archaeologists have reassessed their understanding of the way in which teeth fossilise. The feeling now is that the teeth discovered by the *Challenger* are much older than was first thought. However, fossil megalodon teeth found around Malta (where they are known as 'dragon' teeth because it was thought they had supernatural properties) indicate that megalodon was present in ancient times in the Tethys Sea, the precursor to the Mediterranean.

A second story is even stranger. It appears in D G Stead's *Sharks and Rays of Australian Seas* and relates to events that took place in

Nelson Bay to the north of Sydney, New South Wales, Australia. This is an area that great white sharks are known to frequent, but the shark that the local fishermen encountered was of a quite different order. They were fishing for spiny lobsters, known locally as crayfish, and caught them in lobster traps about 1.07m (3.5ft) in diameter that were placed in deep water. Two to three dozen crayfish would be caught at a time in each pot, and they proved to be irresistible to one giant shark, the like of which the fishermen had never seen before. It took 'pots, mooring lines and all', according to eyewitnesses, and when its size was enquired, the fishermen estimated that it was as long as the wharf that they and D G Stead were standing on: 35m (115ft)! The water 'boiled over a large space' when the shark swam past, they remembered.

The fishermen were familiar with whales – they were on a humpback whale migration route – and they often encountered several species of large sharks, but they were adamant that their monster was a shark. Its head, according to one, was 'the size of the roof of the wharf shed at Nelson Bay', but the thing that struck Stead was their description of its colour. To a man, they agreed it was a 'ghostly whitish' colour. If these Australian fishermen are to be believed – and there's no reason to consider that they were lying – megalodon or a species of shark of colossal proportions could have been patrolling the ocean in biblical times.

Interestingly, a local myth reflects such a monster not that far away from the Nelson Bay monster. In the Torres Strait, between Papua New Guinea and Queensland's Cape York Peninsula, there is the legend of Mutuk, who was delivered from the belly of a shark that had swallowed him. Although accepted as a legend, Mutuk's story is given some degree of credibility by the real events that surrounded Papua pearl diver Iona Asai. In 1937 he was diving in just 3.7m (12ft) of water when he saw a tiger shark (*Galeocerdo cuvier*) swimming rapidly towards him. In an instant, Iona's head was in the shark's mouth, but he survived. He takes up the story:

When I turned I saw the shark six feet away from me. He opened his mouth. Already I have no chance of escape from him. Then he came and bite me on the head. He felt it was too strong so he swallowed my head and put his teeth around my neck. Then he bite me and I felt his teeth go into my flesh.

Iona escaped death by feeling for the shark's eyes and pushing hard until it let go. He made for the mother boat, was pulled aboard and then fainted. His hospital record is there for all to see – he needed two hundred stitches to sew up the two rows of teeth marks in his neck, and three weeks after he left hospital an abscess on his neck produced a tiger shark's tooth. By a strange coincidence, the name Iona is a direct native translation of Jonah, one of Papua Christians' Bible heroes.

Tiger sharks are not common in the Mediterranean, but there are one or two other sharks found here that reach a significant size. In the deeper parts of the sea, the bluntnose sixgill shark (*Hexanchus griseus*) can grow up to 5m (16ft) long. It is a rather slow-swimming, flabby-bodied shark with a broad mouth filled with comb-like teeth, but it can put on a turn of speed to pursue hake, ling and smaller tunas and swordfish. Larger specimens will take animals as large as dolphins. It frequents deep water, from 50m (165ft) to more than 1,800m (5,900ft) deep, and is caught infrequently in the Aegean Sea. In theory, a large specimen could take a small person whole, but as with the great white, the victim would have to pass through the mouth with its rows of sharp teeth. There is a record of one attacking a scuba diver off Caprera Island in the Italian part of the Adriatic, though it was goaded into doing so. It is unlikely that Jonah was swallowed by one of these, though the species can be big and it will scavenge in deep water – where Jonah might have floated down to. It also swims occasionally into shallow inshore waters – exactly where Jonah might have been spewed up.

Stories of sharks spewing up humans also appear in Greek mythology. One involves Cerberus, the three-headed dog, and Delia, daughter of the fisherman Glaucus. Delia had the habit of following her father out to sea in a small boat until he disappeared over the horizon; then, she rowed back to shore. One day a giant shark intercepted her and swallowed her *and* her boat in one enormous gulp. By chance, Cerberus was hunting in those same waters and attacked the shark, biting off his tail. But then he heard the shark scream like a young girl. He quickly realised there was someone inside it, and he bit off the shark's head in order to release its victim. She was taken back to the surface alive and well.

Back in the real world, the basking shark (*Cetorhinus maximus*) is the second-largest fish to swim in the world's oceans and is frequently encountered in the Mediterranean. It grows to 10m (33ft) long and has an enormous mouth. It was probably this gigantic maw that prompted Bishop Erik Pontoppidan of Norway – a prolific writer on sea monsters and the like – to present a lengthy treatise in 1765 suggesting that Jonah was gulped down by none other than a basking shark. The fundamental problem with the theory is that the basker is a filter feeder and eats mainly plankton – certainly nothing bigger than small fish. Its mouth may be broad but its throat quickly narrows and follows a distinct right-hand bend into the stomach. No prophet would get down there.

The largest fish in the sea is the whale shark (*Rhincodon typus*), and, not to be outdone by its smaller cousin, it, too, has been cited in the Jonah tale. This species can grow to 14m (46ft) long, and like the basking shark it has an enormous mouth. When the shark is not in the feeding mode, its mouth resembles a letterbox, but at feeding time it can expand and could easily engulf a man. It is, however, another filter feeder, with a narrow throat down which a person could not travel. This has not stopped the speculation that it is capable of swallowing humans, however.

One tale was published in the *Literary Digest* (4 April 1896). It is remarkably similar to the John Bartley story except that the sea creature doing the swallowing is a whale shark rather than a whale. It tells of an English sailor who was attempting to harpoon a whale shark in the English Channel and fell overboard. The shark turned, swallowed him whole and dived. Fishing boats put to sea and tried to find the fish. Forty-eight hours later, they spotted it and killed it with a shot from a deck gun. The shark was towed to shore and its stomach opened. Inside was the sailor, still alive. He was rushed to hospital, and discharged a few hours later. He was then exhibited in a London museum where the public could gawp at him for the entrance fee of one shilling.

There is, of course, one basic flaw in this story – whale sharks do not occur in the English Channel. Could this be another variation on the John Bartley story? Davis believes that both this and the sperm whale story are one and the same – probably evidence of a young opportunist making a quick buck in a freak show in the wake of the Gorleston Whale exhibition. The story switched from mammal to fish at some stage, an added bonus being that two English boats of 16–20 tonnes (32,000–40,000lb), and both with the name *Star of the East*, were registered with Lloyd's at about the same time as the 234 tonne (468,000lb) barque, giving the story a degree of credibility.

The only other sizeable known sea creature that could possibly take a person whole is the killer whale or orca (*Orcinus orca*), the largest and fastest member of the dolphin family. A large specimen was once found with thirteen porpoises and fourteen seals in its stomach; it had choked on a fifteenth seal. A killer whale shot off the Pacific coast of the USA had eighteen fur seals in its stomach. Killer whales occur in the Mediterranean but they seem to be more interested in the tuna caught by fishermen in the Straits of Gibraltar than in the people themselves.

How about a giant grouper? Groupers have been known to grow to more than 2.4m (8ft) long and weigh nearly half a tonne (1,000lb). There are stories among oilmen of giants such as these actually swallowing oilrig divers whole, and if this sounds fanciful, the experiences of J T L Ponds might make us think again. He and his workmate, named Jake, were inspecting an oil rig in the Gulf of Mexico, and being harassed by an especially large grouper; it was 'big enough to swallow a VW', according to Ponds. Every time it opened its mouth, a strong current would draw in fish, and as it approached the two divers they could feel the movement of the water. As Ponds relates:

> Suddenly I seen Jake's feet sticking out this here fish's mouth . . . So I grabbed his lifelines and started pulling hard. Nothing happened. That fish just remained there without so much as blinking one of those big eyes of his. That gave me a sudden inspiration. I hit him square in the eye with one of my fists. He just spit Jake out.

Exciting as this tale sounds, groupers do not grow to this size in the Mediterranean. The maximum length for the dogtooth grouper (*Epinephelus caninus*) is 1.5m (5ft), while the dusky grouper (E. *guaza*) reaches no more than 1.4m (4.6ft) in length. The wreck fish (*Polyprion americanum*) can reach up to 2m (6.6ft) long. They are long-lived species, so who is not to say that in biblical times, without factory fishing fleets and such like, fish might have been allowed to grow to their natural adult size and that some of them were real giants?

There is an Arabic version of the Jonah story. It is included in an anonymous text from the thirteenth century and is retold in a modern tome (*La Planète des Baleines*) about whales co-authored by Yves Paccalet and the late Jacque-Yves Cousteau. The story tells how Allah rescued Jonah (Yunus or Dhun-Nun in Arabic) from the belly of a fish and cast him ashore at a place 'seven parasangs above Mossul, on the Euphrates, that is now called *Bait*, which means Castaway'. In this version of the Jonah story the fish might well have been a freshwater fish, such as a European catfish or wels (*Silurus glanis*).

The wels has been dubbed 'man-eater' in some parts of Europe, for it grows up to 4.6m (15ft) long and sports a mouth that can be more than 60cm (2ft) across. A fish of this size could easily take a child, and there are stories of it taking larger prey. One tale, for example, features two young Hungarian girls who had gone to the river to collect water when a gigantic catfish took them. Another tells of a wels, caught by a fisherman in Turkey, that contained the body of a young woman.

The interesting thing about these catfish is that they swallow their prey whole. They do not bite off pieces like sharks tend to do, nor do they chew. With a little stretch of the imagination, it is not inconceivable that a giant fish could swallow a modest-sized human whole, and that the victim could be still alive when passing down the throat and into the stomach. There are, however, no records of prey – whether dead or alive – being spewed out again.

Another freshwater predator that could have gobbled up an Arabic Jonah and spat him out is the bull shark (*Carcharhinus leucas*), or *jarjur* in Arabic. It is thought by some authorities to be the most dangerous of all species of sharks, but it differs from most others by regularly entering rivers, including the Tigris and Euphrates, and attacking prey some distance from the sea. The prey could sometimes include people. Which is exactly what happened during the Second World War at Ahwaz in Iran, about 145km (90 miles) from the coast. A British soldier was washing the mud from his ambulance in the River Karun (a tributary of the Tigris) when he stepped down into about a foot of water. Suddenly, a shark grabbed him. He was caught off balance and fell in, and there he fought for his life in water no deeper than that in a bathtub. He defended himself as best he could with his arms and fists, but his right arm was torn open, his hands were slashed and his leg was badly lacerated. The shark was probably a youngster, for bull sharks go into estuaries, rivers and lakes to drop their pups, but the mother must have been there at some time and woe betide anyone who went bathing in deeper water.

Apparently, many rivers entering the Persian Gulf have been the sites of shark attacks. The Danish marine biologists Blegvad and Loppenthin, who studied the fishes of the Iranian Gulf, indicated that there have been many attacks by bull sharks in the region, particularly on children playing in rivers.

Adult bull sharks grow to about 3.5m (11.5ft) long, so even a large specimen would be a little too small to swallow an adult human whole. They also tend to bite chunks off large prey, rather than swallow it whole. Anyway, as with the great white shark, their saw-like teeth would damage anything passing through the mouth and into the throat. That said, could Fergusson's suggestion be relevant here, too? Could a large female bull shark have been caught in a river in the Middle East and her stomach sliced open to reveal parts of a person inside? And could this have given rise to the folk tale of an Arabic Jonah?

4

RED IN TOOTH AND CLAW

Awhole range of powerful meat-eaters – bears, lions, leopards, cheetahs, hyenas and wolves, as well as some of their smaller brethren (wild cats, caracals, lynxes, foxes and jackals) – once inhabited the Bible lands. Miraculously, many of them are still there despite humankind's best endeavours to eradicate them. Down the aeons, people have tried to hunt or poison them, or have inadvertently destroyed their habitat and eliminated their prey, but many species have survived. Only the lion has disappeared altogether from the wild.

LION

Lions were relatively common in the ancient Bible lands, so they would have been part of country people's everyday experience, an animal to be both feared and revered. The lion's roar would have been very familiar among the hills and valleys of the Holy Land, though the lion itself would have been a threat to both people and livestock.

Many references in the Bible, however, tend to be metaphorical more than zoological. The lion is used as a way to describe human qualities that are 'lion-like', such as valiant warriors who have 'the heart of a lion' (2 Samuel 17:10) or the Israelites compared to people who 'rise like a lioness; they rouse themselves like a lion' (Numbers 23:24). Judah – Jacob's fourth son – received a special mention because he was likened to a lion cub; he was strong and had special leadership qualities (Genesis 49: 8–12).

It is this picture of majesty, courage and power that led to the lion being regarded as the universal symbol of sovereignty, the 'King of Beasts' – 'The lion which is mightiest among beasts and does not turn back before any' (Proverbs 30:30).

Down the millennia, many of the ancient cultures in Europe, Africa and Asia have at one time or another credited their leaders with these same qualities. In the New Testament even Jesus was likened to a lion. A roaring lion was a symbol of the kingdom of Judea, and in a dream experienced by John, Jesus is described as 'the Lion of the Tribe of Juda' (Revelation 5:5).

In some cultures fighting a lion was thought to be the ultimate test of leadership, and granted the warrior the right to be sovereign and guardian of the land and the people. Wearing a lion-skin robe or walking on a lion-skin rug was a right reserved for kings. In some African societies the bravery and strength of warriors tested when, armed with no more than a spear, knife or bow and arrow, they come face to face with a lion. In East Africa, for example, Masai and Samburu youths must spear a lion to prove their manhood. Biblical characters have shown their worth by performing similar feats. The first biblical encounter between man and lion involved Samson, who was on his way to marry a Philistine girl at the time:

> So Samson went down to Timnah with his father and mother. As they were going through the vineyards there, he heard a young lion roar. Suddenly the power of the Lord made Samson strong and he tore the lion apart with his bare hands, as if it were a young goat.
>
> Judges 14:5

Later in the Bible, David recalls the time he killed a lion (and a bear) that had been stalking his father's sheep. He did this in order to persuade a sceptical King Saul that he was tough enough to fight Goliath of Gath (1 Samuel 17:35). Goliath, incidentally, was probably the victim of the disease 'multiple endocrine neoplasia, type one', according to doctors at Vanderbilt University in Texas. It is a malignant disorder of the glands, and symptoms include poor eyesight and a softening of the bones. So, when the giant Goliath faced the diminutive David he was unaware that the small, round pebble, carefully chosen from a stream, that David released from his slingshot would smash through the softened bone of his forehead and penetrate his brain. In many cultures lions were invested with divine powers. In Greek mythology, for example, the Nemean lion was a powerful creature with skin that could not be penetrated by arrows or spears. It was defeated eventually by the legendary hero Heracles as the first of twelve labours set by King Eurystheus. It was these legendary powers, attributed to lions, that also inspired the writers of the Bible, and the beast was used to represent the power of evil that could be overcome only with God's help. In Proverbs 28:15 the 'wicked ruler' is as 'dangerous as a growling lion' and in Psalm 57:4 there is a cry for help because 'I am surrounded by enemies, who are like man-eating lions'. Peter even likens the lion to the devil.

> Be sober, be vigilant; because your adversary the devil
> as a roaring lion, walketh about, seeking whom he may
> devour . . .

> 1 Peter 5:8

In other situations the powerful lion became an instrument that delivered the wrath of the Lord. Lions were sent by God to teach the Samaritans a lesson.

They feared not the Lord: therefore the Lord sent lions among them, which slew some of them.

2 Kings 17:25

And there is the story of a pacifist prophet at the time of the Syrian wars.

At the Lord's command a member of a group of prophets ordered a fellow prophet to hit him. But he refused, so he said to him, 'Because you have disobeyed the Lord's command, a lion will kill you as soon as you leave me'. And as soon as he left, a lion came along and killed him.

1 Kings 20:35–36

Similarly, Joshua upset the Lord and was reminded of His power when a lion pulled him off his donkey. Fortunately, neither Joshua nor the donkey was harmed. The lion just stood and waited; it was on God's business, unlike the one that attacked and killed the disobedient prophet who was coming out of Judah on his way to Bethel (1 Kings 23:24).

In the wild, lions tend not to attack and kill people randomly; they are not the all-powerful, fearless predators we tend to think. Cautious, they usually flee when people approach but occasionally they do attack people. One of the earliest records of a man-eating lion appears to be an Assyrian ivory panel from Nimrud dating back to the eighth century BCE, which depicts a man being grabbed at the throat by a lion. The panel is exhibited at the British Museum in London.

One of the most successful man-eating prides ever was the Njombe Man-eaters, a group of seventeen East African lions that went on a fifteen-year rampage at the northern end of Lake Nvasa in Tanzania. They accounted for more than 1,500 human deaths. The most unusual series of fatalities took place between 1896 and 1898 during the building of the Uganda Line, a railway between Mombasa and Kampala, in East Africa. The work had reached the Tsavo River in Kenya, where a bridge was being constructed. Two male lions, each with the sparse mane typical of the region, systematically attacked railway workers camped out along the line. People took to hiding up trees, in stockades, station buildings and even railway carriages but the lions always found their way in, and every night without fail they made a kill. The lions seemed almost mystical and the workers were terrified.

It is quite possible that in biblical times people in the Middle East were exposed to similar dangers, especially those tending flocks of sheep and goats at night. We are reminded of the dangers in Christmas carols, such as 'While Shepherds Watched Their Flocks By Night'. Before he became a prophet, Amos was a shepherd from the town of Tekoa. He lived and preached during the mid-eighth century BCE and in his scriptures he sometimes refers to events that might well have been based on personal experiences.

> Does a lion roar in the forest unless he had found a victim? Does a young lion growl in his den unless he has caught something?

> The Lord says, 'As a shepherd recovers only two legs or an ear of a sheep that a lion has eaten, so only a few will survive of Samaria's people . . .'

> Amos 3:4 and 12

There are several similar references indicating that some of the Bible writers (or friends and acquaintances from whom they obtained their inspiration) had personal experience of wildlife encounters at first hand. Isaiah, for instance, drew upon a field observation when he wrote about God's determination to protect Mount Zion.

> The Lord said to me, 'No matter how shepherds yell and shout, they can't scare away a lion from an animal it has killed; in the same way, there is nothing that can keep me, the Lord Almighty, from protecting Mount Zion. Just as a bird hovers over its nest to protect its young, so I, Lord Almighty, will protect Jerusalem and defend it.'

> Isaiah 30:4

In all, there are about 156 biblical references, 135 of them in the Old Testament. In fact, the lion is mentioned more times than any other wild beast. There are several Hebrew words for 'lion', the most common being *aryeh*, while *cepheer* refers to a young lion and *labi* to an old one. *Laish* indicates an all-powerful, full-grown lion in his prime and is usually the word used in poetry.

The lion had an inauspicious debut and in Hebrew legend it was ill all the time and not very keen on the dry food it was forced to eat. By all accounts it was miserable, and when Noah failed to feed it one day, the lion slashed him on the leg, causing him to be lame for the rest of his life. The deformity meant that Noah could never be a priest.

In zoological terms, there were two types of lion seen in and around the Middle East and the Mediterranean in biblical times. They were the Asiatic lion, *Panthera leo persica*, and the Barbary lion, *Panthera leo leo*, both subspecies of the African lion, so familiar on wildlife films. Each of these lions has its own characteristic features. The Asiatic lion is stockier and has a thicker coat than its African counterpart, and its tail has a longer tassel. The fringe of hair on the belly is more pronounced and the tuft of hair on the elbows is more prominent. On male Asiatic lions the mane is less impressive than their African cousins. There is also the paler-coloured western Asian lion.

Today, the Asian subspecies is confined to the Gir forest, a relatively small patch of land in the northwestern part of India, but it was once more widespread. When Xerxes I of Persia (son of Darius I) made his way through Macedonia in a campaign to conquer the Greeks in 480 BCE, several of his camels were killed by lions. Herodotus (484–430 BCE) noted that lions occurred in large numbers between the River Archelous in Acarnania and the River Nechus in the historical district of Thrace located on the Bulgarian-Turkish border. The Greek philosopher Aristotle mentions wild lions present in Greece in 300 BCE. These may have been related to both the Asiatic and the Barbary races, a genetic intermediary between the two. When they disappeared from Europe is unclear Some experts believe they were all gone by the first century BCE, while others consider they didn't become extinct until some time between CE 80 and CE 100.

The Crusaders frequently encountered Asiatic lions on their Middle East expeditions and the crusading English king was known as Richard the Lionheart. Indeed, they were found across the Middle East to northern India until the end of the nineteenth century. The prevalence of firearms in the region resulted in lions being virtually wiped out. However, zoos and safari parks worldwide have undertaken an intense programme of breeding and today the captive population of Asiatic lions is relatively healthy, though not genetically pure, many captive animals labelled 'Asiatic' actually being hybrids. Hybrid or not, they have been so successful that some zoos have had to put their lions on contraceptives!

The lion that was a favourite in the gladiatorial arenas of ancient Rome was a separate subspecies – the Barbary lion from North Africa, also known as the Atlas, Nubian or Berber lion. Some, but not all, male Barbary lions had the largest and darkest manes and belly fringe of all the subspecies, rivalled only by the mane of the smaller Cape lion, and appeared distinctly noble – most definitely the 'king of beasts'. The long belly fringe extended to the groin and the blond hair around the face gave the male lion a distinctive golden halo.

The Barbary lion was a massive animal. Reports exist of male specimens weighing in excess of 270kg (600lb) compared with today's African and Asian lions weighing in at 160–200kg (350–450lb). It had shorter legs and a longer body, so it would have been several centimetres shorter than its cousins but considerably longer. Sir Alfred Pease, the British big-game hunter and collector and author of *The Book of the Lion*, heard of a Barbary lion in Algeria with a head, body and tail length of 3.25m (11ft). Its head and body alone were about 2.5m (8ft) long, and it stood about 95cm (3ft) at the shoulder. There have been reports of lions 5.2m (17ft) long, though this was thought to be greatly exaggerated.

In the wild, Barbary lions once lived in semi-arid areas of sparsely forested mountains, river courses and oases to the north of the Sahara, in a region stretching from Morocco in the west to Egypt and Sudan in the east. They were less social than those living elsewhere. Food was, and still is, scarce in these parts so the lions behaved much like other solitary cats, living alone or in pairs. Their prey would have included the Barbary stag and gazelle, and domestic sheep, goats and horses. Each lion had a home range centred on a reliable source of water, which it shared with other predators such as the extinct Barbary leopard (see below) and Atlas bear (see below).

Barbary lions were annihilated mainly by hunters and are now extinct in the wild. The last truly wild ones survived in the Atlas Mountains until the early twentieth century. A farmer in Morocco shot the last remaining lion in 1922, though a few animals matching the description of Barbary lions were kept and bred in captivity.

Today, scientists from Oxford University's Wildlife Conservation Research Unit are using DNA analysis of living animals and museum specimens to try to identify lions in zoos and wildlife parks with Barbary blood. Unfortunately, zoos and circuses of the past cared little for the genetic source of their lions and so most in captivity belong to what can only be described as a 'mongrel' breed. The Rabat Zoo in Morocco is the only place where a collection of lions has a pedigree that can be traced directly to nineteenth-century Barbary stock in the Atlas Mountains. In that century the Berbers brought the lions to Morocco as living 'taxes' to the Sultan. They were kept at the royal palaces in Marrakech and Fez, and survived wars and disease. Eventually, the exile of the Sultan deprived them of their palatial living space but in the 1970s some were brought together at Rabat and to ensure a local cataclysm did not wipe them out, individuals were sent to other zoos. There are thought to be about sixty or so surviving worldwide and an International Barbary Lion project managed by WildLink International is co-ordinating efforts to breed and return them to the wild. The offspring of Rabat's royal lions and selected descendants from around the world, including several zoos and private collections in the USA and South Africa, and the Port Lymphe Zoo in England, are to be released into a proposed 400 sq km (155 sq miles) reserve – between the Middle and High Atlas Mountains.

One of the Barbary lion collections is from Ethiopia, where it was the tradition for the head of state to keep lions. One story tells how Emperor Lebna Dengel (1508–40) was forced to move his court from one centre to another, and it is recorded that four lions headed the huge procession of people and animals. This tradition of keeping lions was retained into more recent times. Emperor Haile Selassie I called himself 'The Lion of Judah' and kept a pet lion in his palace at Addis Ababa. More lions languished in cages in the palace grounds and it is these lions that are thought to be of Barbary stock and so able to contribute to the reintroduction programme.

In ancient times, the Barbary lion was undoubtedly the subspecies that was the subject of many sculptures, friezes, mosaics and paintings, featuring strongly in the Roman circus, as well as on many ancient Roman buildings. Caligula had a tame lion that he called Acinaces, meaning 'scimitar', because it could cut off a man's life with one bite to the neck, and Mark Anthony is supposed to have driven two lions in Rome. Across the Mediterranean, Hanno, the Carthaginian general, kept a lion as a pet.

The Barbary lion also featured strongly in European heraldry and classic paintings. In 1144 Henry the Lion, Duke of Saxony, was one of the first to include the lion on a coat of arms and the lion, possibly a Barbary lion, treated by St Jerome in a monastery in Syria (c CE 400) is depicted in a painting with a heavy black mane. In ancient Egypt statues of Barbary lions were placed at the entrances of palaces to protect the king from evil. Some Egyptian kings went even further, their palaces being guarded by the real thing. It is quite possible that when Moses and Aaron paid a visit to the Pharoah's palace in Egypt, Barbary lions protected the grounds. They had to wait for the lion keeper to put away his charges before they could enter. These beasts would have made frightening 'guard-dogs', a fact not missed by many other architects of the great palaces. Solomon's palace, for instance, had a magnificent throne guarded by stone lions.

> The throne had six steps leading up to it, with the figure of a Lion at each end of every step, a total of twelve lions. At the back of the throne was the figure of a bull's head, and beside each of the two arms was the figure of a lion.

> 1 Kings 10:19–20

Images of lions are found in ancient ruins throughout the region, such as on friezes around buildings. On a mural from the Processional Way in Babylon (c 580 BCE), for example, a striding lion with a dark mane, possibly a Barbary lion, is shown baring its teeth. It was in Babylon that the Hebrew prophet Daniel had his famous ordeal in the lions' den. The lions belonged to King Darius I the Great of Persia (550–486 BCE), though whether they were used to guard his palace, execute criminals or bred for hunting is unclear. Many ancient kings are reported to have killed lions from horse-drawn chariots, and it is quite likely that they reared lions for the specific purpose of hunting them.

In earlier times, the Egyptian pharaoh Amenhotep III the Magnificent (ruled 1417–1379 BCE) hunted lions from an open chariot and killed them using just a bow and arrow. He dispatched more than a hundred during his lifetime, a hunting tradition that he took up from his father and grandfather. His son Tutankhamen (1361–1352 BCE) is also depicted hunting lions from a chariot. King Ashurnasirapal II (883–859 BCE) of Assyria hunted specially bred lions, rearing them at a zoological garden in the reconstructed city of Calah (now Nimrud in Iraq). Ashurnasirapal (ruled 668–627 BCE), who was known as the 'Hunting King' and was the last of the great kings of Assyria, continued the sport. He had his image as a great lion hunter immortalised in bas-relief on the walls of the ancient city of Nineveh with the epitaph 'I killed the lion'.

Interest in lions was not confined to hunting them, however. In the ancient world the lion often attained sacred status. The Egyptian goddesses Tefnut and Sekhmet both had lion heads. Sometimes the lion was combined with other animals to create fabulous hybrids: the Egyptian pharaohs were represented as lion-bodied sphinxes; the Assyrian bearded kings were depicted as huge winged lions with human heads; the Sumerian rain god, Ningirsu, was a thundercloud depicted as a black eagle with outstretched wings roaring a thunder-like cry from a lion's head; and the gryphon, a mythological figure with a lion's body and an eagle's head, was a popular decorative motif in the ancient Near East and Mediterranean lands. Indeed, it appears that the lion was used as an icon, with or without additions, throughout the ancient civilised world.

Asian lions and Foo-dogs (lion dogs) stand guard at the entrances of Chinese, Burmese and Japanese shrines and pagodas, while stone lions mount guard outside Hittite fortresses. The Greeks built the Lion Gate at the prehistoric city of Mycenae in around 1250 BCE, and an enormous statue of Fo, a stylised snarling lion that appears on Chinese pottery, set on a large base overlooks the battlefield of Chaeronea, an ancient fortified town that guarded the entrance to the northern plain of Boeotia, where Philip II of Macedon and his son Alexander defeated a Greek army in 338 BCE. Bertel Thorvaldsen's 'Lion of Lucerne' (built 1819–21) is cut into a cliff in remembrance of the heroic stand and sad loss of the Swiss Guard defending the Tuileries in Paris in 1792; in *A Tramp Abroad*, Mark Twain describes this carving of a dying lion as 'the most mournful and moving piece of stone in the world'.

LEOPARD

The Bible lands have been, and still are, home to a second big cat: the leopard *Panthera pardis*. Throughout the ages, it has been known by several different common English names – spotted tiger, panther, pard, pardal or lippard – and at one time or another the word 'leopard' has been applied to lions, pumas, servals, lynx and caracals. The cheetah was known as a hunting leopard and the ounce as the snow leopard. With so many names, there are ample opportunities for the Bible translators to be confused. Topsell spotted the chance for misunderstanding:

> There have beene so many names devised for this one beast, that it is growen a difficult things, either to make a good reconciliation of the authors which are wed to their opinions, or else to define it perfectly and make of him a good and methodical History.

He didn't help things himself. Following the error introduced by the ancient Romans, who thought the leopard was a cross between a lion and a pard or panther, Topsell states that the panther is the female and the pard the male. He compounded the mistake by telling us:

> When the lion covereth the Pardal, then is the whelp called a leopard or libbard; but when the Pardal covereth the lioness, that it is called a Panther.

And, to make matters worse, Topsell continued:

> The Pardal is a fierce and cruell beast very violent, having a body and mind like ravening birds, and some say they are ingendered now and then betwixt dogs and panthers, or betwixt leopards and dogges, even as the Lycopanthers are ingendered betwixt wolves and panthers.

Today, despite all this covering and betwixting, we are still left with the word 'leo-pard' or 'lion-panther'. The former is mentioned in the Old Testament seven times and in the New Testament just once. The Hebrew word is *namer*, which is similar to the Arabic *nimr*, and can be seen in place names mentioned in the Bible, such as Nimrah (Numbers 32:3), Bethnimrah (Numbers 32:36) and 'the waters of Nimrim' (Isaiah 15:6). Solomon's love song also included a place frequented by leopards.

> Come with me from Lebanon, my spouse, with me from Lebanon: look from the top of Amana, from the top of Shenir and Hermon, from the lions' dens, from the mountains of the leopards.
>
> Song of Solomon 4:8

Even today, a number of wadis and springs in Israel bear the name of the leopard, such as Wadi-en-Numeir, meaning 'valley of the little leopard'. It enters the eastern side of the Dead Sea south of the Arnon. In recent times, people who lived in villages with the leopard name were skilled in processing leopard skins. Clearly, the leopard's wonderfully coloured coat has been treasured for centuries, a symbol of power and savagery that has given us an expression that we still use today.

> Can the Ethiopian change his skin, or the leopard his spots? Then may ye also do good, that are accustomed to do evil.
>
> Jeremiah 13:23

The leopard of the Bible was a bigger and paler version of its Asian and African cousins, so large-bodied that even well-informed travellers often mistook its footprints for those of a lion. And, like the lion, it was a danger to shepherds, goat herds and their livestock, and was a big enough threat to be turned into fanciful nightmarish creatures such as the third beast in Daniel's dream (a reference to the invading Alexander of Macedon) and the blasphemous beast that rose out of the sea in the revelation to John.

> After this I beheld, and lo another, like leopard, which had upon the back of it four wings of fowl; the beats also had four heads; and dominion was given to it.
>
> Daniel 7:6

> And the beast which I saw was like the leopard, and his feet were as the feet of a bear, and his mouth as the mouth of a lion: and the dragon gave him his power, and his seat, and great authority.
>
> Revelation 13:2

The leopard was undoubtedly feared in biblical times, and rightly so: it is one of the most wily and dangerous of the big cats. Some wild felines have a penchant for human flesh. The Indian big cat specialist Dunbar Brander once noted that, 'Owing to their knowledge of man's way and being habituated to enter villages at night, [leopards] will enter a hut and drag out their victim from his cot.' He went on to conclude: 'From a man-eating leopard . . . people have no security at all.'

This was borne out by one attack described in big-game hunter Jim Corbett's book *Man-eating Leopard of Rudraprayag*. He describes how a fourteen-year-old orphan boy and his herd of forty goats were locked away in a small room each night by the herd's owner, the boy's master. There were no windows in the room, and the single door was 'locked' with a slither of wood jammed through the catch. The boy placed a stone against his side of the door. One night a leopard came. It clawed at the door, dislodging the wood, and then pushed hard against the rock, shoving the door ajar. Once inside, it ignored the goats, but took the boy as he slept. The goats escaped but none was harmed. In the morning the goats' owner found the boy's remains in a deep ravine close to the village. Despite sleeping immediately above the room, the man had heard nothing.

If this can happen to a person who is supposedly safely locked away, imagine how dangerous it would have been in leopard country for a goat herd or shepherd. Many livestock keepers in biblical times would have had to remain in the open, and would have been constantly afraid of attack. Solomon drew upon this fear. He was reputed to have golden leopards on the steps to his throne, and by some mechanical means or other they could be made to growl as someone approached.

The real leopard of the Bible could have been one of several different subspecies. The largest was the Anatolian leopard (*Panthera pardus tulliana*), of which only a few survived into the twentieth century in the Caucasus and in the Taurus Mountains of Turkey. In North Africa the range of the Barbary leopard (P. *p. panthera*) extended into Egypt, where the last survivors were seen in the Western Desert in 1932. The Arabian leopard (P. *p. nimr*) and Persian leopard (P. *p. saxicolor*) are scarce throughout their range but are still hanging on today.

The Sinai leopard (*P. p. jarvisi*) – probably the main subspecies described in the Bible – was very common at the time the Bible was written, and was still relatively widespread when Tristram visited the region in the mid-nineteenth century. He found traces of leopards at the southeastern end of the Dead Sea, in the forests of Gilead and on Mt Tabor and Mt Carmel. After the great earthquake of Safed in 1837, leopards were seen to search the ruins for dead bodies, and in 1911 leopards were shot close to Jerusalem – killed for their skins, which were valued by officials and the fashion conscious. Today, leopards are still found beyond the Jordan and in the Syrian Desert, despite the well-armed and trigger-happy locals who will blast away at anything that moves.

Despite all this persecution, the leopard is still the most widespread of the big cats. It is a highly adaptable species, living in any habitat from swampy tropical rainforests to hot or cold deserts and rugged mountain areas up to 5,500m (18,000ft) above sea level. It moves silently, though at dusk it might give its presence away with a harsh call like the sound of wood being sawn. It can climb trees with ease, leap 3m (10ft) vertically and accelerate up to a speed of 65km/h (40mph).

The leopard hunts mainly at night, but will be abroad on misty or overcast days. It is an ambush predator, lying in wait in the undergrowth or in a tree for its unsuspecting prey to pass by, and even staking out a village or watering place, waiting for domestic stock to be left unattended. It was a form of behaviour that the Bible writers applied to the prophets and God's judgement of the Jews:

> Therefore I will be unto them as a lion: as a leopard by
> the way will I observe them.
>
> Hosea 13:7

Wherefore a lion out of the forest shall slay them, and a wolf of the evenings shall spoil them, a leopard shall watch over their cities: every one that goeth out thence shall be torn in pieces: because their transgressions are many, and their backslidings are increased.

Jeremiah 5:6

In several of the Bible references to the leopard, the lion is mentioned, too. Leopards and lions would have shared the same living space, just as they do today in East Africa. They would not have been direct competitors, for the lion was more likely to hunt on open ground and the leopard in woodland or rocky areas. Nevertheless, an unlucky leopard could well have had his prey stolen from right under his nose by a powerful lion.

CHEETAH

While most references to the leopard in the Bible are thought to be accurate, there is one passage about the strength and speed of the Chaldean cavalry that may be a mistranslation: 'Their horses also are swifter than the leopards, and are more fierce than the evening wolves: and their horsemen shall spread themselves, and their horsemen shall come from afar; they shall fly as the eagle that hasteth to eat' (Habakkuk 1:8).

The emphasis here on speed seems to suggest not the leopard but the cheetah (*Acinonyx jubatus*), known in some countries, such as India, as the 'hunting-leopard'. The cheetah is not mentioned by name in the Bible, but a subspecies – the Asian cheetah (*A. j. venaticus*, though there is some question about its true taxonomic status) – was present in Bible lands until quite recently. Tristram recorded cheetahs in the neighbourhood of Tabor and in the hills of Galilee in the nineteenth century. He was presented with three cheetah skins by a sheikh whose people had shot the animals in Gilead. In fact, the species was recorded in Syria, Palestine, Iran,

Iraq and the northern parts of the Arabian Peninsula, its range stretching from southern Africa to Bengal in India. Today, the cheetah is very rare outside Africa, though small pockets of animals might still survive in wilderness areas, such as the eastern deserts of Iran. An individual cheetah stalking sheep in the desert not far from the Cairo-Alexandria road was shot in May 1967.

The cheetah is the most streamlined of cats. It relies not on the slow, stealthy stalk of the leopard but on swift pursuit. It has long legs, a flexible spine that enables it to lengthen its stride, a long tail that serves as a counterbalance when turning, and permanently exposed claws that act like spiked running shoes. Its top speed can be in excess of 97km/h (60mph); one individual was timed running at 82km/h (51mph) behind a car for a distance of 55m (183ft).

It was this skill, and the fact that cheetahs can be tamed and trained relatively easily, that attracted 'sports' hunters. A Mesopotamian seal, dated from the third millennium BCE, bears the image of a cheetah being led on a leash. Egyptian tombs and rock temples have representations of tame cheetahs, which suggests that at certain times in ancient Egypt's past they rivalled dogs as hunting companions. The Assyrians also used cheetahs, and the Minoans imported them from Egypt. In Syria and Palestine the Crusaders wrote of how they watched gazelles being hunted with cheetah (though they referred to them as leopards), and one king in Armenia was reputed to have more than a hundred cheetahs kept for hunting. Few European courts in the fifteenth century were without their cheetahs, and in India hunting with cheetahs seems to have been going on since ancient times.

Akbar the Great, who extended the Mughal power on the Indian subcontinent at the time the Authorised Version (AV) was translated, owned countless hunting cheetahs for coursing gazelles, antelope and deer. Abu Fazil, his biographer, recalls one of the hunts:

It chanced that they loosed a special cheetah called Chitr Najan at a deer. Suddenly there appeared in front of them a ravine which was twenty-five yards broad. The deer leapt into the air to the height of a spear and a half and conveyed itself across. The cheetah in its eagerness took the same course, cleared the ravine and seized the deer. On beholding this astonishing occurrence the spectators raised a cry of amazement, and there was a great rejoicing and astonishment. The Emperor raised the rank of that cheetah and made him chief of the cheetahs. He also ordered that as a special honour and as a pleasure to men, a drum should be beaten in front of the cheetah.

SMALL CATS

Other cats present in the region include the Eurasian lynx (*Lynx lynx*) and the caracal or desert lynx (*Felis caracal*); neither is mentioned in the Bible. The lynx is a medium-sized cat with a short tail and tufted ears. It preys on small mammals, such as hares, rabbits and mice, but according to the Tartars of Central Asia it will also take sheep and goats. The lynx hunts at night, yet uses mainly vision to find its prey. A tame lynx kept by Waldemar Lindemann could see a mouse at 75m (250ft), a hare at 300m (1,000ft) and a roe-deer at 500m (1,600ft). Tristram observed one in Palestine and obtained lynx skins from local people. Today, it is found in the wooded areas of Galilee and Jordan, and has also been reported in Iran and the Kurdish Mountains of Iraq.

The caracal or desert lynx, despite its alternative common name, is not related but it has tufted ears like the lynx. It has acquired its name from the Turkish word *garahgulak*, meaning 'black-ear'. This cat is the origin of the expression 'to put the cat among the pigeons', because in India caracals were once taken into an arena with a flock of pigeons. Two caracals were pitted against each other, and bets were taken as to how many birds each caracal could bring down before the flock escaped; ten to a dozen was the usual number.

Like the lynx, the caracal is widespread from southern Africa to central India, but avoids the more barren parts of hot deserts. It is found in the Naqab Desert and the Dead Sea Depression. The caracal is a solitary, nocturnal hunter and is adept at climbing if necessary; it can jump well, too, and will knock down fleeing birds before they have time to gain height. In the Middle East sand rats, jerboas and hares might be on the menu. In Iran and India it has been trained for hunting.

Of the smaller cats, the domestic cat (*F. domestica*) was tamed by the Egyptians. There is only one biblical reference to it, in the Apocrypha, and it is surprising that although the Jews had a historical connection with Egypt there should not be a single mention in the rest of the Bible. Similarly, the classical authors of Greece and Rome did not mention it, yet today it has the same worldwide distribution and popularity as the domestic dog, and is common throughout the Bible lands.

The single reference is in the Apocrypha of Baruch the son of Neriah, secretary to and companion of the prophet Jeremiah. It was written about CE 100, after the destruction of Jerusalem, and questions the relationship between God and man. The relevant passage occurs in the Epistle of Jeremy: 'Upon their bodies and heads sit bats, swallows, and birds, and the cats also' (Baruch 6:22). These are thought to be wild cats rather than domestic or feral cats, and there are several contenders for their identity. First and foremost is the ancestor to the domestic cat, the African wild cat (*F. sylvestris lybica*). It is larger and stockier than its tame relative, but resembles a pale striped tabby. The patterning is paler in cats living in more arid environments, though this species is not a desert cat. Its more northerly relative is the more burly European wild cat (*F. s. silvestris*), whose range is known to extend to the Caucasus. Then, there is a distribution gap between the African and European wild cats that coincides with the Holy Lands. Here

Arabia and Palestine have been home to another subspecies, *F. s. iraki*, which is closely allied to the African wild cat. This cat thrives in almost any kind of country, but it is rarely seen. It hides in a tree or a rock crevice by day, preferring to hunt at night. For food it takes mainly rodents and hares, but when a drought hits the area it will turn to lizards, beetles, grasshoppers and crickets, and may even try a date or two. Although wild cats shun people, they often live alongside homesteads and villages, and people in the recent past have taken them from the wild and introduced them to captivity. Georg Schweinfurth, a nineteenth-century botanist and explorer, encountered the practice in the country south of Bahr el Ghazal in Sudan. In *Heart of Africa* he wrote:

> One of the commonest animals hereabouts was the wildcat of the steppes. Although the natives do not breed them as domestic animals, yet they catch them separately when they are young and find no difficulties in reconciling them to a life about their huts and enclosures, where they grow up and wage their natural warfare against the rats. I procured several of these cats, which, after they had been kept tied up for several days, seemed to lose a considerable measure of their ferocity and to adapt themselves to an indoor existence so as to approach in many ways to the habits of the common cat. By night I attached them to my parcels, which were otherwise in jeopardy, and by this means I could go to bed without further fear of any depredation from the rats.

Schweinfurth was witnessing a process that must have taken place thousands of years previously in Palestine and Egypt. Archaeological evidence indicates that tabbies roamed the streets of Jericho in the late sixth millennium BCE, and at a similarly dated site at Hacilar in western Turkey statuettes of women playing with cats have been found. The cat appeared in Egypt about 2000 BCE.

African wild cats and domestic cats have been found as mummies in Egyptian tombs, a fate shared by another species, the jungle or reed cat (*F. chaus chaus*). Its colour is similar to that of the Abyssinian breed of domestic cat, which brings into question the ancestry of the domestic cat. The jungle cat was tamed and trained in ancient times to hunt wildfowl. It is much larger than the African wild cat, however, and has a colour range from sandy-brown to reddish or grey-brown. The jungle cat has no flank markings, but has brown stripes on the legs. The ears are reddish and have lynx-like tufts. It has a short, ringed tail with a black tip. The kittens are striped for camouflage, but these colours are lost when they grow up. Jungle cats are found from Egypt to India, including Lower Egypt, Israel, Jordan, Syria, Iraq and Iran. They live in swampy areas with reed beds in Egypt and Iraq and in woodlands, scrub or agricultural areas in India. In the Jordan Valley they favour dense tamarisk woodlands.

Jungle cats hide in dens – usually the disused burrow of a badger, fox or porcupine – and do not restrict their hunting to night time. They move slowly and deliberately, stalking hares and game birds. Rats, mice, frogs and snakes appear in the diet, and they will even have a go at porcupines. They sometimes raid chicken coops.

Another species of small cat to be found in the Holy Land is the sand or sand-dune cat (*F. margarita*). Its scientific name derives from Commandant Margueritte, the leader of a French party that explored the Ouargla Oasis in the northern Sahara in 1855–56. The sand cat is one of the most widespread small cats in the world, yet it is also one of the rarest. It has the large ears so characteristic of small desert mammals, and its dense soft coat is the colour of pale sand with just a hint of stripes. The ears are a reddish-brown colour with black tips and a reddish streak runs from the eyes and across the cheeks. Its feet have pads of thick hair that prevent them from burning and provide traction on the hot, loose sand. The sand cat lives in burrows by day, and emerges to hunt at night, locating prey using its highly acute hearing. Little is known about its natural food, but from research carried out in Turkmenia it is thought that rodents make up 80 per cent of its diet. There are several subspecies that live in the deserts and semi-deserts from the Sahara to Pakistan, but the desert cat of the Middle East is *F. m. harrisoni*.

DOG

The domestic dog – *keleb* in Hebrew – was not liked in biblical times. In the countryside dogs were kept by shepherds to help watch flocks, and townsfolk tolerated dogs in the streets and at local rubbish tips, where they removed rotting meat. At night they kept up an incessant howling and barking, and the psalmist tells how packs of dogs often scavenged outside the city walls: 'They return at evening: they make a noise like a dog, and go round about the city' (Psalms 59:6).

The passage is from a prayer for deliverance from one's enemies, but it sets the tone for the way dogs were depicted in the Old Testament. They were not quite the lowest of the low, for that honour was left to the pig, but they were pretty close. In cities, apparently, they even devoured human bodies: 'Him that dieth of Jeroboam in the city shall the dogs eat'; 'Him that dieth of Baasha in the city shall the dogs eat'; 'Him that dieth of Ahab in the city the dogs shall eat' (1 Kings 14:11, 16:4, 21:24). They were also given any foods unfit for human consumption: 'And ye shall be holy men unto me: neither shall ye eat any flesh that is torn of beasts in the field; ye shall cast it to the dogs' (Exodus 22:31).

As a consequence, the word 'dog' became synonymous with the adjectives cowardly, lazy and dirty and was an extreme term of abuse. 'Beware of dogs', advised St Paul (Philippians 3:2); 'Am I a dog's head?' asked Abner (2 Samuel 3:8); and Mephibosheth said to King David: 'What is thy servant, that thou shouldest look upon such a dead dog as I am?' (2 Samuel 9:8). When applied to the speaker himself or herself, as in the latter case, the term 'dog' is a term of abject humility, but more usually it was used to show absolute disdain. Abishai the son of Zeruiah used 'dog' in unflattering terms: 'Why should this dead dog curse my lord the king? let me go over, I pray thee, and take off his head' (2 Samuel 16:9). Indeed, in the forty or so references to dogs in the Bible, there is scarcely a mention in which the animal is not spoken of with little more than contempt. It is said in Hebrew legend that when the Israelites looked back at the waters of the Red Sea closing on the Egyptians, dogs were gnawing the feet of their enemy's dead bodies – the final indignity.

In the New Testament dogs (or at least people referred to as dogs) were excluded from God's city. They appear in the last chapter of the last book of the Bible.

> Blessed are they that do his commandments, that they may have right to the tree of life, and may enter in through the gates into the city. For without are dogs, and sorcerers, and whoremongers, and murderers, and idolators, and whosoever loveth and maketh a lie.

Revelation 22:14–15

The dogs with which the Bible writers would have been familiar were pariah dogs, a breed of dog peculiar to the Middle East and southern Asia. In the company of people, they were used for herding stock or as guard dogs, but many of them simply wandered the countryside or the streets of towns in a wild or semi-wild state, living as scavengers. Some authorities believe they were feral dogs – that is, domestic dogs (*Canis familiaris*) that have been abandoned or have escaped and are living wild, some of them interbreeding with wild canids such as jackals and wolves. Others suggest that the pariah dog was a truly wild dog, like the dhole of India, and that only some were domesticated for flock-guarding duties. Tristram records that they resembled jackals, with 'short, sharp-pointed ears, sharp snout, generally a tawny coat and tail, scarcely bushy'. Whatever their origin, their history goes back thousands of years, and their images can be found on ancient monuments throughout the Bible lands. Today, public health campaigns have resulted in their numbers dwindling in the wild or semi-wild state.

In the 1930s, however, the pariah dog made something of a comeback to respectability when the Haganah (Jewish Defence Force) asked dog-breeder Professor Rudophina Menzel to set up a military dog division. Dogs traditionally used by the military elsewhere in the world would not have fared well in the arid climate of the region, so Menzel turned to the pariah dog, a breed that is able to survive with little food and water, and is well adapted to desert conditions. From several distinct types of pariahs she chose 'collie-like' dogs for her primary stock, and created what is now known as the Canaan dog. The pariah dog was first used by the military as a 'watch-dog' rather than as an attacking 'guard dog'. It is wary of strangers, will circle an intruder, and bark a warning. The dog is considered highly intelligent, is extremely alert and loves digging: the gardens of Canaan dogs kept as pets are always full of holes. The dog is also used in Israel as a guide dog for the blind. Today, it is Israel's national dog.

The Jewish people did not hunt with dogs, so the tradition of breeds specially bred for the chase was not evident in Palestine. Elsewhere in the Middle East, hunting with dogs, either as 'sport' or to gather food, was more common. As a consequence, the ancient Egyptians and other nations had several breeds of hunting dog, and these were probably the first dogs to be selectively bred. They included the Persian greyhound, which was used to hunt and bring down gazelles. The pharaohs and the rulers of Mesopotamia kept the greyhound, certainly from the fourth millennium BCE on, and its image was carved into tombs.

This greyhound was not the ultra-slim, short-haired animal we see at racetracks today, but a larger and stronger dog with long silky hair on the ears and belly, and a fringe of the same hair on the tail. It was similar to the saluki, a highly prized breed, though in ancient times it was not bought and sold but changed hands only when presented to visiting dignitaries. The Persian greyhound was not as swift as today's racing animals, but it had incredible endurance, and was highly prized by desert sheikhs. The greyhound appears in the AV as one of four things that are impressive to look at: "There be three things which go well, yea, four are comely in going: A lion which is strongest among beasts, and turneth not away for any; A greyhound; an he goat also, and a king, against whom there is no rising up' (Proverbs 30:29–31).

There is some debate over whether the AV translators have got this right, however. A marginal note offers 'horse' as an alternative, indicating they were unsure. The Septuagint suggests 'strut of the cock', which has been adopted by several modern translations. The Hebrew is *zarzir*, meaning 'girt in the loins', but it is not at all clear to which animal this refers. Some commentators suggest that it could refer to a warhorse with its ornamented girth, bridle and saddle; others have opted for the wild ass, which has a striped pattern about its loins. Whatever it is, it must be an animal that has 'stateliness and majesty of gait' rather than speed.

WOLF

References to the dog's wild ancestor are not ambiguous. Known as *zeeb* in Hebrew, *deeb* in Arabic and *lukos* in Greek, the wolf (*Canis lupus*) was not liked. It was, after all, one of the main predators of livestock and gained a less-than-flattering reputation as a consequence. Of the thirteen references in the Bible, the word 'wolf' is used mainly as a metaphor for greed and destructiveness: 'Benjamin shall ravin as a wolf: in the morning he shall devour the prey, and at night he shall divide the spoil' (Genesis 49:27); 'Her princes in the midst thereof are like wolves ravening the prey, to shed blood, and to destroy souls, to get dishonest gain' (Ezekiel 22:27). Benjamin – Jacob's youngest son – had the wolf as his emblem, and the tribes of Israel were compared to wolves, lions and serpents because they were unassailable.

In the New Testament Jesus used the wolf to illustrate the dangers confronting people who follow Him. He also gave us another expression that endures to this day: 'Behold, I send you forth as sheep in the midst of wolves: be ye therefore wise as serpents, and harmless as doves' (Matthew 10:16); 'For I know this, that after my departing shall grievous wolves enter in among you, not sparing the flock' (Acts 20:29); 'Beware of false prophets, which come to you in sheep's clothing, but inwardly they are ravening wolves' (Matthew 7:15).

Like any part of the world where the wolf is a threat to a person's livelihood, or even his life, the wolf has featured strongly in folklore. Hebrew legend is no exception. It is told that the Lord sent a plague of wolves into Egypt, because the captive Israelites had been forced to catch wolves (and lions) for the circus.

At the time of the AV translation, the wolf was alleged to have all manner of mystical powers, particularly if it was dead. Topsell recorded some of the claims:

> The brains of a wolf do decrease and increase with the moon. The neck of a wolf is short, which argueth a treacherous nature. If the heart of a wolf be kept dry, it rendereth a most pleasant and sweet-smelling savour . . . If any labouring or travelling man doth wear the skin of a wolf about his feet, his shoes shall never pain or trouble him. He which will eat the skin of the wolf well tempered and sodden will keep him from all evil dreams and cause him to take his rest quietly. The teeth of a wolf being rubbed on the gums of young infants doth open them whereby the teeth may the easier come forth.

Topsell's wolf and the wolf of the Bible were grey or timber wolves (*Canis lupus*), the largest wild member of the dog family and the species most widespread in the northern hemisphere of both the Old and New World. It varies considerably in size from the icy north to the balmy south, the wolf of the Bible lands being about a third the size of that in the Arctic. About 32 subspecies have been described at one time or another and two subspecies – *C. l. pallipes* and *C. l. arabs* – are present in Israel. These are divided into three distinct populations: a *pallipes* population that enjoys the Mediterranean-type climate to the north of the Judaean Hills and another in the deserts of the Negev, and an *arabs* population in the far south. Those in the north, where the rainfall is higher, are significantly larger than those in the deserts. The southern wolves have significantly smaller heads and bodies and their coats are a pale fawn.

Their food varies with location, and nowhere are they dependent on just a few prey species as wolves are in North America. These wolves are opportunists, taking hares (*Lepus capensis*), jirds (*Meriones* spp.), chukar partridges (*Alectoris chukar*), domestic stock, scavenging at rubbish tips and nowadays taking advantage of road kills. They will also take gazelles. There's even a report of three wolves that were seen one morning bringing down a Dorcas gazelle after a chase over about 1 km (0.6 miles).

The larger *pallipes* wolves will go for livestock, but the practice is uncommon. In scenes reminiscent of Bible times, a small pack was observed hunting sheep to the southeast of Haifa in the 1970s. They focused on this prey once or twice a week, but always hunting in different places. Two individuals in the pack were the known sheep killers and generally they killed no more than one sheep at a time. The hunt usually took place in late afternoon while the sheep were still grazing or returning to their night enclosure. On one occasion the wolves got among the fold and, like foxes in a chicken coop, killed sixteen sheep in one night. Tristram discovered that wolves like these were so stealthy that they could bypass the guard dogs:

When we encamped in a glen in North-western Galilee, we were often startled by the discharge of firearms at intervals through the night, and, on inquiring the cause, were told by the shepherds that they fired in order to frighten any wolves that might be prowling near the fold undetected by the dogs.

Other small packs have still been operating today in Golan and to the southwest of Jerusalem. Here sheep are taken, too, but the main livestock in this area are cattle that range free on the grasslands. This is beef country, and the wolves take their share by killing calves and scavenging on calf carcases. A few packs may be eight or more strong, yet, as with the packs in the north, only a couple of individuals do the killing. Both beef and zebu cattle are present but the wolves avoid the zebu mothers as they defend their offspring vigorously. On one of his journeys, Tristram was taken by surprise by a wolf intent on stealing a calf:

> In the open Plain of Gennesaret my horse one day literally leapt over a wolf, which started from under the bank of a narrow ditch I was crossing, but allowed us to leap before he started, when he ran with all speed across the plain. He was, no doubt, secreted under the bank, which was certainly no more than three feet in depth, waiting, wolf-like, for an opportunity of seizing his victim out of a herd of cows and calves, which were grazing in charge of a Bedouin boy, not a 100 yards further on.

In the desert wolves go for the small black goats of the Bedouin rather than sheep, and they will also enter settlements. They pass through cowsheds but do not attack the inmates, even small calves; instead, they break into the hen houses and kill chickens. These desert wolves do not seem so dependent on readily available water as other wolves for they are found up to 50km (30 miles) from the nearest watering hole.

Wolves will drive griffon vultures (*Gyps fulvus fulvus*) away from carcasses, but larger scavengers are avoided. The wolf's main rival is the hyena (*Hyaena hyaena syriaca*), and an uneasy truce between the two exists at rubbish dumps. The wolves tend to back down – hyenas are bigger and more powerful. Their main period of activity is at dusk and during the night, a fact that did not go unnoticed in the Bible: 'Wherefore a lion out of the forest shall slay them, and a wolf of the evenings shall spoil them, a leopard shall watch over their cities: every one that goeth out thence shall be torn to pieces' (Jeremiah 5:6); 'Her princes within her are roaring lions; her judges are evening wolves; they gnaw not the bones till the morrow' (Zephaniah 3:3).

Wolves are not as widespread in the region as they once were, and they have been replaced in many places by feral dogs, mainly crossbreeds between pariah dogs and German shepherd dogs. These mongrels survive by raiding rubbish dumps, and killing sheep, lambs and goats. They might kill many animals in a killing spree, one feral dog pack accounting for seventy kids and goats in a single night. They bite their victims in the throat but do not eat all those they have killed. Blame, though, usually falls squarely on the wolves.

Tristram was once followed closely by a wolf and the event proved considerably unnerving:

> Their boldness is remarkable. When camping at desolate Moladah, on the southern frontier of Simeon, I had one evening wandered alone three or four miles from the tents. In returning before sunset I suddenly noticed that I was followed at an easy distance by a large tawny wolf. The creature kept about 200 yards behind me, neither increasing nor diminishing his distance. I turned upon him, when he too turned. In vain I endeavoured to close with him, for he always exactly accommodated his pace to mine. We continued respectively to advance and retreat without coming close quarters. The wolf's

evident intention was to keep me in sight until evening, when he hoped to steal upon me in the darkness unperceived. He never uttered a sound of any kind, and walked as if quite unconscious of my presence. When it was nearly dark, I found him rapidly closing upon me, and, thinking him within shot, I halted, slipped down a ball, and took deliberate aim without his moving. The bullet struck a rock between his legs, and then he turned and trotted very quietly away.

Many of Tristram's encounters involved just a single wolf, a situation that seems to prevail to this day. The large packs so characteristic of northern lands are rarely present in the Holy Land. Wolves are more usually seen alone or in pairs, though several large groups have been recorded. It is thought that this could indicate that wolves in the region have ready access to sufficient food so they do not need a large pack to bring down prey. Increased agricultural activity might well have helped wolves – it has resulted in an increase in the small mammals that eat crops and so there is more prey for the wolf. When the harvest is ready, wolves even abandon their normal fare and feast on fruits and other cultivated plant products.

JACKAL AND FOX

Of all the wild dog-like animals present in the Holy Land, the commonest by far are jackals and foxes, yet the jackal fails to get a single mention in the AV. This, however, might be another translation error. The Hebrew word *Iyim* means 'howler', and is similar to an Arabic word meaning 'sons of howling'. In the AV it is translated as 'wild beast': 'And the wild beasts of the islands shall cry in their desolate houses, and dragons in their pleasant palaces' (Isaiah 13:22).

The passage also mentions 'dragons'. It is thought the Hebrew word *tan*, translated in the AV as 'dragon', also refers to the jackal. Dragons and wild beasts appear again in God's revenge:

And thorns shall come up in her palaces, nettles and brambles in the fortresses thereof: and it shall be an habitation of dragons, and a court for owls. The wild beasts of the desert shall also meet with the wild beasts of the island, and the satyr shall cry to his fellow.

Isaiah 34:13–14

Identifying this animal as 'jackal' instead of 'dragon' does seem appropriate for *tan*, when mention is made of the noise it makes: 'Therefore I will wail and howl, I will go stripped and naked: I will make a wailing like the dragons, and mourning as the owls' (Micah 1:8).

The interpretation seems to be fitting for such a vocal animal, but its howling has probably contributed to its bad press. Tristram drew attention to the nightly wailing of jackals around his camp, and recalled how ruins were a favourite haunt of these creatures:

About the ruins of Baalbek the packs of jackals secrete themselves by hundreds: there their sudden howl would break the dead stillness of the night, as we lay under those towering columns, and, caught up from the pack to pack, was echoed back from the cavernous temples below, till the air seemed filled as if with the wailing of a thousand infants.

Despite this focus on night-time activity, jackals are actually active both day and night, especially early and late in the day. Nevertheless, many Bible references do link the animal with the dark or times of desolation, bleak ruins and doomed cities, with *tan* or *tannim* used often in the context of a desert wilderness along with ostriches and 'wild beasts': 'I am a brother to dragons and a companion of owls' (Job 30:29); 'And I hated Esau, and laid his mountains and his heritage waste for the dragons of the wilderness' (Malachi 1:3); 'And I will make Jerusalem heaps, and a den of dragons', 'Behold, the noise of the bruit is come, and great commotion out of the north country, to make cities of Judah desolate, and a den of dragons', 'And Hazor shall be a dwelling for dragons, and a desolation for ever' (Jeremiah 9:11, 10:22 and 49:33).

Jeremiah seemed to like jackals. He continues in a similar vein in his Lamentations, but here the Hebrew word is *shu'al*, which the AV translators have translated as 'fox': 'Because of the mountain of Zion, which is desolate, the foxes walk up on it' (Lamentations 5:18).

Modern thinking is that *shu'al* also should be translated both as 'jackal' and 'fox'. In a psalm for David, when he was in the wilderness of Judah, the psalmist draws attention to the way in which the 'foxes' will clean up the battlefield, a task more usually associated with the jackal: 'But those that seek my soul, to destroy it, shall go into the lower parts of the earth. They shall fall by the sword: they shall be a portion for foxes' (Psalms 63:9–10).

After a battle, jackals rather than foxes are more likely to turn up and scavenge on dead bodies. The jackal of the Bible is the golden jackal (*C. aureus*), a species with a striking yellow to pale gold coat that can change with the seasons. Like all jackals, it is a slender dog-like mammal with large, erect ears, a fox-like face, long legs and a bushy tail. It is a nimble, muscular runner.

Despite its reputation as a scavenger, it is actually an opportunistic omnivore. Scavenging accounts for less than 20 per cent of its diet. It will eat almost anything edible, including fruits (all sorts, like dates and grapes), insects, reptiles, frogs and toads, birds, and small mammals ranging in size from mice to baby gazelles. Hunting is often cooperative, a pair of jackals having considerably more success than a solitary animal. The two jackals quarter patches of taller grass and bushes in order to flush out hiding fawns. If they find nothing, they will stand and look for another herd of gazelles and then head off in search again. Adults will carry food in their stomachs and regurgitate it at the den site for cubs or a suckling mother. Food might also be cached, an insurance policy for lean times.

Widely distributed species can be found today throughout Africa, southeast Europe, and southern Asia to Burma. In Africa the golden jackal's range overlaps with that of other jackal species, but they rarely meet, for each has its own preferred habitat. The golden jackal inhabits arid grasslands and deserts, where it might have a home range of up to 2.5 sq km (1 sq mile). Tristram found jackals denning in old quarries and caves in Syria, but elsewhere they were 'content with the cover of brushwood', visiting built up areas under the cover of darkness:

> They sweep the desolate ravines of the Dead Sea, and secrete themselves in the hermit's caves by Jericho. They nightly visit the walls of Jerusalem, and provoke a defiant chorus from the swarming pariah dogs, as intolerant of them as the hound is of the fox. I have known them enter not only villages but walled towns. A pack one night entered the town of Caiffa, through a gap in the wall, and scoured the place unmolested.

Today, of course, jackals are less likely to visit modern cities, but whatever the landscape or cityscape, their territories are scent marked, the male and female of a pair scenting together. Jackals are monogamous, so they leave a message for intruders that says 'this territory is occupied'. And the pair may not be alone. Young jackals often do not leave their parents immediately but become 'helpers'. In this way, they learn the best ways to survive and bring up a family, and share in the spoils of the hunt. They also wander outside the family territory, enabling them to prospect for unoccupied or badly defended ranges while still having a secure home base. An extended family pack might number up to eight individuals, and in this respect jackals differ from the mainly solitary foxes.

In certain circumstances, very large numbers will gather

together, such as at rubbish dumps where food is plentiful. At a rubbish tip in Israel, for instance, a group containing twenty animals was seen to tolerate each other's company. One of the breeding males was accepted as the dominant male, and they all defended the rubbish tip as a communal territory. Another group, living among coastal sand dunes near a kibbutz, contained seventeen individuals. Unrelated jackals, mostly young unmated females, followed the mated pairs, though in one case an unrelated male took advantage of the situation: he fed persistently on the mated couples' pups! In Old Testament translations this grouping activity has led commentators to substitute 'jackal' for 'fox' in Samson's fire attack on the Philistine crops:

> And Samson went and caught three hundred foxes, and took firebrands, and turned tail to tail, and put a firebrand in the midst between two tails. And when he had set the brands on fire, he let them go into the standing corn of the Philistines, and burnt up both the shocks, and also the standing corn, with the vineyards and olives.

Judges 15:4–5

It is reasoned that Samson was more likely to catch 300 jackals than 300 foxes, though the argument is slightly flawed because red foxes are sometimes found in groups, too – a male with up to five vixens in tow.

As social animals, jackals need to communicate with others of their kind, and they have a wide repertoire of calls, including howls, barks, growls, whines, cackles and yelps, golden jackals being among the most vocal of species. They locate each other by howling, much like wolves, and use the call to advertise that their territory is occupied. Howling can be infectious, with groups starting up one after the other at dusk until the area echoes with their wailing.

They also communicate with touch, a pair often grooming each other. A nibble around the face is a common greeting ceremony. Body language is used in aggressive stand-offs with strangers, along with typical canine facial expressions such as lifting the lips to reveal the canine teeth.

Unfortunately, jackals and people do not seem to get on well, so the former are persecuted mercilessly by the latter. In Jewish legend the jackal mother is said to dislike its young, and suckling mothers would eat their own offspring if God had not veiled their faces so they cannot see them.

Jackals are clearly unloved. The consequence is that numbers are far less than they were in Bible times, owing partly to an extermination programme organised by the Plant Protection Department of Israel's Ministry of Agriculture in 1964 and partly to rising standards of hygiene that have denied the jackal waste from the table; but these animals are so resourceful that their numbers are slowly building again.

While jackals are rare, their close relatives the foxes are more common, and several species are found in the region. In the southern and eastern deserts and steppe of Palestine is the reddish-grey Egyptian fox (*Vulpes niloticus*). This is replaced by the similarly coloured Palestine fox (*V. palaestina*) in the north and lands closer to the Mediterranean. The Galilee region has an intruder from Iran, the light yellow-coloured tawny fox (*V. flavescens*). This fox is larger than the other two and it has black ears. The distribution of the familiar red fox (*V. vulpes*) also extends into the Middle East and North Africa, its southern limit being Sudan. Tristram came across two subspecies, in the south of the region. He describes the slightly paler Egyptian fox (*V. v. niloticus*), with a greyer belly and tawny back, and in the north the larger and stronger Syrian fox (*V. v. flavescens*).

Characterised as scheming in the literature of many countries, the fox's reputation is partly based on its natural behaviour. Foxes are resourceful, the red fox being the most widespread of vulpine species. Some commentators argue that it is probably the most adaptable of all the carnivores. The Bible writers noted the animal's cunning and applied the word 'fox' not only to false prophets – 'O Israel, thy prophets are like the foxes in the desert' (Ezekiel 13:4) – but also to the hypocrisy of Herod: 'Go ye, and tell that fox . . .' (Luke 13:32).

It is through this wiliness, however, that foxes get their food. As meat-eaters all foxes catch small mammal prey, such as rodents, and they all adopt the 'mouse leap' that involves jumping upwards and forwards and then diving on the prey with the front paws. Invertebrates, such as beetles and grasshoppers, will appear in the diet, and earthworms may be extricated from their burrow by a tugging that is so gentle it does not tear the worm in half. Prey is sometimes cached for lean times. In fact, foxes will forage for or scavenge just about anything in season, including fruit; something that Solomon alluded to in his love poem: 'Take us the foxes, the little foxes, that spoil the vines: for our vines have tender grapes' (Song of Solomon 2:15).

Mention of little foxes suggests several small desert foxes. There is the rare fennec or desert fox (*V. [Fennecus] zerda*), the smallest of the dog-like predators that is found in the deserts of Palestine and Sinai. Recognised by its tiny body – it weighs just 1.5kg (3.3lb) – long whiskers and oversize ears, the fennec is a true desert fox. It does not sweat or pant to lose heat like the domestic dog, but instead tiny capillaries bring the warm blood close to the skin in the ears and it is here that heat is lost. The ears also act like huge receiving dishes that can pick up the quietest of scrabbling sounds, such as a beetle larva moving under the sand. Moving *over* the sand, the fennec has hairy soles, an adaptation to prevent it from sinking into soft sand. It lives sometimes in small groups consisting of up to ten animals led by a dominant male, so it, too, could be a candidate for Samson's firebrands (though maybe it is a bit small for that kind of job). Unfortunately, this fox has been hunted extensively and in certain parts of its range, such as the

Arabian Peninsula, it is extremely rare. But in captivity it fares well and breeds easily, and is exhibited in many zoos today.

Another desert specialist in the region is Ruppell's fox (*V. ruppeli*), which occurs in the Naqab Desert, as well as parts of Egypt, Sinai and the Arabian Peninsula. There is also Blandford's, cliff or Afghan fox (*V. carta*), which is small and lives on the steep slopes in desert canyons. Blandford's fox is nocturnal, feeding mainly on insects and often raiding vineyards for grapes and groves for melons and other fruits. It is hunted for its pelt, notably in the Central Asian part of its range, and is considered an endangered species. Blandford's fox was not discovered in Palestine until 1982, when it was spotted at Ein Geddi. Today, it is frequently seen on the cliffs at dusk or illuminated by the light from streetlights.

HYENA

The hyena is one of the larger predators in the region. It is not mentioned in the AV, but many commentators believe some of the 'wild beasts' in the Bible could be identified as hyenas. Modern versions introduce it as a logical identity for the term 'wild beasts of the islands'. The Good News Bible, for example, translates this passage as 'The towers and palaces will echo with the cries of hyenas and jackals'. The Hebrew word is *tzebua* or *zevoa*, meaning 'howling creature'. Jeremiah mentions it but the AV translators identify the animal as a bird: 'Mine heritage is unto me as a speckled bird, the birds round about are against her' (Jeremiah 12:9).

Tristram believes this to be not a 'speckled bird', in fact, but the striped hyena (*Hyaena hyaena*), which was once common in the region. The Arabic word for hyena is *dhubba*; another allusion to it is the Valley of Zeboim, known to the Arabs as the 'valley of hyenas'; 'And another company turned the way to Beth-horon: and another company turned to the way of the border that looketh to the valley of Zeboim toward the wilderness' (1 Samuel 13:18).

Today, Wadi-ul-Qelt, a valley to its north known as Shaqq-ud-Diba (meaning 'cleft of the hyenas') and Wadi-Abu-Diba (also meaning 'valley of the hyenas') are all possible locations for the biblical Valley of Zeboim. Hyenas, though, are not confined to specific locations, and can be found in many different habitats. A favourite place for den sites in Tristram's time was the old rock-hewn tombs that were found throughout the Holy Land. He observed how the hyena brought the bones they scavenged to these caves:

> I have found in an old quarry tenanted by these beasts, heaps of bones of camels, oxen, and sheep, and no less than seven camels' skulls together, which had baffled the gnawing powers even of an hyaena. We met with hyaenas in the Jordan Valley, near Beersheba, at Jerusalem, Nazareth, Mount Carmel, and Tabor.

They even dug up bodies from graves, and if an enterprising family member covered the grave with boulders to prevent hyenas from taking the body, the hyenas simply dug into the side. They were not only scavengers, however, but also accomplished predators:

> Its food is carrion, but especially bones, and, when pressed by hunger, it will attack large animals. The ass of one of my servants was once devoured by the hyaenas in the night, while he was sleeping close by.

It is a wonder Tristram's servant did not lose his life, too, for hyenas have been known to attack people, albeit rarely. None other than Teddy Roosevelt wrote about the way hyenas 'enter native huts and carry away children or even sleeping adults'. Roosevelt was probably writing about the spotted hyena (*Crocruta crocruta*). which is not present in the Middle East, but the striped hyena is just as wily. It is quite capable of attacking a person who is very young, injured or alone in the wilderness at night. Hyenas have been known to kill people when they are sleeping, biting the face with bone-crushing teeth and ultra-strong jaws. In fact, the hyena has the most powerful jaws of all the carnivores, its massive cheek teeth quite capable of cracking and splintering bone. In India striped hyenas are thought to have accounted for many deaths. In 1962, for example, nine children from the town of Bhagalpur in the Bihar District were thought to have been taken by hyenas during a six-week period.

Although superficially dog-like, the hyena is more closely related to civets. It has characteristically powerful forequarters and sloping back. The striped hyena has a longer coat than some of its more southerly relatives, with black stripes on the body and legs and a black-tipped mane. It is mainly a scavenger, but will take insects and eggs, and even fruit and vegetables. If a corpse is discovered, the hyena will slice off and cache portions for eating later.

Today, hyenas are not very common. There are roughly 150 in Palestine and they are often involved in road traffic accidents – about twenty animals are known to be killed each year. Nevertheless, the population is thought to be on the increase.

BEAR
Our last big meat-eater or carnivore is the bear. It is often listed along with the lion, as these two powerful predators were a serious threat to shepherds, goat herds and their flocks in biblical times. Bears especially were ferocious and unpredictable. David told how he dealt with an attack by a bear (and a lion) on his flock of sheep in order to impress King Saul.

> And David said unto Saul, Thy servant kept his father's sheep, and there came a lion, and a bear, and took a lamb out of the flock: And I went out after him, and smote him, and delivered it out of his mouth: and when he arose against me, I caught him by his beard, and smote him, and slew him.
>
> 1 Samuel 17:34–35

The shepherd Amos also reflected on an encounter with these animals, particularly if you ran from one straight into the path of the other – a biblical version of out of the frying pan and into the fire – 'As if man did flee from a lion, and a bear met him' (Amos 5:19). The bear in question was the light-furred Syrian bear *Ursus arctos syriacus*, a subspecies of the familiar Eurasian brown bear *U. arctos* (or grizzly in North America). It was considerably smaller than its more northerly relatives. A Kodiak Island grizzly – the largest living kind of brown bear – can weigh up to 750kg (1,656lb), whereas a Syrian bear is no more than 205kg (450lb). The Syrian bear was hunted extensively by German officers during the First World War, but it survived in the region until the 1940s, one of the last wild bears being shot in 1945. It was more common in biblical times, and was encountered in the montane forests of the region by stock minders. The bear often invaded vineyards and fruit groves, and it is especially fond of *chummuc* or chickpeas planted in upland fields. The most aggressive bears would have been females with cubs, and not surprisingly it is the 'she-bear' or sow that features strongly in the Bible. It was a custom in biblical times to capture cubs, which were subsequently hand-reared and trained for a life performing in captivity, but woe betide any hunter who should come face to face with their mother. It was good material for a proverb: 'Let a bear robbed of her whelps meet a man, rather than a fool in his folly' (Proverbs 17:12).

> I will meet them as a bear that is bereaved of her whelps, and will rend the caul of their heart, and there will I devour them like a lion: the wild beast shall tear them.
>
> Hosea 13:8

The bear and the lion again, but it was a couple of she-bears that were on the Lord's business when they sorted out some young delinquents who were throwing insults at Elisha:

And he went up from thence unto Beth-el: and as he was going up by the way, there came forth little children out of the city, and mocked him, and said unto him, Go up thou bald head; go up, thou bald head. And he turned back, and looked on them, and cursed them in the name of the Lord. And there came forth two she bears out of the wood, and tare forty and two children of them.

2 Kings 2:23–24

The death of 42 children is perhaps a bit harsh for a bit of name calling, but if a lesson is to be taught there is no doubt that the image of a marauding bear will reinforce it. It is the stuff of nightmares, or at least, one of Daniel's dreams: 'And behold another beast, a second, like to a bear, and it raised up itself on one side, and it had three ribs in the mouth of it between the teeth of it: and they said thus unto it, Arise, devour much flesh' (Daniel 7:5). The image was all the more frightening when the bear or the lion was unseen, waiting to pounce: 'He was unto to me as a bear lying in wait, and as a lion in secret places' (Lamentations 3:10).

In all, the bear – known in Hebrew as *dobh* or *dohv* – is mentioned about thirteen times in the Old Testament and once in the New Testament. One story from Hebrew legend still survives today. It suggested that the mother bear was created without teats, so God encouraged the cubs to suck their claws until they were ready to leave their mother and go their separate ways. The story has endured for centuries. Both Aristotle and Pliny recorded it. Pliny described how bear cubs are 'born a shapeless mass of white flesh, but little larger than mice, their claws alone being prominent. The mother then licks them into proper shape.'

The naturalist Bartholomew summarised it thus: 'The whelp is a piece of flesh little more than a mouse having neither eyes nor hair and having claws someadeal burgeoning and so this lump she licketh and so shapeth a whelp with licking.' Shakespeare included a reference to the fable: 'Like to a Chaos, or an unlick'd bear whelp,/That carries no impression like the dam' (*Henry VI, Part 3*, III.ii).

This was still considered genuine behaviour up until the seventeenth century, and it was down to observers such as Sir Thomas Browne to castigate purveyors of the tale:

> that a bear brings forth her young informous and unshapen, which she fashioneth after licking them over, is an opinion not only vulgar, and common with us at present, but hath been of old delivered by ancient writers.

He went on to disprove it, quoting Matthiolus, who wrote about hunters who had cut open a pregnant bear and discovered perfectly formed, bear-shaped embryos inside, not lumps of tissue without shape. So, the paw-sucking story may have been disproved eventually but it has left us today with the expression 'to lick into shape'.

5

BEASTS OF THE FIELD

At some point in the distant past, people began to settle down and change from a migratory to a sedentary life. Something that helped them do this was the taming and rearing of what were previously wild animals. It was an insurance policy for hard times, when 'wild foods' were difficult to find. Ironically, the first animals to be domesticated were probably pigs. The remains of semi-domesticated pigs have been found by University of Delaware scientists at an early Neolithic site at Hallan Cemi in eastern Turkey, dated to about 10,000 years old. The ancients, who were probably at an intermediary stage in the progression from foraging to farming just after the end of the Ice Age, chose wisely. The pig converts food more efficiently than most other domestic stock, turning 35 per cent of food energy into meat, compared to 13 per cent for sheep and 6.5 per cent for cattle. Yet pigs are taboo in Mosaic law.

PIG
Pigs or swine, however, do appear in the Bible with six entries in the Old Testament and fourteen in the New, always with an accompanying hint of revulsion. In Hebrew the word is *chazir* and there is no debate about its meaning. Pigs are most definitely

'unclean' – in some cases so unclean that a dim view is taken of even mentioning them. In the theatre a certain Shakespeare play is referred to traditionally as 'the Scottish play' and in a similar way some people in the Holy Land refer to the humble hog not as a 'pig' but as 'that unclean thing'. The pig's problem is that it has cloven hoofs but it does not chew the cud: 'And the swine, though he divide the hoof, and be clovenfooted, yet he cheweth not the cud; he is unclean to you' (Leviticus 11:7).

In ancient times, people noticed the way in which pigs stretch out their feet when lying down and considered it to be the pig's attempt at being accepted as 'clean'. It was good fodder for maxims: 'As a jewel of gold in a swine's snout, so is a fair woman which is without discretion' (Proverbs 11:22).

Why the pig should be singled out in this way is a bit of a mystery. At one time or another, scholars have blamed parasites and disease. They say that pigs' flesh is more likely to harbour parasites in a hot climate, but this has not stopped people feasting on pigs elsewhere in the tropical world. In the South Pacific, for example, pig is a delicacy. Islanders roast it on hot stones in earth ovens, the flesh no more cooked than a rare steak. In fact, entire cultures have grown up in several parts of the world based on the pig as a main food item.

The answer to this enigma might not be in the realms of food hygiene, but in legend. In ancient Egyptian folklore it was thought that the souls of the wicked transferred to pigs and that the wickedness could be inherited by eating the contaminated flesh. It was a theme picked up by Jesus in a well-known incident. He and his disciples arrived by boat on the southeast side of the Sea of Galilee (the district of Gadara according to some manuscripts, but referred to as Gerasa or Gergesa in others). They had just disembarked when a violent mad man who lived in the burial caves near by confronted them. Jesus spoke to the devils in him and they begged that they not be sent away but into a herd of swine close by:

And forthwith Jesus gave them leave. And the unclean
spirits went out, and entered into the swine: and the
herd ran violently down a steep place into the sea, (they
were about two thousand;) and were choked in the sea.

Mark 5:13

With enormous pig herds like that in the countryside, there must
have been a market for pigs or pig products. This notion is
supported further by the parable of the prodigal son. During his
time away from home, the young lad spent some of his time
looking after pigs in a far country: 'And he went and joined
himself to a citizen of that country; and he sent him into his fields
to feed swine' (Luke 15:15). Somebody must have been eating
them.

Nevertheless, eating pork was a taboo among devout Jews;
indeed, swine were 'the most unclean of the unclean', to quote
Canon Tristram. The strength of this feeling is illustrated by a
passage in one of the books called Apocrypha.

Eleazar, one of the principal scribes, an aged man, and
of a well favoured countenance, was constrained to
open his mouth, and to eat swine's flesh. But he,
choosing rather to die gloriously, than to live stained
with such an abomination, spit it forth, and came out of
his own accord to the torment.

2 Maccabees 6:18–19

Pigs even featured in Jesus's Sermon on the Mount: 'Give not that
which is holy unto the dogs, neither cast ye your pearls before
swine, lest they trample them under their feet, and turn again and
rend you' (Matthew 7:6).

The last few words demonstrate that people considered the
domestic pig potentially dangerous, a trait associated more

commonly with its untamed relative, the wild boar (*Sus scrofa*). Until the nineteenth century, it was common in the Bible lands. In fact, a Hebrew legend joked that God rearranged nature every seven years and that the wild boar was so numerous that it must have been transmogrified from mountain mice.

Wild boar in the Middle East frequented reedy marshes and thickets by rivers and lakes, where they rooted about for roots, tubers, bulbs, fungi, fallen fruits, ferns, the eggs and chicks of ground-nesting birds, frogs and even small mammals if they could catch them. They were even found in the desert wilderness near Beersheba, where they fed on the roots of asphodels, irises and crocuses that carpeted the slopes.

Tristram encountered them in the thickets along the banks of the River Jordan, from Ariha (Jericho) to the Sea of Galilee (Lake of Gennesaret or Lake Tiberias), though the river valleys with permanent water and a 'rich fringe of oleander' that descend to the Jordan or the Dead Sea were occupied by the greatest number of animals. From here, 'whence dogs nor man can dislodge them', they would make their nightly forays into the land cultivated by local villagers. When crops were ripening, men had to wait up all night in order to drive them away. But when the Jordan broke its banks and flooded the thickets, the boars were driven out into the open and the villagers got their own back.

Tristram's party shot a few. He describes its taste as 'bearing the same relation to pork as venison does to mutton'. It was also useful to have wild boar steaks in the larder in order to stop pilfering, as their local guides would not risk getting anywhere near 'the unclean thing'.

Common though it was, the wild boar receives but a single mention in the Bible. Its claim to fame is as a spoiler of vineyards: 'The boar out of the wood doth waste it, and the wild beast of the field doth devour it' (Psalms 80:13).

It is thought that the 'boar' in this context could actually be a reference to the Roman legions, for the legion based in Palestine had a boar on its standard. It was an appropriate emblem, for the wild boar is a particularly vicious animal. What it lacks in beauty it makes up for in strength, intelligence and tenacity. A female with her striped piglets is particularly fierce. She struts out fearlessly with her nose in the air to confront any threat to her offspring, and will not hesitate to attack a person who should wander too close.

Male boars are even more formidable. They stand with all their strength in the shoulder, and sport upwardly pointing tusks that can do serious damage to man and horse. The largest specimens might weigh 320kg (704lb), but more usually they average 175kg (385lb) and are up to 1.85m (6ft) long. They can and do attack people, though not usually deliberately. If they do take umbrage, they can slice up a person in minutes, and there is little left behind as evidence – they take flesh, skin, bones, the lot. Down the ages, they probably fed alongside wolves and other scavengers on the corpses left on battlefields.

Their main natural predator was the leopard, and as leopards declined, wild boar numbers increased and agricultural lands, particularly orchards and vineyards, were seriously damaged. In the nineteenth century Tristram noted that wild boar could wipe out an entire crop in a single night, the animals taking both fruit and root stock. Today, the wild boar still has a foothold in the Holy Land, though numbers are considerably less than in Tristram's time.

SHEEP AND GOAT

Stock rearing was a key livelihood at the time the Bible was written. People kept the same assortment of domestic animals that we see today – sheep, goats, cattle, camels, horses, asses and mules. It was a hard life in this especially dry region, with herdsmen travelling sometimes hundreds of miles away from their families to find what little pasture there might be, an aspect of rural life illustrated in the story of Joseph and his brothers.

And his brethren went to feed their father's flock in Shechem. And Israel said unto Joseph, Do not thy brethren feed the flock in Shechem? come, and I will send thee unto them. And he said to him, Here am I. And he said to him, Go, I pray thee, see whether it be well with thy brethren, and well with the flocks; and bring me word again. So he sent them out of the vale of Hebron, and he came to Shechem. And, a certain man found him, and, behold, he was wandering in the field: and the man asked him, saying, What seekest thou? And he said, I seek my brethren: tell me, I pray thee, where they feed their flocks. And the man said, They are departed hence; for I heard them say, Let us go to Dothan. And Joseph went after his brethren, and found them in Dothan.

Genesis 37:12–17

Sometimes entire families travelled with the flocks and herds, sleeping in tents just as the Bedouin have been doing in recent times. The animals they raised were not only for the needs of the family but also used to barter for other goods.

The domestic sheep was the first domestic animal in the Bible to be mentioned by name, Adam and Eve's son Abel being the first shepherd and the first butcher: 'And Abel was the keeper of sheep, but Cain was the tiller of the ground' (Genesis 4:2); 'And Abel, he also brought of the firstlings of his flock and of the fat thereof (Genesis 4:4).

Each farmer usually did his own butchering, though there were specialist butchers who traded in the larger cities. There was no prescribed way to dispatch an animal, but there were rules about how it should be eaten: 'It shall be a perpetual statute for your generations throughout all your dwellings, that ye eat neither fat nor blood' (Leviticus 3:17).

Dead or alive, the sheep was an animal of great economic

importance. The number of sheep a person possessed often established his worth – even the status of a prophet. Job had about 14,000 sheep, while Isaac had so many that the Philistines were envious. It was also *the* animal of sacrifice. The lamb was often selected as it represented the pure and innocent, and a male would be superfluous to the needs of the flock, but they were only killed on special occasions. Loss of such a valuable possession was a serious event, and several predators were ready to snatch a sheep from the flock:

> And David said unto Saul, Thy servant kept his father's sheep, and there came a lion, and a bear, and took a lamb out of the flock: And I went out after him, and smote him, and delivered it out of his mouth: and when he arose against me, I caught him by his beard, and smote him, and slew him. Thy servant slew both the lion and the bear . . .
>
> 1 Samuel 17: 34–6

Wolves and leopards were also more prevalent in those days, so shepherding could be a dangerous occupation. In a conversation between Jacob and Laban, his uncle, the hardships are outlined clearly.

> This twenty years have I been with thee; thy ewes and thy she goats have not cast thy young, and the rams of thy flock have I not eaten. That which was torn of beasts I brought not unto thee; I bare the loss of it; of my hand didst thou require it, whether stolen by day, or stolen by night. Thus I was; in the day the drought consumed me, and the frost by night; and my sleep departed from mine eyes.
>
> Genesis 31:38–40

For protection from wild animals, the sheep were often kept at night in a sheepfold. This was a corral of stones topped with thorn bushes to keep predatory animals out and the sheep in. Any that were prone to straying had one leg tied to their tail, for the breeds favoured in Bible lands had unusually large tails, from 13cm (5in) wide at the narrowest part to 38cm (15in) across at the widest. In the New Testament Jesus likened himself to the gate of the sheepfold, and spoke of his love for his people – the flock: 'Then said Jesus unto them again, Verily, verily, I say unto you, I am the door of the sheep' (John 10:7); 'I am the good shepherd: the good shepherd giveth his life for the sheep' (John 10:11).

In fact, throughout the Bible, people are likened to flocks of sheep, and the authorities, whether they be God or earthly kings, have been described as shepherds. In one case the kings of Israel were taken to task for neglecting their flock:

> Thus saith the Lord God unto the shepherds; Woe be to the shepherds of Israel that do feed themselves! should not the shepherds feed the flocks? Ye eat the fat, and ye clothe you with the wool, ye kill them that are fed: but ye feed not the flock . . . And they were scattered, because there is no shepherd: and they became meat to all the beasts of the field, when they were scattered.

> Ezekiel 34:2–5

Sheep were kept principally for milk. Their wool was secondary, though sheep were sheared twice each year. In more recent times, though, mutton has become more valued than beef. Young rams can be seen being stuffed with food, like geese in France. Mulberry leaves might be forced into the ram's mouth, with one of its handlers working its mouth to help it chew and swallow the food. The ram is also bathed in cold water each day. The result is fat and tender meat from an animal known as a *ma'luf*, from the root word meaning 'manger'.

Like sheep, goats were very important animals in the lives of people in the Middle East. Both provided milk, cheese, semn (a clarified butter used in cooking), hides, wool and meat. A kid goat was also a favoured meat dish at most feasts: 'Go now to the flock, and fetch me from thence two good kids of the goats; and I will make them savoury meat for thy father, such as he loveth' (Genesis 27:9); 'And Gideon went in, and made ready a kid, and unleavened cakes of an ephah of flour: the flesh he put in a basket, and he put the broth in a pot, and brought it out unto him under the oak, and presented it' (Judges 6:19).

Although there were few restrictions on how and when it could be cooked and eaten, there were some: 'Thou shalt not seethe [cook] a kid in his mother's milk' (Exodus 23:19).

A goat produces 2–5 litres (0.4–1.1 gallons) of milk per day, and goats' milk was drunk regularly in many households: 'And thou shalt have goats' milk enough for thy food, for the food of thy household, and for the maintenance for thy maidens' (Proverbs 27:27).

Goat skins were sewn together to make portable wine, oil, semn and water carriers, and to provide provision sacks that hold wheat and rice. Saddlebags were made of the same material. A rolled-up strip made a bolster for the head when sleeping. Skins were (and still are) used occasionally as simple clothes: 'They wandered about in sheepskins and goatskins' (Hebrews 11:37).

Goat skins indicate extreme poverty. Today, members of some sects wear goat skins or sheep skins to demonstrate their renunciation of worldly goods. Goats' hair was spun to make essentials, such as tent ropes, and weaved into cloth to make rugs and tents, for it swells when wet to exclude rain and shrinks when dry, helping the air circulate more easily. It was spun in a unique way – when the hair was still on the animal's back. Goats' haircloth also provided one of the coverings of the tabernacle (the portable tent in which the Israelites carried the Ark of the Covenant, the sacred chest that held the Ten Commandments):

And thou shalt make curtains of goats' hair to be a covering upon the tabernacle: eleven curtains shalt thou make. The length of one curtain shall be thirty cubits, and the breadth of one curtain four cubits: and the eleven curtains shall be all of one measure.

Exodus 26:7

An ancient cubit was about six palms or 45cm (18in), making the curtains 13.5 x 1.8m (44 x 6ft). Goats' hair was also used to stuff pillows: 'And Michal took an image, and laid it in the bed, and put a pillow of goats' hair for his bolster, and covered it with a cloth' (1 Samuel 19:13).

Goat skin, hair and blood have at one time or another been used to deceive. Goat skin was placed on Jacob's smooth hands and neck to make him hairy to the touch, like his brother Esau, and by this deception gain the blessing of his blind father Isaac. The blood was smeared on Joseph's multicoloured coat to deceive his father into thinking he had been killed by wild beasts.

Goats were also used for sacrifice: a kid goat was sacrificed at the dedication of the Tabernacle. It was a golden goat that stood on the third step of Solomon's grand throne, along with a leopard. In all, there are just over 120 references to the goat in the Bible.

The Authorised Version (AV) translators, though, would have had a very strange view of the goat. In Topsell's *Four-Footed Beasts*, for example, the great man credits the animal with the most extraordinary qualities: 'There is no beast that heareth so perfectly and so sure as a goat, for he is not only holp in this sense with his ears, but also hath the organ of hearing in part of his throat.'

Goats' fat, according to Topsell, also makes the best candles, wine can be prevented from going sour by the addition of a goat's milk, and goats' blood cleans up rusty iron. He continues with more mystical claims: 'The lodestone draweth iron, and the same, being rubbed with garlic, dieth, and loseth that property, but, being dipped again in goat's blood, reviveth and recovereth the former nature.'

Females predominated in flocks of sheep and goats, the ratio being about ten to one, at least according to the present that Jacob gave to his brother Esau: 'And he lodged there that same night; and took of that which came to his hand a present for Esau his brother; two hundred she goats, and twenty he goats, two hundred ewes, and twenty rams' (Genesis 32:13–14).

Sheep and goats were ideal animals to keep in the arid conditions of the Holy Land, for they could make use of land unsuitable for any other form of agriculture. They also descended from wild stock that was adapted to live in the particular conditions that prevail in the region.

A main difference between wild goat and sheep is the way in which they overcome the difficulties of the wild places in which they live. Goats are cliff dwellers, while sheep occupy the more open land close to the cliffs. Both have predators that stalk them among the rocks, but goats escape to inaccessible ledges, while sheep clump together and simply run.

At first wild sheep and goats were of little economic value to early man as game, but during the Neolithic period they were domesticated in the Middle East, where their ability to thrive in wilderness areas where the vegetation is sparse was of great value. It is thought the two groups were domesticated in the same region, the Eurasian wild sheep (*Ovis amnion*) giving rise to the domestic sheep, and a subspecies of the common wild goat native to Asia Minor, known as the pasang (*Capra hircus aegagrus*), yielding the domestic goat, which was first recorded in Persia.

The wild goat that was the ancestor to the domestic goat was long extinct before the Old Testament was written. Its remains have been found in Stone Age deposits. Yet there are several references to 'wild goats' in the Bible. The meat of the wild goat was considered 'clean', and therefore could be eaten. Psalmists celebrated its habitat: 'The high hills are a refuge for the wild goats' (Psalms 104:18). Wild goats also get a mention when Saul went in pursuit of David: 'Then Saul took three thousand chosen men out of all Israel, and went to seek David and his men upon the rocks of the wild goats' (1 Samuel 24:2).

But if wild goats were extinct, to which animal could the Bible writers be referring? The Hebrew words used were *aqqo* in the list of 'clean' animals in Deuteronomy and *ya'el* elsewhere. The general feeling today is that *ya'el* was the Nubian ibex (*C. ibex nubiana*). This is a goat antelope species that once lived from the Syrian Mountains, across North Africa and south to Sudan and Eritrea, but was hunted extensively for the medical properties of its body parts; only small, isolated populations exist today. One group is found in the crags behind Ein Gedi on the western shore of the Dead Sea, the very place where David hid from Saul.

The ibex is a goat-like rock climber. It is very agile and surefooted, sometimes walking or jumping from one narrow ledge to the next on almost vertical rock faces. Males and females segregate into same-sex groups for most of the year, meeting up in the autumn during the rut. Pregnant females (females are recognised by their smaller horns) leave their main groups when ready to give birth. Babies follow their mothers within hours of being born, and rejoin the herd with them. Mature males then head off in one direction and mothers with offspring and immature males go in the other. They give a whistling snort when alarmed, and run away, though not quickly.

Male ibex horns are massive and thick, and less curved than those of its domestic relative. Its coat is a more even colour, and it has a smaller chin beard. The ibex is the most advanced of all the wild goat species.

There is one mention in the Bible of the chamois (*Rupicapra rupicapra*). It is one of the 'clean' animals, according to the AV translation: 'The hart, and the roebuck, and the fallow deer, and the wild goat, and the pygarg, and the wild ox, and the chamois' (Deuteronomy 14:5).

The chamois is one of the most primitive of the living wild goats and sheep, but its mention presents us with something of a problem, for the chamois has never lived in the Bible lands. The AV translators must have got it wrong. The Hebrew word is *zetner*, which is similar to the Arabic word *zamar*, meaning 'leaping', which probably indicates a mountain goat or sheep. Tristram opts for one of the wild mountain sheep – the Barbary sheep (*Ovis tragelaphus*), which is called *kebsch* in Arabic and *aoudad* in North Africa. As evidence, he states that the Arabs tell of a kebsh or 'ram' living in the mountains of Sinai, though he knew of no skins, horns or other trophies or actual sightings by Europeans. The Barbary sheep is similar to the mouflon (*O. musimon*), the smallest of the wild sheep and an inhabitant of Asia Minor, Iran, Sardinia and Corsica.

CATTLE

Wild oxen or cattle appear in the Bible just twice, but there is a big question mark over these two entries, for some authorities do not believe them to be cattle at all. The first reference is in the list of 'clean' animals: 'These are the beasts which ye shall eat: the ox, the sheep, and the goat . . . and the wild ox' (Deuteronomy 14:4–5). Here the cattle are mentioned twice, as both 'ox' and 'wild ox'. The ox is clearly the domestic version, but the 'wild ox' is grouped with deer and antelope, so could it actually be something altogether different?

'Thy sons have fainted, they lie at the head of all the streets, as a wild bull in a net: they are full of the fury of the Lord, the rebuke of thy God' (Isaiah 51:20). This second mention seems to suggest a violent and untameable creature. Some scholars have suggested the buffalo. The domesticated water buffalo (*Bubalis arnee [bubalus]*) was kept in Palestine, especially in low-lying marshy areas, but there is no evidence to suggest that their wild relatives were present, for they are not written about nor depicted on ancient monuments. Indian buffalo are to be found today in some parts of the Holy Land, such as around the Sea of Tiberias, the

Jordan Valley and the plain of Coele. They were thought to have been introduced into these areas in relatively modern times. Some are domesticated, while others are feral.

The European bison or wisent (*Bison bonasus*) is another contender for the identity of the 'wild ox', for it lived in the Lebanon, but it is felt that it was not sufficiently known further south to have appeared in the list of 'clean' animals.

Tristram champions one of the antelopes and not the wild ox for the identity of what is known in Hebrew as the *teo*, in particular, the Arabian oryx (*Oryx leucoryx*). The animal was close to extinction in the wild not that long ago, but historically it would have been found on the Arabian and Sinai peninsulas, and into Jordan, Syria and Iraq. It is recognised by its white coat with black markings on its face and chocolate legs. Its horns are almost straight.

The oryx lives in stony deserts where rain may not have fallen for years, sand storms scour the land, and the air temperature can vary by 20°C (36°F) every day. Summer shade temperatures can reach 50°C (122°F) and the winter drop to 6°C (43°F) is made to feel even colder by the strong bitter winds. It is a place of extremes, and the oryx is built to survive them: it is the ultimate desert specialist.

The animal's white coat reflects the rays of the sun in summer, while in winter the hairs stand erect to absorb the warmth, giving the coat a velvet look and feel. Its feet are splayed to help it walk on sandy surfaces, and its ability to walk long distances is remarkable. It might trek up to 30km (19 miles) in a single night in search of the meagre vegetation that grows in the desert.

The fate of the oryx was sealed immediately after the Second World War: motorised hunting and automatic weapons hastened its decline. Just a handful were left in the wild, but fortunately herds were reared in captivity and some individuals have now been returned to the wild.

While the wild ox is in doubt, its domestic cousin is not. Domestic cattle are descended from the aurochs (*Bos primigenius*

primigenius) of Eurasia, with apparently several centres of domestication, including eastern Europe, central Asia and southeast Asia. They are mentioned 450 times in the Bible, albeit not always by the same name. Just as we have 'ox', 'cow', 'bull' and 'cattle' in the English language, there are six Hebrew alternatives, and by whichever name they were known the animals were very important to Jewish farmers. They hauled the plough, helped tread the corn, pulled carts, and were employed as beasts of burden: 'Thou shalt not plough with an ox and an ass together' (Deuteronomy 22:10); 'Thou shalt not muzzle the ox when he treadeth out the corn' (Deuteronomy 25:4); 'they brought their offering before the Lord, six covered wagons, and twelve oxen; a wagon for two of the princes, and for each one an ox' (Numbers 7:3); 'Moreover they that were nigh them . . . brought bread on asses, and on camels, and on mules, and on oxen, and meat, meal, cakes of figs, and bunches of raisins, and wine, and oil, and oxen, and sheep abundantly' (1 Chronicles 12:40).

Although the oxen mentioned in the last passage were being carried as meat, they were rarely killed or sacrificed, except on very special occasions. In the main, though, cattle were too valuable for sacrifice or even eating, and beef was served only for special celebrations, such as a homecoming. This is probably why the elder brother of the prodigal son was so miffed. In Jesus's parable he complained strongly to his father:

> Lo, these many years do I serve thee, neither trans-
> gressed I at any time thy commandment: and yet thou
> never gavest me a kid, that I might make merry with my
> friends: But as soon as this thy son was come, which
> hath devoured thy living with harlots, thou hast killed
> for him the fatted calf.

Luke 15:29–30

The return of the prodigal son aside, cattle were mainly offered in sacrifice by the wealthier elite. Abram was one of the special few. When he grumbled to God that he had no heir, God asked him to sacrifice a whole host of produce, including a cow: 'Take me an heifer of three years old, and a she goat of three years old, and a ram of three years old, and a turtledove, and a young pigeon' (Genesis 15:9). Abram did so, slicing in half all the animals, though not the birds, but when he placed them on the ground the vultures arrived and he had to chase them off.

The master of sacrifice, however, must have been Solomon: 'And Solomon offered a sacrifice of peace offerings, which he offered unto the Lord, two and twenty thousand oxen, and an hundred and twenty thousand sheep' (1 Kings 8:63); 'Also king Solomon, and all the congregation of Israel that were assembled unto him before the ark, sacrificed sheep and oxen, which could not be told nor numbered for multitude' (2 Chronicles 5:6).

In everyday life cattle were not slaughtered at the drop of a divine hat, but were exceedingly well looked after. Mosaic instructions even made special provision for them, putting them on a footing not far removed from the farmers themselves. It meant that they had a day off each week: 'Six days thou shalt do thy work, and on the seventh day thou shalt rest: that thine ox and thine ass may rest, and the son of thy handmaid, the stranger, may be refreshed' (Exodus 23:12).

It also meant that a farmer had not only to look after his brother, but also his brother's cattle: 'Thou shalt not see thy brother's ox or his sheep go astray, and hide thyself from them: thou shalt in any case bring them again unto thy brother' (Deuteronomy 22:1).

This also went for his brother's donkeys, and if any of them should fall over or become trapped in a ditch, the farmer must help them get to their feet. What is more, the care lavished on these animals should be extended to enemies as well: 'If thou meet thine enemy's ox or his ass going astray, thou shalt surely bring it back to him' (Exodus 23:4).

Curiously, despite the respect with which cattle were given as animals of value to people, they were subjected to some very strange laws. If an ox should gore a person to death or badly injure them, it was not slaughtered ritualistically as other animals, but stoned to death itself. And it was forbidden to eat the miscreant afterwards.

> If an ox gore a man or a woman, that they die: then the ox shall be surely stoned, and his flesh shall not be eaten; but the owner of the ox shall be quit. But if the ox were wont to push with his horn in time past, and it hath been testified to his owner, and he hath not kept him in, but that he hath killed a man or woman; the ox shall be stoned, and his owner also shall be put to death.

> Exodus 21:28–29

So, any farmer who ignored a tetchy bull could be in trouble. The bull is allowed one serious assault, but any more and it could be fatal. A nudge with the horns was less risky: 'If the ox shall push a manservant or a maidservant; he shall give unto their master thirty shekels of silver, and the ox shall be stoned' (Exodus 21:32). The cattle of yesteryear were not the breeds we see today. They would have been much scrawnier, and like their sheep and goat counterparts would have to have survived on poor pasture and the occasional handout of grain, beans or barley straw. Some were brought in and fattened for special occasions: 'Better is a dinner of herbs where love is, than a stalled ox and hatred therewith' (Proverbs 15:17).

The cattle in this context were also known as 'fat oxen', animals that were were mostly brought inside and stall-fed during the winter. They were particularly succulent, and a delicacy at those special feasts of the wealthy elite.

Many cultures used cattle as currency. The Romans, for example, called cattle *pecus* and a herd was known as a *pecunia*.

Eventually, *pecunia* became the general word for money – hence the English adjective 'pecuniary', meaning 'of money'. Similarly, *fee* was the Old English name for cattle, and in Hindi *rupa* was the word for a herd of zebu cattle, giving rise to the currency name 'rupee'.

Another word that has some relationship with cattle is 'kine'. In modern physics the kine is a unit of velocity in the centimetre-gram-second (CGS) system, and derives from the Greek *kinein*, meaning 'to set in motion'. Kine is also a pidgin language in Hawaii, but in the seventeenth-century Bible it means something completely different. Many kine appeared in a dream told to Joseph by the Pharaoh. In the dream the Pharaoh is standing by a river.

> And, behold, there came up out of the river seven well favoured kine and fatfleshed; and they fed in the meadow. And, behold, seven other kine came up after them out of the river, ill favoured and lean-fleshed; and stood by the other kine upon the brink of the river. And the ill favoured and leanfleshed kine did eat up the seven well-favoured and fat kine.

> Genesis 41:2–4

Joseph went on to interpret the dream. Easton's *Bible Dictionary* of 1897 attempted to interpret the beast, and concluded that the Pharaoh's kine are buffalo, perhaps the domesticated form of the water buffalo (*Bubalis arnee [bubalus]*) that would feed on the grasses and sedges along the edge of the river. There are two breeds – river and swamp buffaloes – and both have been used in various parts of the world, including Asia and North Africa, to perform agricultural tasks. In another passage kine are needed to haul a cart to move the Ark of the Covenant:

Now therefore make a new cart, and take two milch kine, on which there hath come no yoke, and tie the kine to the cart, and bring their calves home from them: And take the ark of the Lord, and lay it upon the cart; and put the jewels of gold, which ye return him for a trespass offering, in a coffer by the side thereof; and send it away, that it may go.

1 Samuel 6:7–8

The mention of 'milch' here gives us a clue, for milch is an old English word for 'giving milk'. Whatever the breed, it is female. The 'buffalo' explanation, however, fails to reflect the nature of the animal in other passages in the Bible. Earlier in the book of Genesis, Jacob presented kine to his brother Esau: "Thirty milch camels with their colts, forty kine, and ten bulls, twenty she asses, and ten foals' (Genesis 32:15).

Kine here are mentioned alongside 'bulls', which suggests that kine are 'cows'. In fact, modern versions translate kine in all these passages simply as 'cows', i.e. adult female cattle. The Hebrew is *paroth*, plural of *parah* and the feminine of *par*, meaning 'young cow' or 'heifer'. Elsewhere in the Bible, other Hebrew words are used, such as *alaphim* and *baqar*, which also mean 'ox' or 'cow', and these are translated as 'kine' in the AV:

And he will love thee, and bless thee, and multiply thee: he will also bless the fruit of thy womb, and the fruit of thy land, thy corn, and thy wine, and thine oil, the increase of thy kine, and the flocks of thy sheep, in the land which he sware unto thy fathers to give thee.

Deuteronomy 7:13

Later in Deuteronomy, the *alaphim* version of kine is used again.

> Blessed shall be the fruit of thy body, and the fruit of thy ground, and the fruit of thy cattle, the increase of thy kine, and the flocks of thy sheep.

Deuteronomy 28:4

Here 'kine' and 'cattle' are used in the same passage, so perhaps the 'fruit of thy cattle' refers to the fecundity of a breeding bull, and 'kine' to a milk-producing cow. This seems to add up when we consider another reference later in the same book, this time referring to the *baqar* version of kine:

> He made him ride on the high places of the earth, that he might eat the increase of the fields; and he made him to suck honey out of the rock, and oil out of the flinty rock; butter of kine, and milk of sheep, with fat of lambs, and rams of the breed of Bashan, and goats, with the fat of kidneys of wheat; and thou didst drink the pure blood of the grape.

Deuteronomy 32:13–14

Quite a collection of natural foods mentioned here, with the kine clearly producing milk that was turned into butter. Another kine (*baqar* version) product is mentioned when David arrived at Mahanaim, and the people brought out a wealth of food:

> [Shobi, Machir and Barzillai] brought beds, and basons [basins], and earthen vessels, and wheat, and barley, and flour, and parched corn, and beans, and lentiles, and parched pulse, and honey, and butter, and sheep, and cheese of kine, for David, and for the people that were with him, to eat.

2 Samuel 17:28–29

The only conclusion we can reach without causing too much controversy is that a kine is simply a domestic cow.

Interestingly, in biblical times, cattle west of the River Jordan were generally stall-fed, whereas those on the plains and hills to the south were kept in a semi-wild state, including the famous 'bulls of Basan or Bashan'. This district produced an especially large breed of cattle: 'Hear this word, ye kine of Bashan, that are in the mountain of Samaria, which oppress the poor, which crush the needy, which say to their masters, Bring, and let us drink' (Amos 4:1).

Although 'kine' is not a household word in English today, it would have been familiar to the seventeenth-century translators of the AV. They would have known about kine-pox, for example, a disease of cows that is similar to smallpox but less virulent. It was not until the nineteenth century that kine-pox vaccine was used to help protect people against smallpox.

CAMEL

The most recognisable domestic animal of the Middle East must be the camel. It is *gamal* in Hebrew, meaning 'to repay' and *dromos* in Greek, meaning 'a runner', and it is from the Greek that we get the common name of the local species – dromedary. The Arabian one-hump camel or dromedary (*Camelus dromedaries*) is the quintessential desert animal, yet there are no truly wild dromedaries living today. There are wild Bactrian or two-hump camels living in the colder parts of Central Asia, which were discovered by the Russian naturalist A G Bannikov in a remote part of the Gobi Desert in 1945. But the dromedary is only found as a domestic or feral animal.

It was once native to India, the Middle East and North Africa and was domesticated in central or southern Arabia around 4000 or 2000 BCE or between the thirteenth and twelfth centuries BCE, depending on which school of thought you believe. From there the practice of camel-rearing spread north into Egypt and North Africa, east to

India and south into East Africa. The first known records of camels in Egypt were decorations on pottery from the sixth dynasty, dated to about 3500 BCE.

Nowadays, most dromedary camels belong or once belonged to somebody. Feral camels that appear to be wild, such as those in the Australian outback and near Pisa in Italy, were once domestic stock. Today, dromedaries may be allowed to run loose in a semi-wild state to forage but they depend on people for access to water. Any unguarded camels return to their wild roots and form into stable groups. There may be exclusively bachelor herds or herds with a dominant male, ten to fifteen females and their young, but come the rut their owners guard them closely.

In some places camels are encouraged to fight as sport during the rut. It was an indulgence of the ancient Greeks, and is still practised in the province of Aydin in Turkey. Today's fighting camels are crossbred from dromedaries and Bactrian camels and are known as *tulus*. They are bred for their aggressiveness, and fed with wheat, barley and oats during the summer to turn them into heavyweight contestants. The fights last for about fifteen minutes, during which time the camel tries to bring down and suffocate his opponent.

Camels have their origins not in the Old World but the New. Fossil evidence indicates that they first appeared about 40–45 million years ago in North America and then dispersed throughout Asia as recently as 2–3 million years ago. They are very well adapted to desert conditions, thriving on a meagre diet of dry vegetation, thorns and saltbush that other plant-eating mammals avoid. They can survive long periods without water–up to ten months in the semi-wild state – and can gulp it down rapidly when available. They can take in about 115 litres (25 gallons) in ten minutes and conserve water by producing dry droppings and very little urine. Camels have sweat glands all over the body, just as we have, but the camel will allow its body temperature to rise by as much as 6–8°C (11–14°F) to reduce the need to sweat and cool by evaporation. The nostril cavities reduce water loss further by moistening incoming air and cooling exhaled air. The nostrils can be closed to prevent blown sand from entering, and the eyes have a double row of protective eyelashes. The ear openings are also thickly haired. The dromedary is recognised by its one hump or hunch, while the Bactrian has two. In the AV the humps were referred to as 'bunches': 'they will carry . . . their treasures upon the bunches of camels' (Isaiah 30:6).

The dromedary's single hump is not a water reservoir, as was once believed, but a fat store enabling the camel to go for long periods without food. A day's food might be a single feed of beans or some dates or small balls of barley meal. Also, they do not store water in the so-called 'water-cells' in the stomach.

Thick fur and underwool keep the animal warm on cold desert nights and provide some insulation against the daytime heat. The dromedary and the other cameloids (the Bactrian camel from Mongolia, and the guanaco, alpaca, llama and vicuna from South America) differ from other animals with hoofs in that their bodyweight rests not on the hoof itself but on the sole pads, so only the front part of the hoof touches the ground. Camels' hoofs are wide and splayed to help them walk on sand, and they run with a characteristic gait with the legs on each side moving together. They were recognised by the Bible writers for their swiftness: 'thou art a swift dromedary traversing her ways' (Jeremiah 2:23).

The dromedary has become an important animal in the Middle East, not only as a beast of burden, but also for its meat, wool and milk. One camel can provide about 6 litres (1.3 gallons) of milk per day nonstop for up to 18 months, and in the Western Sahara camel milk is one of the main food sources for desert nomads. It remains fresh much longer than cows' milk, and is drunk thinned with water. It is also made into a sour-tasting cheese, and is an ingredient in cosmetic face cream. There's one oblique reference in the Bible of a gift from Jacob to his brother: 'And he lodged there that same night; and took of that which came to his hand a present for Esau his brother . . . thirty milch camels with their colts' (Genesis 32:13–15).

The camel's coat consists of long, coarse, outer protective fibres up to 40cm (15in) long and an inner insulating layer of finer hairs. The shorter fibres are used to make sleeping mats, coats and blankets. The wool is not plucked but collected as the coat is shed, and an animal might provide up to 2.25kg (5lb) during the course of a year. World production is more than 1,500,000kg (3,500,000lb) a year. People known as 'trailers' follow camel caravans and collect the hair in baskets.

There is one reference in the New Testament to John the Baptist's attire, but that reference tells us a great deal about his social level: 'And John was clothed in camel's hair, and with a girdle of skin about his loins; and he did eat locusts and wild honey' (Mark 1:6). This distinguished John from the wealthy, who had softer coats of camel hair. Elijah most probably wore a rough camel-hair coat, too: 'He was an hairy man, and girt with a girdle of leather about his loins' (2 Kings 1:8).

It is also thought that 'sackcloth' mentioned in several places in the Bible meant a rough coat of camel hair: 'In the streets they shall gird themselves with sackcloth' (Isaiah 15:3).

Camel dung is collected to light cooking fires, but camel meat is consumed only by certain members of the community. Although Arabs may eat camel meat, it is forbidden to Israelites; one legend tells how fallen angels (so not to be copied) ate a thousand camels a day. The skin, however, was used to make sandals.

The camel's main use, though, has been for riding or as a beast of burden. As with horses, different breeds have particular functions. The largest camels are used for carrying goods, while the *hajin* is a dromedary used mainly for riding. The dromedaries or *heirie* are classified by the distance they can cover in a day compared to that of a pack camel. The *talatayee* can go three days' journey in one, the *sebayee* seven days, and the exceptional and rare *tasayee* nine days' journey in one. These fast 'ships of the desert' were legendary: 'When thou shall meet a heirie, and say to the rider, "Salem aliek" ["Peace be between us"], ere he shall have answered thee "Aliek salem" ["There is peace between us"], he will be afar off, and nearly out of sight; for the swiftness is like the wind' (*Illustrated London News*, 7 March 1846).

As the main means of desert transport, even in today's automobile age, camels in caravans walk about 30km (19 miles) a day, and carry loads weighing up to 100kg (220lb). They are also valuable as wedding dowries and other major gifts – particularly white or pale coloured camels. Their future depends totally on that of the desert nomads. If they settle, there will be little need for working camels.

There are several references in the Bible to nomads and camels as pack animals. When his brothers sold Joseph, for instance, it was to a passing caravan: 'and they lifted up their eyes and looked, and, behold, a company of Ishmeelites came from Gilead with their camels bearing spicery and balm and myrrh, going to carry it down to Egypt' (Genesis 37:25).

That camels were a sign of wealth is evident from some of the earliest passages in the Bible. Abraham had many camels (in fact, he had lots of everything, including 'flocks, and herds, and silver, and gold, and menservants, and maidservants, and camels, and asses' – Genesis 24:35) and they featured when his servant was sent to find a wife for Isaac:

> And the servant took ten camels of the camels of his master, and departed ... And he made his camels to kneel down without the city by a well of water at the time of the evening . . . And when she [Rebekah] had done giving him drink, she said, I will draw water for thy camels also, until they have done drinking ... And the man came into the house: and he ungirded his camels, and gave straw and provender for the camels.
>
> Genesis 24:10–32

An amusing postscript to this particular passage comes a little later in the story. In the AV there is a line in Genesis 24:61 that reads, 'And Rebekah arose, and her damsels, and they rode upon the camels', but an unfortunate printing error in an edition published in 1823 read 'And Rebekah arose, and her camels'. It became known as 'The Camels' Bible'.

Abraham was not alone, though, in amassing considerable wealth. Jacob also had his fair share after he cleverly hoodwinked Laban: 'And the man increased exceedingly, and had much cattle, and maidservants, and menservants, and camels, and asses' (Genesis 30:43).

Curiously, camels feature less as Israelite possessions later in the Old Testament. Other than Solomon's and David's animals, it was mostly other nations that possessed the camel. The Queen of Sheba, for instance, showed her wealth when she visited Solomon: 'And she came to Jerusalem with a very great train, with camels that bare spices, and very much gold, and precious stones' (1 Kings 10:2). But the ultimate camel herd must have been that of the Midianites and Amalekites: 'and their camels were without number, as the sand by the sea side for multitude' (Judges 7:12).

Camels were used both for peaceful purposes and in war, and they were even used to pull chariots: 'And he saw a chariot with a couple of horsemen, a chariot of asses, and a chariot of camels' (Isaiah 21:7).

In the New Testament there are two references to the camel, both by Jesus. He uses the animal to make moral points. On one occasion he criticises the establishment, the scribes and Pharisees: 'Ye blind guides, which strain at a gnat, and swallow a camel' (Matthew 23:24). This refers to the way a Jew will filter his wine to ensure that he will not inadvertently eat an 'unclean' insect that has fallen in. In this context it was used to highlight people in authority who carefully avoided inconsequential faults but did not hesitate to commit the worst sins.

On another occasion Jesus used the camel once more to warn

the wealthy: 'And again I say unto you, It is easier for a camel to go through the eye of a needle, than for a rich man to enter into the kingdom of God' (Matthew 19:24). The passage is very well known but there is a question mark over whether the AV translation got it right. The medieval theologians would argue that Jesus was referring to a small gate, known as the 'eye of the needle', which was big enough for people to enter but not for a camel. That a city architect could make such a mistake is stretching a point, so the alternative interpretation suggests that Jesus has been misquoted. It is more likely that Jesus referred to a thick piece of rope, which contrasts more logically with a piece of thread. In fact, in St Luke's account the Greek translation clearly uses the word *belone*, meaning a 'surgeon's needle', and in St Matthew's version the word is *rafic*, meaning a 'sewing needle'. Neither mentions a city gate. So the problem may have come later. The Greek for 'rope' or 'cable' is *kamilos*, which when translated into Latin might well have been confused with *kamelos* meaning 'camel', and the mistranslation has persisted ever since.

The camel was also known, albeit not well known, in Europe at the time of the AV translation. Shakespeare mentions it several times, and the natural historian Bartholomew points out that it shares with humans the afflictions of baldness and gout. Whatever the context, it is often portrayed as aloof and disgruntled, a reference no doubt to the way it holds its head and nose up high (compared to the arched neck of the horse) and to its unfortunate habit of spitting when upset.

In Mosaic law the camel is considered unclean despite being a ruminant that chews the cud like a cow or sheep. It has a divided hoof, but the toes are not separated completely, which might account for the description in Leviticus 11:4: 'these shall ye not eat of them that chew the cud, or of them that divideth the hoof: as the camel, because he cheweth the cud, but divideth not the hoof; he is unclean unto you'.

Camels, along with horses and asses, were fed *se'irim* and

tebhen, identical with the *shar'ir* (barley) and *tibn* (straw) that Arabs feed to their horses to this day: 'Barley also and straw for the horses and dromedaries brought they unto the place where the officers were, every man according to his charge' (1 Kings 4:28). *Tibn* is straw that has been broken into small pieces during threshing; hay is practically unknown in the area. The *tibn* is a coarse fodder or roughage, and it is mixed with barley or other grains, or even peas, for without the additions the animals will refuse to eat it.

Well-fed animals will sometimes nose about in the mixture eating the grains that settle to the bottom and leaving the straw. Any *tibn* left over is thrown on to the floor as bedding. *Tibn* is also used with clay to plaster walls or for making sun-dried clay bricks. There is *qashsh* too, meaning 'dried up', which refers to the stalks left in the wheat or barley field. Camels and other domestic stock are sometimes allowed to graze on it, as a roughage supplement to the regular food.

HORSE

While the camel was an everyday work animal, the horse was the mount of kings and warriors, more involved in warlike activities than in sport and agriculture. The horse is mentioned in the Bible 149 times, and several Hebrew words are used for it, the most common of these being *sus*, meaning 'horse', and *paras*, meaning 'horseman', though this is sometimes used for 'horse', too.

Unlike the ass, which was probably tamed in the Middle East, the domesticated horse had its origins in Central Asia and eastern Europe. In the early days, the Canaanites had horses and chariots, and the Israelites would have been familiar with horses in Egypt. Recent archaeological excavations on the edge of the Nile delta, about 100km (60 miles) northeast of Cairo, have uncovered the world's oldest known stables. They consist of six rows of buildings covering an area of more than 17,000 sq m (183,000 sq ft) that would have housed at least 460 horses used by the soldiers of Rameses II to pull chariots. The stable floors were sloped to channel and collect the horses' urine and dung that was used to fertilise surrounding fields.

The first mention of horses in the Bible relates how the animals were bartered for food during Egypt's great famine. Joseph acquired them on behalf of the Pharaoh: 'and Joseph gave them bread in exchange for horses' (Genesis 47:17). The Israelites were forbidden by God to own any themselves: 'But he [a chosen king] shall not multiply horses to himself, nor cause the people to return to Egypt, to the end that he should multiply horses' (Deuteronomy 17:16).

God had good reason to impose a ban. By trading with other countries for horses, they were liable to import their vices and idols, too. And if they had well-trained warriors on horseback, they would have less need of God's protection:

> Woe to them that go down to Egypt for help; and stay on horses, and trust in chariots, because they are many; and in horsemen, because they are very strong; but they look not unto the Holy One of Israel, neither seek the Lord!
>
> Isaiah 31:1

Nevertheless, by the time Solomon was on the throne, imported horses from Egypt and Assyria were amassed to form an elite cavalry:

> And Solomon gathered chariots and horsemen: and he had a thousand and four hundred chariots, and twelve thousand horsemen, which he placed in the chariot cities, and with the king at Jerusalem ... And Solomon had horses brought out of Egypt ... And they fetched up, and brought forth out of Egypt a chariot for six hundred shekels of silver, and an horse for an hundred and fifty: and so brought they out horses for

all the kings of the Hittites, and for the kings of Syria, by their means.

2 Chronicles 1:14–17

And, despite the protestations of the prophets, the horse became a symbol of power and speed.

> Hast thou given the horse strength? hast thou clothed his neck with thunder? . . . the glory of his nostrils is terrible. He paweth in the valley, and rejoiceth in his strength: he goeth on to meet the armed men. He mocketh at fear, and is not affrighted; neither turneth he back from the sword. The quiver rattleth against him, the glittering spear and the shield. He swalloweth the ground with fierceness and rage: neither believeth he that it is the sound of the trumpet. He saith among the trumpets, Ha ha; and he smelleth the battle afar off, the thunder of the captains, and the shouting.

Job 39:19–25

In some cases the horse – together with chariots – was actually worshipped. In the Middle East in Old Testament times, there were many cults that held the horse and chariot in high esteem. They were the horses of the sun, a form of sun worship that had horses dedicated to the sun. As part of the cult, horses and chariots were placed outside the temple in Jerusalem. King Tosiah did away with this pagan worship:

> And he took away the horses that the kings of Judah had given to the sun, at entering in of the house of the Lord, by chamber of Nathan-me-lech the chamberlain, which was in the suburbs, and burned the chariots of the sun with fire.

2 Kings 23:11

In some cults the horses and chariots were actually sacrificed to the sun. It was not uncommon in ancient times. One of the grandest of the Vedic religious rites in India was performed by the king to celebrate his supremacy. A fine stallion was chosen and allowed to roam freely for a year. A royal guard protected him and wherever the horse went, the king claimed sovereignty, sometimes having to fight for it. If the horse was not captured, it was brought back at the end of the year to the king's capital. It was then sacrificed to the sun, a rite known as *asvamedha* in Sanskrit. Part of the ritual was that the king's number-one wife had to lie alongside the dead horse. It was said that the horse's wanderings were like the sun passing over the world, and this represented the power of the king over the entire earth. The king could then take on the title of *cakravartin*, meaning 'universal monarch', and the kingdom would have prosperity and fertility.

In ancient lore horses were given different roles, depending on their colour: a white horse symbolised victory and conquest, for example, while a red horse represented war and bloodshed. When John was trying to give his readers hope and encouragement at a time when Christians were being persecuted, he was forced to use symbolism that only other Christians at that time would understand:

> And I saw when the Lamb opened one of the seals, and I heard, as it were the noise of thunder, one of the four beasts saying, Come and see. And I saw, and behold a white horse: and he that sat on him had a bow; and a crown was given unto him: and he went forth conquering, and to conquer. And when he had opened the second seal, I heard the second beast say, Come and see. And there went out another horse that was red: and power was given to him that sat thereon to take peace from the earth, and that they should kill one another: and there was given unto him a great sword. And when he had opened the third seal, I heard the third beast say,

Come and see. And I beheld, and lo a black horse; and he that sat on him had a pair of balances in his hand. And I heard a voice in the midst of the four beasts say, A measure of wheat for a penny, and three measures of barley for a penny; and see thou hurt not the oil and the wine. And when he had opened the fourth seal, I heard the voice of the fourth beast say, Come and see. And I looked, and behold a pale horse: and his name that sat on him was Death, and Hell followed with him. And power was given unto them over the fourth part of the earth, to kill with sword, and with hunger, and with death, and with the beasts of the earth.

Revelation 6:1–8

In layman's terms, this imagery represents the 'four horsemen of the apocalypse'.

ASS, DONKEY AND MULE

While the horse was for special occasions and the camel for the wealthy, the beast of burden adopted by the 'man in the street' was the ass. Asses were domesticated in the Middle East by about 4,000 BCE, but their wild ancestor is a subject of continued debate.

The Bible lands were home to two types of wild ass, known in Hebrew as *pere*, meaning 'to run'. One had its origins in Asia and the other in Africa. The Asian wild ass, or onager (*Equus hemionus*), once had a wide distribution with six subspecies distributed from Palestine east to Mongolia and south to India. In the Middle East the Syrian onager, or achdari (*E. h. hemippus*), inhabited Syria, and the Persian onager, or ghor-khan (*E. h. onager*), was found in Iran. All were hunted and shot for their meat and skins.

The German monk Felix Fabri reports seeing a herd of Syrian onagers close to Jericho in the fifteenth century, and later, in the seventeenth century another traveller wrote of seeing wild asses near El Gedi. These two accounts are the only known references to the Syrian onager being in Palestine, but the English naturalist Tristram reported wild ass in the Eastern Hauran, the basaltic volcanic region in Syria now famous for its vineyards, and there were reports of a live ass being captured in the Syrian Desert and shipped to Vienna Zoo in 1909. It died there in 1927, and was quite possibly the last known individual of this subspecies.

The onager is still to be encountered in largish numbers in Turkmenistan; nevertheless, the International Union for the Conservation of Nature and Natural Resources (IUCN) has listed it as 'endangered'. Just three other small, isolated populations survive today, in northern Iran, southern Mongolia and northwest India.

In Iran the scattered groups in the sand and gravel desert of Dasht-i-Lut in the south – one of the hottest deserts on earth – and the vast saline desert of Dasgt-i-Kevir in the north are the remnants of once-vast herds that migrated seasonally across the Persian plains and steppe. They live in a land of extremes with maximum and minimum temperatures reaching 42°C (108°F) and -20°C (-4°F). In much of the region rainfall is less than 10cm (4in) a year. In order to avoid the worst of the heat and cold, the onagers head for the desert highlands in summer, returning to the lowland areas during winter. As recently as 1910, the Swedish explorer Sven Hedin found onagers not far to the east of Teheran. Today, they are protected, but still hunted illegally.

Some onagers were imported into Israel from Iran in 1969, and placed in the Hai-Bar Reserve (see below). These were bred successfully and onagers were released into the wild, in the Ramon Crater Region of the Negev highlands in 1982 and 1992. There are about a hundred in the wild in Israel today, where they can be seen visiting watering places at Ramon Crater and Nahal Paran in the summer, plus a further forty at Yotvata Hai-Bar.

The Persian onager stands about 1.2m (4ft) high at the shoulder. It has a rusty-brown back and legs, white belly, black tail tuft, a short, stiff black mane and a black stripe (the list or eel-stripe) down its back with a white drop-shadow on either side.

The African wild ass (*E. africanus [asinus]*) has two known modern subspecies – the Nubian wild ass (*E. a. africanus*) and the Somali wild ass (*E. a. somaliensis*). These animals were hunted, too, the Somali ass having the unfortunate habit of stopping every so often and looking back, an easy target for a hunter with a rifle. Today, it is one of the world's most endangered large mammals. A few scattered groups survive in Somalia and Ethiopia, but the wild animals breed so readily with domestic and feral donkeys that the wild stock is becoming gradually diluted. It is hard to tell which is pure and which is a hybrid.

The African species of wild ass stands about 1.25m (4ft) at the shoulder, and is either grey or brownish, becoming reddish in summer, shading into white underparts. There is usually a black stripe down the back, and the Nubian race has a traverse stripe on the shoulders (the shoulder-cross). The Somali race has bands on the legs. The hooves are long and narrow. They were once found throughout the northern part of Africa, the Nubian breed living between the Sahara Desert and the southern shore of the Mediterranean, and the Somali breed reaching as far south as the Somali/Ethiopia-Kenya border. A dwarf breed of the Somali wild ass was to be found on the island of Socotra.

All types of wild ass are strong, possess immense stamina and are fast. 'It has feet,' says Ossian, the Celtic warrior bard, 'like the whirlwind' and according to the Roman teacher Aelian, who wrote about the characteristics of animals, it moves as if 'it were carried forward by wings like a bird'. An unidentified traveller on horseback once tried to approach a herd of sixty to seventy wild asses, known as khurs, in the Cutch region of northwest India. He galloped towards them, but could approach no nearer than 'twenty yards'. In fact, onagers can reach 72km/h (45mph) at top speed and sustain a pace of up to about 50km/h (30mph), making them the fastest of all the wild members of the horse family

Equidae. The African wild ass has a 50km/h top speed. Despite this swiftness, the wild ass's foot and leg are more designed for surefootedness over rocky ground.

With these attributes, in biblical times the wild ass was held up as a symbol of power, freedom and wild nature: 'Who hath sent out the wild ass free? or who hath loosed the bands of the wild ass? . . . The range of the mountains is his pasture, and he searcheth after every green thing' (Job 39:5–8); 'And he was driven from the sons of men; and his heart was made like beasts, and his dwelling was with the wild asses' (Daniel 5:21); 'And the wild asses did stand in high places, they snuffed up the wind like dragons' (Jeremiah 14:6).

The Bible writers clearly recognised the robustness of the African wild ass. It is a large mammal that has adapted to the rigours of arid, stony regions with no trees to offer shade, and where temperatures may soar to 50°C (122°F) or more during the day and fall to 15°C (59°F) at night. The wild ass can survive water losses of more than 30 per cent of its body weight, while most other mammals would peg out after losing 12–15 per cent. It restricts sweating and reduces the water content of its droppings in order to retain moisture. On reaching a water supply, it drinks rapidly, downing 24–30 litres (5–7 gallons) in one go, restoring water loss in less than five minutes.

This toughness and the animal's extraordinary strength and surefootedness were attributes that were greatly appreciated. People living about 6000 BCE in the Middle East put them to good use, though the wild ass was hunted for food at first. Rock drawings at Wadi Abu Wasil, in Upper Egypt's Eastern Desert, depict hunters bringing down wild asses. There are pictures of bowmen accompanied by saluki hounds hunting ostrich, wild ox and wild asses, and there are tethered asses. Are they animals caught in a 'treadle' trap (a trap with a wooden spring mainly used for catching deer on the leg), stool-pigeons to bring in other animals, or the first signs of domestication? No one is sure. What is clear is that the tethered animals have long ears, and therefore resemble the African subspecies.

In later rock pictures from the same area, dated before 3000 BCE – that is, before the first of the pharaohs – there are clear images of asses carrying goods. The wild ass had been tamed, and the result was the domestic ass or donkey (from the Flemish *donnekijn*, meaning 'small dun-coloured animal'), and it has been the dependable pack animal for centuries. It can work under hot and difficult conditions, and is so sturdy it can keep going for days on poor-quality food. It will eat just about any type of vegetation. An individual can carry a load of more than 100kg (220lb), and can travel for much longer without water than a horse.

Initially, the donkey was more than just a means of transport. In ancient Egypt it trod grain, pulled the plough, and the mares were milked. Donkey mares' milk has a higher sugar and protein content than cow's milk, and was used by the ancient Egyptians for food, medicine and as a cosmetic for the skin; Cleopatra was said to have bathed in asses' milk. In Israel it was listed as 'unclean' so people were forbidden to eat it.

Of the several species and subspecies of wild ass, it is not clear which was the direct ancestor of the domestic donkey. The Nubian race of the African wild ass was once the favoured subspecies for the honour, but archaeologists have since unearthed the remains of asses, both wild and domesticated, at Neolithic sites in Palestine. The dentition and leg bones of these animals indicate that they were not onagers, but more closely related to the African wild ass, which evidently had an ancient distribution that included lands outside Africa.

Onagers were also thought to have been domesticated or used to revitalise donkey stock. The Syrian achdari (*E. hemionus hemippus*), for example, may have been tamed in Mesopotamia (modern-day Iraq). The Sumerians used it not for donkey-like carrying tasks but for horse-like purposes. The Royal Standard of Ur (in the British Museum) depicts onagers being attached to and pulling four-wheeled war chariots. They played the role of horses, as there were no horses in Mesopotamia until the first millennium BCE.

What are thought to be onagers also appear on wall paintings in the tombs of Thebes in New Kingdom Egypt. In one picture skewbald Arab-type horses pull a chariot, while another has a team of thin-maned, dun-coloured animals that could be either onagers or mules from onager mares. Herodotus writes about the Persian army led by Xerxes invading Europe with the help of chariots pulled by onagers. There is one reference in the Bible to the ass (whether the onager or another domesticated species is not known) pulling a chariot: 'And he saw a chariot with a couple of horsemen, a chariot of asses, and a chariot of camels' (Isaiah 21:7).

One unusual mode of transport, which the Jews probably learnt from the time they were in Egypt, also involved asses. It was a litter in which the passenger sat on a chair set between a pair of asses. The gait of the ass is suited to this means of transport, and it goes some way to explain events when the Levite went to Gibeah, 'and there were with him two asses saddled' (Judges 19:10).

This was probably not a common sight, for most asses were ridden in the normal way with a saddle on the back. In Persia there were two types – slow and heavy animals used for carrying goods, and sleek and glossy ones that carried their head high and raised their feet well. These latter animals were kept solely for riding. Their saddles were round on one side and flat on the other, the rider sitting closer to the crupper or rump than the neck. They were broken like horses but were taught only to amble. Their trainers would tie their fore- and hind legs with a short rope of cotton to shorten the stride. Normally, when these asses were running at top speed, a horse would have had to gallop to keep pace.

The goods-carrying asses were not slouches either. Across the desert, they were more expeditious than even the camel. On the

Arabian Peninsula heavily loaded camels would take two nights to complete the journey between Djidda and Medina, resting at Hadda during the day. A group of more lightly loaded asses carrying the same quantity of goods made the journey in fifteen or sixteen hours. It was an ass-caravan that made the daily mail run between the two towns.

In Hebrew the domestic she-ass is *athon*, named for its slowness, and the male or jackass known as *hamor*, a reference to its dun reddish colour. With such a reliance on donkeys, people of the Bible lands had quite a technical vocabulary. *Anah*, for example, was the general word for ass, while *hamor* meant 'working ass' (the same as the Arabic *hamal*, meaning 'porter'). This gave rise to the Greek *onos*, then the Latin *asinus*, followed by the French *âne*, and the Celtic *asal* that was still used in Ireland until quite recently.

It was the ass that carried the goods and chattels of Moses and his band when they set out for their forty-year trek in desert country. Donkeys carried the Ark of the Covenant and the portable Tabernacle of Jehovah across the Sinai and Negev Deserts, and when Moses came down from Mt Sinai with his stone tablets, one of the Ten Commandments specifically mentions the domestic ass: 'Thou shalt not covet thy neighbour's house . . . nor his ox, nor his ass, nor anything that is thy neighbour's' (Exodus 20:17). The ass was clearly a valuable animal (there was no mention of horses and camels), and the wild variety helped Moses extricate himself from a particularly awkward situation. Legend has it that Moses was an especially accomplished desert navigator and water-diviner, and stories of his feats of navigation are still told today among the Bedouin. On one occasion, when the Children of Israel were down to their last drop of water and Moses's sixth sense was about to let them down, a dust cloud appeared on the horizon. By its speed, Moses knew that it must be a herd of wild asses, so he decided to follow. After a while, they came across the asses' watering hole, a rock from which a freshwater spring gushed. They were saved.

It was this admiration for the ass that led to a certain faction of the Israelites indulging in donkey worship. The cult took the ass as its totem, and some time later, when the Jews were the enemies of Rome, they were described rather pejoratively as 'donkey-worshippers'. The Christians in Rome shared the same offensive label.

However, of the 83 other Bible references to the domestic ass, the animal is placed firmly in the 'beast of burden' category. At its first mention we discover that Abraham not only rode his steed but also used it to carry wood to make a burnt offering in the land of Moriah:

> And Abraham rose up early in the morning, and saddled his ass, and took two of his young men with him, and Isaac his son, and clave the wood for the burnt offering, and rose up, and went unto the place of which God had told him.
>
> Genesis 22:3

The sons of Jacob loaded their asses with corn (Genesis 42:26–7), and Joseph in Egypt sent a plethora of gifts loaded on asses to his father: 'And to his father he sent after this manner; ten asses laden with the good things of Egypt, and ten she asses laden with corn and bread and meat for his father by the way' (Genesis 45:23).

Food brought to David when he was proclaimed king over all Israel confirmed the ass as a reliable beast of burden alongside other domestic breeds:

> Moreover they that were nigh them . . . brought bread on asses, and on camels, and on mules, and on oxen, and meat, meal, cakes of figs, and bunches of raisins, and wine, and oil, and oxen, and sheep abundantly: for there was joy in Israel.
>
> 1 Chronicles 12:40

The reference to the mule here might be considered odd because it was forbidden to breed from animals of different species: 'Thou shalt not let thy cattle gender with a diverse kind . . .' (Leviticus 19:19).

The mule is a nonfertile hybrid, a cross between a mare and a jackass and known for its swiftness and good temper (the hinny is a cross between a stallion and she-ass, known to be slow and stubborn); yet it is mentioned 21 times. The only explanation is that in order not to have broken Mosaic law, the mule must have been bred elsewhere, such as Armenia, and imported into Israel: 'They of the house of Togarmah traded in thy fairs with horses and horsemen and mules' (Ezekiel 27:14). The Hittites were horse and mule breeders. They published the first manual on horseracing and introduced price regulation on the stock they bred. Horses commanded the price of twenty sheep, but mules cost sixty sheep. It was an expensive beast due to its triple value – useful for pack transport, ploughing and riding. In ancient times, when the horse was not far removed from the wild tarpan, a relatively short-legged beast, the hybrid mule stood out. This is the result of 'hybrid rigour' in which the outcross is larger and stronger than its parents. It enabled generals and standard bearers to rise above the crowd, giving the former a wide view of the battle and making the latter conspicuous to the rest of the army.

The first mule breeder could well have been Anah. He was not a Hebrew but a Hivite, so his life was not governed by Mosaic law. It seems he was an enterprising stockman: 'this was that Anah that found the mules in the wilderness, as he fed the asses of Zibeon his father' (Genesis 36:24).

Here we must look at the AV translation. In *Donkey: The Story of the Ass from East to West*, Anthony Dent suggests that 'mules' in the plural are an unlikely thing to come across by chance in the desert, and that maybe the translators mixed things up a little. He proposes that it would make more sense if it read 'invented' instead of 'found', and points out that the Latin (from which the AV was translated) for both 'invented' and 'found' is *invenuit*. Coincidence? Could it be that Anah, probably a resourceful donkey breeder, somehow got hold of some mares and bred them with his donkeys to 'invent' the mule? Interestingly, Anah's name is an old Semitic word for 'ass'. On the other hand, there may be nothing in it at all. Modern versions of the Bible suggest that Anah chanced upon 'hot springs' but no mules.

Whatever the truth, the mule was a firm favourite by King David's time, and whether imported or bred locally, several dignitaries rode the animal. Solomon rode his father's mule when King David declared him King of Israel, and he received gifts of mules: 'The king also said unto them, Take with you the servants of your lord, and cause Solomon my son to ride upon mine own mule' (1 Kings 1:33); 'And they brought every man his present, vessels of silver, and vessels of gold, and garments, and armour, and spices, horses, and mules, a rate year by year' (1 Kings 10:25).

Absalom had a less dignified ride. He rode a mule into war, though in retrospect he might have considered it to be safer on foot:

> For the battle was there scattered over the face of all the country: and the wood devoured more people that day than the sword devoured. And Absalom met the servants of David. And Absalom rode upon a mule, and the mule went under the thick boughs of a great oak, and his head caught hold of the oak, and he was taken up between the heaven and the earth; and the mule that was under him went away.
>
> 2 Samuel 18:8–10

A mule also caught out the Babylonians. Cyrus the Great, Emperor of the Medes and Persians, had blockaded Babylon, which had rebelled, but the city was well prepared with ample provisions to wait out a long siege. The walls of the city were high, thick and almost impregnable, and one day a soldier shouted down from the ramparts, 'Cyrus will never take Babylon – not till mules have foals!' The inevitable happened. In the Persian camp a mule did indeed give birth, and not long afterwards Babylon fell.

In reality less than 1 per cent of female mules form ova and are fertile. The female achieves this when the genes in her egg cells separate out into either horse or ass ova. So if she mates with a horse she will give birth to a horse and with an ass she will produce an ass. Under normal circumstances she will give birth to neither for she is effectively a sterile hybrid. Nevertheless, the mule was (and still is in some parts of the world) valued because it possessed some of the best features of the horse and the ass – endurance, surefootedness in rough terrain and an ability to carry heavy loads. During the Trojan war, mules dragged the combustible materials to the funeral pyre of Patroclus and pulled the chariot of Priam to the tent of Achilles. Pelias had mules pull his chariot in the chariot race, and at the time of Homer mules ploughed the plains of Greece.

The Welsh gypsies, incidentally, knew the ass as *mokhio*, from the Romany word *moila* or *meila*, which can be traced back to the Latin *mulus*. It has been suggested that the Romany word was the result of inflated sales patter – they 'talked up their asses' to have the qualities of the larger and stronger mules!

Mules aside, the ass was the main form of transport in many places in the Middle East. Many of the prophets and their families rode on a domestic ass, but perhaps one of the most famous riders was Jesus in the New Testament. He entered Jerusalem on the back of an ass, an event that fulfilled a prophecy in the Old Testament.

> Rejoice greatly, O daughter of Zion; shout, O daughter of Jerusalem: behold, thy King cometh unto thee: he is just, and having salvation; lowly, and riding upon an ass, and upon a colt the foal of an ass.

> Zechariah 9:9

The entry into Jerusalem has frequently been used to illustrate how meek Jesus was, given that he rode an ass rather than a horse. The real reason for his choice of transport, however, was probably quite different. Asses were respectable mounts for important people at that time, and Jesus was certainly not humbling himself by riding one. Horses were reserved for the military. A conquering hero would ride to victory on a horse. Jesus was coming as a man of peace, so he arrived on a donkey.

> And when they drew nigh unto Jerusalem, and were come to Bethphage, unto the mount of Olives, then sent Jesus two disciples, Saying unto them, Go into the village over against you, and straightway ye shall find an ass tied, and a colt with her: loose them, and bring them unto me. And if any man say ought unto you, ye shall say, The Lord hath need of them; and straightway he will send them. All this was done, that it might be fulfilled which was spoken by the prophet, saying, Tell ye the daughter of Sion, Behold, thy King cometh unto thee, meek, and sitting upon an ass, and a colt the foal of an ass. And the disciples went, and did as Jesus commanded them, And brought the ass, and the colt, and put on them their clothes, and they set him thereon.
>
> Matthew 21:1–7

Legend has it that the cross-shaped mark on the ass's back appeared after Jesus rode into Jerusalem. It's a nice story, but ancient Egyptian bas-reliefs that predate Christ clearly show the mark on the back. Jesus, however, was in noble company in riding an ass. Judge Abdon was accompanied by an extraordinary procession of asses: 'And he had forty sons and thirty nephews, that rode on threescore and ten ass colts: and he judged Israel eight years' (Judges 12:14). Similarly, Judge Jair had his entourage. He judged for 22 years, 'And he had thirty sons that rode on thirty ass colts' (Judges 10:4).

Abigail, wife of Naban, also rode an ass, and she prepared quite a feast for David and his followers that was carried on the back of a large number of asses:

> Then Abigail made haste, and took two hundred loaves, and two bottles of wine, and five sheep ready dressed, and five measures of parched corn, and an hundred clusters of raisins, and two hundred cakes of figs, and laid them on asses . . . And it was so, as she rode on the ass, that she came down by the covert of the hill, and, behold, David and his men came down against her; and she met them.
>
> 1 Samuel 25:18–20

Large numbers were also used as pack animals in war. According to a quote in the Apocrypha, Holofernes, chief captain of the Assyrian army, was a devotee:

> And he mustered the chosen men for the battle, as his lord had commanded him, unto an hundred and twenty thousand, and twelve thousand archers on horseback; and he ranged them, as a great army is ordered for war. And he took camels and asses for their carriages, a very great number.
>
> Judith 2:15–17

Inevitably, given its personality, the ass or donkey has featured in Jewish legend and humour. It was noted that the ass had the habit of smelling its dung and then urinating. This behaviour, according to the legend, arose at the time the donkey grumbled to God that it did not receive a fair wage when working for humans. God said that it would receive fair recompense when its excrement smelled like flowers and its urine flowed sufficient to turn a watermill. So the donkey constantly checks both to see if it has made the trade.

6

IVORY, APES AND BADGER SKINS

The Authorised Version (AV) of the Bible includes several animals with strange-sounding names and the 'pygarg' is one such beast. What could it be? The pygarg, or 'white buttocks', is mentioned just once in the Old Testament and not at all in the New. It is included in the list of animals that it is permissible to eat: 'These are the beasts which ye shall eat: the ox, the sheep, and the goat. The hart, and the roebuck, and the fallow deer, and the wild goat, and the pygarg, and the wild ox, and the chamois' (Deuteronomy 14:4–5).

The Hebrew word is *dishon or diyshon*, meaning 'springing' or 'leaper', and this seems to indicate a member of the antelope subfamily. Indeed, modern translators opt simply for 'antelope', but it is possible we can be a little more precise and focus on the addax (*Addax nasomaculatus*), a desert antelope that was once common throughout the Sahara and parts of the Holy Land. A largish, horse-like antelope, the addax stands more than a metre (3.3ft) at the shoulder and has a greyish-white coat with a white rump, belly and legs, and a tuft of chestnut hair on its head, like a wig. Its most impressive feature is its pair of metre-long horns, which are spirally twisted. The addax is thought also to have been the *strepsiceros* or 'twisted-horn' mentioned by the ancient writers, and the pygargus –

an antelope with a white rump – described by Herodotus. Pliny knew it by its African name *addaca*.

The addax is a true desert animal. It lives in both stony and sandy deserts, including dune areas, where it is well adapted to the searing heat, coarse vegetation and lack of water. It is often seen some distance from any source of water, obtaining moisture both from the minuscule amounts in plants on which it feeds and from dew. It is said to be able to detect patches of vegetation from several kilometres away, and is able to move towards it over the sand without sinking in, by virtue of its broad hooves.

At one time it was safe in its remote and inhospitable desert environment, but the introduction of firearms and four-wheel-drive vehicles changed all that. Today, residual populations of addax are confined to parts of the western Sahara, southern Algeria and western Sudan. A small population in the Hai-Bar Reserve is a part of the international effort to save the species.

There is also a quite separate pygarg – the *pargargue a queue blanche*, or white-tailed eagle (*Haliaeetus albicilla*) that once bred in Syria and Israel – but this is not the pygarg of Deuteronomy.

ROEBUCK

Another antelope-like creature to appear in the Bible is the 'roebuck' or 'roe', which gets seventeen mentions. The word 'roebuck' is usually reserved for the male roe deer, but the general feeling today is that this was an AV mistranslation. The Hebrew word is *tsebhi*, which should be more appropriately translated as 'gazelle' (Tribe: Antilopini). The word 'gazelle', though, would have been new to seventeenth-century AV translators, as it had only been introduced to the English language from the Arabic *ghazal* in about 1600.

The gazelle in question was probably Dorca's gazelle or jebeer (*Gazella dorcas*), which nowadays roams the high semi-desert plains of the Holy Land feeding on artemisia and steppe grass. In Tristram's time, gazelles were seen just about everywhere in the Holy Land, with herds of a hundred or more animals in more southerly parts of the region. Tristram recalls seeing them visiting a freshwater spring near a salt mountain at the southern end of the Dead Sea. They were also in the hills at Ein Geddi in the deserts near Beersheba, and in the wooded areas of Mt Carmel. He even saw a small group feeding on the Mount of Olives, close to Jerusalem. They can still be found near the city today, but more usually in groups of three to seven animals, though groups of up to twenty gazelles can be seen in the Naqab Desert.

In the Bible the gazelle with its long neck and legs and slender body was considered a thing of beauty. Its swiftness and grace are mentioned frequently: 'And there were three sons of Zeruiah there, Joab, and Abishai, and Asahel: and Asahel was as light of foot as a wild roe' (2 Samuel 2:18). Similarly, the Gadites who were with David in the wilderness were likened to gazelles: 'And of the Gadites there separated themselves unto David into the hold to the wilderness men of might . . . whose faces were like the faces of lions, and were as swift as the roes upon the mountains' (1 Chronicles 12:8).

The scribes also picked up on the gazelle's timidity, a characteristic that was used to illustrate how the world would feel if the Lord were angered: 'And it shall be as the chased roe, and as a sheep that no man taketh up'(Isaiah 13:14).

The female form of the Hebrew word for 'gazelle' and the Greek equivalent 'Dorcas' was used to express prettiness and also gave rise to a popular name – Tabitha: 'Now there was at Joppa a certain disciple named Tabitha, which by interpretation is called Dorcas: this woman was full of good works and almsdeeds which she did' (Acts 9:36).

While Dorca's gazelle was the most commonly encountered, there were several more species present in the region. The goitered gazelle (G. subgutturosa) inhabited the semi-deserts and desert steppe, and the slender-horned gazelle (G. leptoceros) was found in Egypt. Tristram also describes a local form of gazelle that he considered was more beautiful than all the rest – the ariel gazelle or cora (*G. gazella arabica*) – which he found in the oak forests near Gilead. It was slightly darker than Dorca's gazelle, with almost black markings, including a dark marking along the flanks. The creature blended beautifully into its background. Today, we know it as the mountain gazelle (*G. gazella*), which was once found commonly in the hills of the Arabian Peninsula and Palestine, but is now encountered more usually in other parts of the Middle East, such as the mountains and deserts north of the Emirates, Abu Dhabi and Dubai.

All gazelles share a bouncing gait (known as 'stotting' or 'pronking'), especially when alarmed. They leap vertically with stiff legs, all four feet landing together. Several interpretations have been offered – the animal is communicating alarm, it is attempting to get a better view of the predator, or it is demonstrating to the predator that it is fit and able to get away.

The gazelle is permitted food, and is hunted, but it is also in competition with domestic and feral goats and sheep for the sparse vegetation of the wilderness and has not fared well. Several species are endangered, owing not only to habitat destruction but also to hunting. Tristram describes how in the nineteenth century gazelles were either staked out at their watering places or herded into a huge enclosure with a pitfall at its end. The Bedouin, however, hunted with greyhound and falcon. The falcon would fly at the head of the gazelle, carefully avoiding the horns; the delay this caused enabled the dogs to catch up and bring it down. Tristram describes the flesh as 'very dry and lean' but not as 'savoury as that of the wild goat'.

In Hebrew folklore God specifically protects the gazelle. It is said to give birth on the highest mountain pinnacle where the fawn is caught and prevented from falling to its death by an eagle – a more comfortable interpretation, perhaps, of a predation event that must have occurred regularly in ancient times! Large eagles have a penchant for gazelle fawns.

DEER

Deer are similar in appearance to antelope and gazelles. The word 'deer' is found in the AV only twice, as in 'fallow deer', but there are several references to animals that could only be deer – eleven mentions of 'hart', the adult male deer, and ten of 'hind', the adult female deer. Whatever their identity, they were considered 'clean': 'These are the beasts which ye shall eat . . . The hart, and the roebuck, and the fallow deer' (Deuteronomy 14:4–5). The 'hart' here could refer to either the red deer (*Cervus elaphus*) or the (real) roe deer (*Capreolus capreolus*). Along with the fallow deer (*Dama dama*), the red and roe deer were once common in the Holy Land, and King Solomon took full advantage of them. The feasting table for a single day included a fine selection: 'And Solomon's provision for one day was . . . Ten fat oxen, and twenty oxen out of the pastures, and an hundred sheep, beside harts, and roebucks, and fallowdeer, and fatted fowl' (1 Kings 4:22–23).

Quite a spread. But table decoration aside, the hart, known as *ayyal* in Hebrew, was known not only for its athletic ability, but also its vulnerability: 'Then shall the lame man leap as an hart' (Isaiah 35:6); 'And from the daughter of Zion all her beauty is departed: her princes are become like harts that find no pasture, and they are gone without strength before the pursuer' (Lamentations 1:6); 'As the hart panteth after the water brooks, so panteth my soul after thee, Oh God' (Psalms 42:1).

The hind, known as *ayyalah* in Hebrew, seems also to have served as a symbol of strength and agility: 'He maketh my feet like hinds' feet: and setteth me upon my high places' (2 Samuel 22:34 and Psalm 18:33).

She also must have been considered the kind of animal that is so devoted to her young that she will not abandon them unless things get really bad, such as in times of extreme drought: 'Yea, the hind also calved in the field, and forsook it, because there was no grass' (Jeremiah 14:5).

Evidence that deer were common in Palestine can be seen in

place names. Ajalon, meaning 'deer pasture', appears as the name of a Levitical city in the tribe of Dan, and of another in Zebulon and there is Mount Ajlun in Gilead: 'Aijalon with her suburbs' (Joshua 21:24); 'And Elon the Zebulonite died, and was buried in Aijalon' (Judges 12:12).

Of the three species of deer present in the Holy Land, the hart and hind references could have been to any one or all of them. The red deer was the biggest, and the stag or hart would probably have been considered the most magnificent, especially when his antlers were fully formed. Walt Disney used the image as the climax to his animated masterpiece *Bambi*.

In the wild, the range of the European red deer once extended into Lebanon, and a closely related subspecies was found in North Africa. Images of the red deer have been found in ancient Egyptian temples. It is the largest of the three species, standing up to 1.27m (4.1ft) at the shoulder, males being bigger than females. This deer gets its name from the red to reddish-brown coat, which becomes darker and greyer in winter.

The fallow deer is picked out for special mention in the Bible. It is *jahmur* in Hebrew, which is thought to be a subspecies of fallow deer (*Dama dama mesopotamica*) that was a native of Persia and was relatively common in the more fertile areas and wooded areas of the country. Unfortunately, there are no more than a hundred animals surviving today in areas of floodplain forest in western Iran. In Tristram's time, it was still found wild in Palestine to the west of the Sea of Galilee, on Mount Tabor, and in the woods between Tabor and the gorge of the River Litany. Today, the fallow has all but vanished because of intensive hunting.

Until around the time of the Shah of Iran's deposition, in 1979, the last wild population was to be found in the willow thickets, Euphrates poplars and tamarisks that grew in the valleys of the Dez, Karcheh and the Uper Karun rivers in western Iran. The locals here called them *yakhmur*, which is also the ancient Hebrew name mentioned in the Bible. They are smallish deer, standing about 90cm

(3ft) at the shoulder, and retain throughout adulthood the spots that most deer lose when mature, meaning that they are camouflaged in the dappled light of a forest. The deer's common English name comes from an Old English word meaning 'brownish-yellow'; fallow deer are said to have been taken to England from the Levant by the Phoenicians.

The third species is the roe deer, and although the 'roebuck' or the 'roe' are mentioned in the Bible (see above), the reference is not thought to be to this deer; rather, it must be included in the general 'hart and hind' deer references. Roe deer are a little smaller than fallow deer, stags standing about 85cm (34in) at the shoulder, and have a characteristic patch of white hairs on the rump that can be erected when the animals are alarmed.

Roe deer were once common in the forests of the Holy Land. Until the nineteenth century, they were present in the mountains of Ramah and Beth-El, in the Jordan Valley, on Mt Carmel and in the Naphtali Mountains near Qedesh. The ancient tribe of Naphtali, whose hilly lands overlooked the Hula Valley, had the roe deer as its emblem. In some places roe deer fawns were raised as pets, and the antlers were used by *fellah* (Egyptian peasant women) to comb the wool of sheep and camels. In the vicinity of Safed alone, Dr Israel Aharoni – the first modern Jewish zoologist – records having seen hundreds of pairs of horns being used in this way at the beginning of the twentieth century In local hotels they were used as coat hangers. Inevitably, the species has been seriously threatened in the region by hunting. Animals have been forced into the mountains, where their agility has enabled them to survive among the rocks.

BADGER
Of the smaller wild mammals, several familiar creatures – badgers, weasels, moles and mice – are mentioned in the Bible, but like many biblical animals they are sometimes not what the seventeenth-century translators thought they were. Take the

badger, for example. On the surface, it might seem obvious to include the animal – after all, there are several species of badgers living in the Holy Land. References in the Bible, however, are not to the animal itself but to its skin.

In ancient times, 'badger skin' appears to have all manner of uses. There were badger skins for sacrifice:

> And the Lord spake unto Moses, saying, Speak unto the children of Israel, that they bring me an offering . . . And this is the offering which ye shall take of them; gold, and silver, and brass, And blue, and purple, and scarlet, and fine linen, and goats' hair, And rams' skins dyed red, and badgers' skins, and shittim wood.

Exodus 25:1–5

Then there were skins for making leather footwear: 'I clothed thee also with broidered work, and shod thee with badgers' skin, and I girded thee about with fine linen, and I covered thee with silk' (Ezekiel 16:10). The simple sandal consisted of a sole made of wood or palm bark fastened by leather straps.

Finally, it was used as a covering for the Ark of the Covenant: 'And thou shalt make a covering for the tent of rams' skins dyed red, and a covering above of badgers' skins' (Exodus 26:14). What sort of badger this could have been is unknown, and to collect enough skins to make a large tent would have been quite a task. Badger leather was on sale in the Middle East when Canon Tristram visited in the nineteenth century, and badger skin rugs, sporrans (the Black Watch regiment changed from badger skin to goat skin or buff leather sporrans in 1769), pouches and other items are made and sold to this day, so the notion of a badger-skin marquee is not total nonsense.

The familiar Eurasian badger (*Meles meles*) has the characteristic black upper parts with white ear tips, and a white face and neck with a pair of black stripes running from the nose, through the eyes to the back of the ears. The honey badger (*Mellivora capensis*) has a 'punk haircut' with white upper parts and black sides and under parts. It could have been this black-and-white pattern of either species that the Ark builders found attractive.

There is, however, another more rational explanation. The Latin *taxus*, meaning 'badger', might well have been confused with the Hebrew word *tachash*, which refers to the skin or fur of a 'clean' animal that has been treated in a particular way, such as 'blue-processed skins'. In fact, the earliest Aramaic translation comes up with an equally cryptic word, *sas-gavna*, from *sas* meaning 'worm' and *gavna* meaning 'colour', suggesting that the word does indeed refer to a process that renders the hide colourful. But which animal is involved? At one time or another, *tachash* has been identified with all sorts of animals – ermine, badger, antelope, okapi, giraffe and an imaginary animal known as a *keresh*. It was a one-horned, unicorn-like animal conveniently thirty cubits long whose hide had six colours. According to legend, it was hidden away after the Tabernacle covers had been completed, so we cannot see it today.

The word *tachash*, though, is remarkably similar to the Arab word *tucash*. The people of the Sinai Peninsula apply the name *tucash* to the skins of seals, porpoises and dugongs (sea cows). It is known that seal and sea cow skins were once used as covers. Pliny notes that they were good for roofs, as it was believed that lightning would not strike them. So it is quite conceivable that porpoise or dolphin skins, or even seal or sea cow skins, could have covered the Ark, and not badger skins.

The monk seal (*Monachus monachus*) was once common in the Mediterranean. Several different species of dolphins and porpoises are there, too. The dugong or sea cow (*Dugong dugon* – from the Malay *duyong*) lives not far away, in the Red Sea.

Monk seals are the only seals that inhabit warm, tropical seas, and the Mediterranean monk seal was probably the source of stories of nymphs and sirens who lay on the rocks and enticed passing sailors to their doom. The seals once hauled themselves out on to beaches and into caves in large numbers, but the population has now decreased substantially – from abundance to near extinction during the course of a human lifetime. They were hunted for blubber and skins. On the Turkish Black Sea coast, for example, monk seal skins were sent to big cities to turn into leather, but locally shoes known as 'carik' were made from seal skins, as were leather harnesses for ploughing oxen. Now the problem is that monk seals are especially vulnerable to disturbance, and the increase in tourist traffic on Mediterranean coasts has meant they have nowhere to go.

The dugong was recorded by the ancient Greeks, Egyptians and Phoenicians, and in more recent times it has been hunted so intensely that it is considered endangered throughout its range, from Australia to Africa. Most parts of its body have uses. The blubber is rendered into oil for cooking, caulking boats and medicinal purposes (it has been used as a cod-liver oil substitute and was thought to be effective against tuberculosis and rheumatism); the meat is said to be like tender veal or pork, and the thick skin makes fine leather that is turned into shoes and shields. The larger teeth of the male are turned into knife handles and other ivory artefacts, and the bones make an excellent charcoal for refining sugar. The eye secretions are considered by some cultures to make a good love potion. Curiously, a previously used scientific name for the population living in the Red Sea is – appropriately, given the biblical context – *Halicore tabernaculi*.

Whether 'badger skin' should be interpreted as a different animal altogether is a mystery unlikely to be solved, but badgers are not the only members of the Mustelidae family present in the region. The stone marten (*Martes foina*) is still found in the hills and mountains of Palestine. In the recent past, skins could be bought in the markets of Jerusalem. The marbled polecat (*Vormela peregusna*) is relatively common, inhabiting the hills and the coastal plain. It has gained a bad reputation on account of its habit of killing chickens but it also catches rats and mice. The common European otter (*Lutra lutra*) is present, albeit in smaller numbers than in the nineteenth century. Today, the upper part of the River Jordan still has otters but the seasonal lowland streams are too polluted.

WEASEL, MOLE AND HEDGEHOG

The weasel is listed with the unclean animals but is mentioned nowhere else in the Bible: "These also shall be unclean unto you among the creeping things that creep upon the earth; the weasel, and the mouse, and the tortoise after his kind' (Leviticus 11:29). Its inclusion is possibly related to the belief – at least according to Hebrew legend – that the female weasel is impregnated via the ears and gives birth through her mouth. It was a story that persisted into the seventeenth century, and it had to be rebuffed by the naturalists of the day, such as Bartholomew: 'their opinion is false that mean that weasels conceive at mouth, and kitteneth at the ear.'

Like most animals, the weasel has medicinal value. The Bavarian scientist, philosopher and theologian Albert Magnus (*c* 1206–80) refers to its efficacy: 'If the heart of a weasel be eaten, while still palpitating, it makes a man know future events.'

Its identification as a 'weasel' in the AV, however, is questionable. Although the common weasel (*Mustela nivalis*) and its larger cousin the polecat (*M. putorius*) are both found in the region, modern translators have suggested various alternatives. The Hebrew word *holedh* might be translated more appropriately as mole rats (*Spalax* spp.), for these are also common throughout the Holy Land.

Mole rats live in tunnels in arid environments and are so well adapted to an underground life that they are essentially blind but have touch-sensitive spines on the face with which they can feel the sides of tunnels. They also use a form of echo-location, banging their heads on the tunnel roof and listening for the echoes bouncing off obstacles in their path. Mole rats' huge incisor teeth protrude from the mouth so that the creatures can dig the earth without opening their mouth. Each mole rat digs its own burrow, which maybe as long as 350m (1,150ft). There are several species, including the Palestine mole rat (*Spalax ehrenbergi*), and they all feed on fleshy roots, bulbs and tubers. They can be a crop pest, but fortunately they are just 13–25cm (5–10in) long, and their subterranean existence means that they do not travel far.

The more familiar mole (*Talpa* spp.) is mentioned twice. The first reference in the AV comes in the list of unclean animals: 'And the ferret, and the chameleon, and the lizard, and the snail, and the mole' (Leviticus 11:30). The Hebrew word in this passage, however, is *tinshemet*, which, according to some Bible naturalists, refers to the desert monitor lizard (*Varanus griseus*) rather than the mole. The second mention is in Isaiah's prophecy of a time of desolation when arrogance and sin will be destroyed before everlasting peace: 'In that day a man shall cast his idols of silver, and his idols of gold, which they made each one for himself to worship, to the moles and to the bats' (Isaiah 2:20).

Here the mole is *chepho-peroth* in Hebrew, referring, appropriately enough, to a burrowing animal. Its identity, though, is more probably the mole rat (see above) because the more familiar moles, such as those from Europe, are not present in the region, even though they are found in neighbouring lands, such as Greece and Turkey, which border the Mediterranean.

Hedgehogs are not mentioned in the Bible at all, even though they are numerous, and several species are present in the Holy Land. The long-eared hedgehog (*Hemiechinus auritus*) is found in the Naqab and on the northern coastal plain, and the Palestine hedgehog (*Erinaceus sacer*) is common in the hills. As its name suggests, the long-eared hedgehog has larger ears and shorter spines than the common European hedgehog. It eats mainly insects and other invertebrates but will feast on fallen grapes on summer evenings. Several hedgehogs together will usually be heard more than seen for they fight noisily with loud, low growls. The Bedouin roast and eat them.

BAT

Bats make very few appearances in the Bible, and in two mentions seem to have been confused with birds. In the list of clean and unclean animals, the bat has been grouped with the unclean birds: 'And these are they which ye shall have in abomination among the fowls . . . And the stork, the heron after her kind, and the lapwing, and the bat' (Leviticus 11:13 and 19).

Bats, of course, are not birds but mammals that fly. They differ in form from birds in having a membrane stretched across the wing rather than feathers. In birds the wing is held across the arm only, whereas in bats it stretches from extended hand bones back to the hind legs. Bats and their fellow flyers – birds, pterodactyls and insects – are a good example of convergent evolution, in that the skill of powered flight evolved independently several times, albeit many millions of years apart. But in Bible times, writers and scholars did not have the classification system devised later by the Swedish naturalist Carl Linnaeus, which grouped together animals with similar anatomical, physiological and behavioural characteristics. Ancient scholars saw bats as flying animals, but categorised them as birds ('fowl' in the AV), along with certain insects, such as butterflies. In Hebrew the term for such creatures was *owph*, meaning 'cover with wings' or 'flying creature'. If the extinct pterosaurs had been around at that time, they would have been grouped with the birds, too, even though today we classify them with the reptiles. In old Hebrew the grouping is similar to that which we use to describe, for example, drifting animal life in the sea or a lake: we call it all 'plankton', even though the animals included come from unrelated animal groups.

The bat has what can only be described as a bad reputation. It has been considered a magical creature, often associated with evil. At the time of the AV translation, it was thought to cohabit with witches and warlocks, and to possess demonic powers. Signs that the tradition had even older roots can be seen in the bat's role in the desolation of the last days: 'In that day a man shall cast his idols of silver, and his idols of gold, which they made each one for himself to worship, to the moles and to the bats' (Isaiah 2:20).

But spare a kind thought for the bat, an extraordinary flying machine that is on the wing at dusk and is able to detect, home in on and snatch a small insect from midair, and all in the dark using echo-location, i.e. bouncing very high frequency sounds off objects in its path and listening for the returning echoes.

The bat in the Bible is named *atalef* or *ataleph*, which refers to the diminutive insect-eating 'microbats' of the suborder Microchiroptera that are usually on the wing at dawn and dusk. There are about twenty species living in the Bible lands, including the short-tailed bat (*Pipistrellus kuhlii*) that Tristram found in caverns under the Temple of Jerusalem and in the Cave of Adullam in Judah. The populations roosting here were so great that they made it difficult for Tristram's party to keep their naked torches alight when crawling through the tunnels. It is a species that nowadays stakes out streetlights and grabs the moths that are attracted to the glow.

There are also fruit bats present in the region. These are the so-called 'mega-bats' of the suborder Megachiroptera, known also as 'flying foxes'. Fruit bats can be agricultural pests, stripping apricot and other trees of their fruit, which they take to a distant perch to eat. Farmers counter this by protecting the crop in plastic bags or even enclosing the entire tree in a net. Fruit bats fly during the day, whereas the microbats are mainly on the wing at night.

Being about at night, and roosting in damp and dark places such as caves, bats have inevitably been aligned with the devil and witches, and, like many of the animals mentioned in the Bible, they were thought to have unusual medical properties. In *Of Wonders of the World*, Albert Magnus points out a way in which bats might be useful to bedtime readers:

If you wish to see anything submerged and deep in the night, and that it may not be hidden from thee than in the day, and that you may read books in the dark night – anoint your face with the blood of a bat and that will happen which I say.

CONEY

Another small creature on the 'unclean' list is a rabbit-like character called the coney: 'And the coney, because he cheweth the cud, but divideth not the hoof; he is unclean unto you' (Leviticus 11:5).

At the time of the AV translation, 'coney' was a name for the rabbit, from the Latin *cuniculus*, but rabbits are not present in Palestine. In Hebrew it is *shafan* or *shaphan*, meaning 'one that hides'. Whatever its true identity, the coney lived in the more remote parts of the Holy Land, and although it was a little creature, it was considered one of four (together with the ant, locust and spider) to be wise.

Its habitat was rocky landscape: 'The high hills are a refuge for the wild goats; and the rocks for the conies' (Psalm 104:18); 'The conies are but a feeble folk, yet make they their houses in rocks' (Proverbs 30:26). Any number of small mammals – mice and rats, for example – could make their home in the rocks of a mountain wilderness, but the favourite for the identity of the coney is not the rabbit but the Syrian hyrax (*Procavia capensis syriaca*), a subspecies of the rock hyrax or dassie. It is a bit of an enigma among small mammals, for at first naturalists thought it was related to guinea pigs (*Cavia* spp.) (hence the scientific name), but it later became apparent that its nearest living relatives are elephants and aardvarks, collectively known as the 'primitive ungulates'.

The Bible's reference to the coney 'chewing the cud' is not altogether correct. The rock hyrax has relatively primitive features. It feeds mainly on coarse grasses, cropping with the molar or cheek teeth, rather than the front incisors. It does not ruminate, but it has a complex gut with three separate areas where microbial digestion takes place, and so can deal effectively with fibres just as more advanced ruminants, such as cattle, do. It constantly moves its jaws, however, so to the untrained eye it could look as if it is chewing the cud.

The rock hyrax makes up for its less advanced digestive system by having several anatomical and physiological features that equip it for a life in the rocky wilderness. The creature has rubber pads on the bottom of its feet that are lined with many sweat glands. As the animal runs, its feet sweat, the moist layer giving it better traction, enabling it to climb more easily over rocks. It also has tactile hairs distributed over the body that help it find its way in dark holes and clefts.

Unlike other desert animals, however, the rock hyrax is very poor at regulating its body temperature. Therefore several will huddle together for warmth at night and on cold days, and bask in the sun each morning before foraging. The rock hyrax has super-efficient kidneys, so it is able to survive with little water intake; it also produces very concentrated urea and excretes large quantities of calcium carbonate. As individuals tend to urinate in the same places, splashes of white crystals form over time and local people have used them as medicine.

The rock hyrax's natural predators are leopards, lions, jackals and eagles, to which we must add man. The hyrax is prized by the Arabs for its flesh, and, true to form, Tristram tried it and found the meat dark and rather like hare. Hyrax are hard to catch, however, as they tend to post guards and warn each other of danger with a high-pitched scream. Another nineteenth-century wandering cleric, the Reverend F K Holland, made the following observation:

> Once, when crossing a mountain pass, I was startled by a shrill scream near me, but could see nothing. On my return in the evening, I approached the place cautiously, and saw eight conies out, playing like rabbits. I watched

them for some minutes before they saw me. At length one caught sight of me, and immediately uttered its scream, and all at once rushed to their holes.

Nowadays, hyraxes often hide among the fallen rocks at the edge of a kibbutz cultivation. They wait for the coast to be clear before raiding the crops. Where food was once scarce and cultivation has expanded, rock hyraxes have increased dramatically in numbers. A similar increase in numbers due to an expansion of agriculture is true for the porcupines, such as the crested porcupine (*Hystrix indica*) of wetland areas, which do not get a mention in the Bible. Squirrels, which are also left out, have not been so successful. The Syrian squirrel (*Sciurus anomals syriacus*) was once common in the scrub forest south of Mt Hermon and the Lebanon, around Damascus and in Gilead, and the forest of Galilee. The only known population to survive today is in the lower region of Wadi Assal (Nahal Siyon).

HARE

While there are no rabbits in the Holy Land, there *are* hares. The hare (*Lepus europeus syriacus*) in this region is a smaller and paler subspecies of the common European or brown hare. It has two entries in the Bible, in the list of unclean animals: 'Nevertheless these shall ye not eat of them that chew the cud, or of them that divide the hoof: . . . the hare, because he cheweth the cud, but divideth not the hoof; he is unclean to you' (Leviticus 11:4 and 6).

The error here is that the hare – *arnaheth* in Hebrew, *arneb* in Arabic – does not chew the cud. Moses' mistake could be forgiven because hares tend to grind their incisor teeth to keep them at a manageable length and this movement, like that of the coney, strongly resembles chewing the cud. Their inclusion on the unclean list, though, might still be relevant because they recycle their droppings in order to extract every ounce of water and nourishment.

Hares are animals of open country, with long rear legs adapted for a quick escape when danger threatens. Brush-like hairs on the feet pads help with grip and cushion the feet on hard ground. Some hares can reach speeds in excess of 80km/h (50mph). The ears are large to help pick up audible signs of danger and also help in heat regulation – blood can be directed to the ears when it is hot and in this way lose heat, or directed away from the ears to retain heat when it is cold.

In Hebrew folklore the hare was afforded magical properties, such as its ability to change sex. This attribute was alleged to have followed an unfortunate disaster that occurred when the female hare escaped from the Ark, only to drown. Subsequently, the male was reportedly given the power to have offspring. As a consequence, the stomach of a male hare was considered a cure for infertility. It was a legend that influenced the seventeenth-century translators, and was recorded as a 'reality' by Topsell. He also suggested that the beast was magical, stating that a person could get a harelip just by looking at a hare! Lupton, another seventeenth-century natural historian, proposed in his *A Thousand Notable Things of Sundry Sorts* (1627) that the brain of the hare had unusual dental properties that mothers could make use of: 'boys' gums are cleansed; for it has the power to make the teeth come quickly and without pain'.

The hunting of hares was depicted on Assyrian reliefs, and the animal also appeared on wall paintings in ancient Egypt. To the Romans, roast rabbit meat and embryos were a delicacy, and hares and rabbits were kept in fenced areas known as 'leporaria'. During the time of the Roman Empire, the practice was introduced to the rest of Europe, where escapees from monasteries and other establishments that kept rabbits invaded the countryside and became a serious agricultural pest, a situation that exists in some places, such as the British Isles, to this day.

Tristram recognised several subspecies in the region. Apart from the Syrian hare, which has slightly shorter ears than its

European cousin, there is a southern version (*Lepus europeu aegyptiacus*) that is no bigger than a rabbit but with ultra-long ears – it lives in the southern region of Judaea and the Jordan Valley. In the southeast *L. e. sinaiticus* inhabits the Arabian Peninsula, and in Egyptian deserts there is *L. e. isabelinus;* both subspecies may be distinguished by their small size and buff colour.

MOUSE AND OTHER SMALL MAMMALS

Mice receive six mentions in the Bible, but none is becoming. As one might expect, the mouse is considered unclean: 'These also shall be unclean unto you among the creeping things that creep upon the earth; the weasel, and the mouse, and the tortoise after his kind' (Leviticus 11:29).

The Hebrew word here is *akbar* or *akhbar*, and the Arabic *far ah*, meaning 'corn eater' and it is a broad term that refers to all manner of small, brown, fluffy rodents living in the region. The choice is considerable, and includes field mice, voles, dormice, shrews, jerboas and gerbils. In order to narrow down the selection, scholars have tried to assign species to different passages. In the Old Testament, for example, there is a reference to the way in which certain people have gone away from the true faith by eating forbidden foods: 'They that sanctify themselves, and purify themselves in the gardens behind one tree in the midst, eating swine's flesh, and the abomination, and the mouse, shall be consumed together' (Isaiah 66:17).

It is quite possible that the 'mouse' in this context was actually one of three species: the jerboa or desert rat (*Jaculus orientalis*) with its long back legs made for leaping; the golden hamster (*Mesocricetus auratus*) – the very species that people keep these days as pets, which originated in Syria (all the pet hamsters today were bred from a male and two females that were caught in 1930 by Dr Israel Aharoni of the Hebrew University in Jerusalem); and the edible dormouse (*Glis glis*), an animal famed for its deep hibernation, a characteristic that led to the French expression translated as 'to sleep like a dormouse'.

In ancient times, many of these species were considered a delicacy and eaten. The Arabs were not so circumspect as the Jews and they ate jerboas, dormice and the large fat sand rat or fat jird (*Psammomys obesus*). In about 100 BCE the Romans bred dormice for the pot, rearing them in special gardens, known as *gliraria*, that were planted with oak and beech trees. The animals were kept first in large enclosures and then fattened up with acorns and chestnuts in small earthenware vessels known as *dolia*. They were served up as 'one of the greatest delicacies on the table of rich gormandisers'.

In the wild, all are animals well adapted for the dry conditions of the Middle East. The desert jerboa, for instance, does not drink water but manufactures what is known as 'metabolic water' from its food. It has tufts of hair around its ear openings to prevent sand from entering and a thickened fold of skin that can be drawn down to protect its nostrils when the jerboa is digging. The golden hamster ('hamster' derives from the German word *hamstern*, meaning 'to hoard') survives on desert vegetation that would be inedible to other creatures, such as the autumn crocus (*Colchicum*) that contains high levels of colchicines, poisonous alkaloids that are nevertheless useful in the treatment of gout.

Other species present in the region include sand rats (*Psammomys* spp.) and gerbils (*Gerbillus* spp.), including the bushy-tailed gerbil (*Sekeetamys calurus*), and jirds (*Meriones* spp.). They burrow about the roots of desert plants and in among the rock in hilly districts. According to Tristram, one species is 'as large as a squirrel and much heavier'. He also describes porcupine mice (*Acomys* spp.) as a common rodent in the ravines and wilderness close to the Dead Sea and in the southern deserts at the time of his journeys in the mid-nineteenth century. Their backs are covered with long, grooved hairs, not unlike those of hedgehogs. One population feeds exclusively on bat droppings carpeting the Aswan tombs.

The other Bible references to the mouse are in the story of the return of the Ark of the Covenant from Philistia. The Philistine priests thought it appropriate to send a gift to repay the sin of having stolen it and kept it. Part of the gift was gold statuettes of mice, a reminder of the mouse plagues that ravaged the country: 'Wherefore ye shall make . . . images of your mice that mar the land' (1 Samuel 6:5). The 'mice' on this occasion were probably the European vole (*Microtus arvalis*), a species prone to sudden population explosions that could wreak havoc in agricultural lands. Similar plagues have occurred in Spain and Italy in the distant past, and in Australia in recent times. Herodotus described a similar event. On that occasion the armies of Sennacherib were having a go at the Egyptians, but an army of mice nibbled at their bowstrings, quivers, shield covers and leather harnesses and they had to withdraw. In thanksgiving for their rescue, the Egyptians similarly created a golden statue of a mouse and presented it to their gods.

In some modern editions of the Bible, the Philistia experience is attributed not to mice but to rats. The other appeasement gifts accompanying the Ark were gold models signifying another plague that hit the Philistines, described in the AV as 'emerods' and translated in modern versions as 'tumours'. The plague was described by the first-century CE Jewish priest, scholar and historian Flavius Josephus as 'sore distemper', which eventually killed anybody inflicted with it. This is reminiscent of bubonic plague, which is transmitted by the fleas that live on rats, particularly the black rat (*Rattus rattus*), which originated in India but quickly made it to other parts of the world when international trade increased. In about CE 100 Rufus of Ephesus, the legendary Greek physician who lived in the Roman Empire during the reign of Trajan, published accounts of 'deadly bubonic outbreaks in the Levant about 300 BCE'.

At the time of the AV translation in the seventeenth century, mice had almost the same reputation as rats. Bartholomew said of the mouse that: 'His urine stinketh and is contagious; and his biting is venomous and his tail venomous.' Nevertheless, he conceded that the mouse had something going for it, though who would consent to be treated by such foul methods is a mystery: 'Mice dirt bruised with vinegar keepeth and saveth the head from falling of hair. His new skin laid about the heel, healeth and saveth kibes [chapped skin] and wounds.'

IVORY AND APE

At the other end of the size range is the elephant, the largest living land mammal. Elephants as such are not mentioned in the Bible, but their ivory is. The Hebrew word is *shen*, meaning 'tooth': 'Moreover the king made a great throne of ivory, and overlaid it with the best gold' (1 Kings 10:18). Solomon was the king in this instance, but he was not the only ivory connoisseur: 'Now the rest of the acts of Ahab, and all that he did, and the ivory house which he made, and all the cities that he built, are they not written in the book of the chronicles of the kings of Israel?' (1 Kings 22:39).

In God's judgement against Israel, however, ivory houses were among the first structures to be removed: 'And I will smite the winter house with the summer house; and the houses of ivory shall perish' (Amos 3:15).

Ivory was used also on Tyrian ships, along with hulls built from fir trees from Senir, masts of Lebanese cedar and Bashan oak oars: 'the company of the Ashurites have made thy benches of ivory, brought out of the isles of Chittim' (Ezekiel 27:6).

The only references to elephants themselves occur in the books of the Aprocrypha. A couple of centuries before the Christian era, in 190 BCE, there were records of elephants being used in warfare by the Romans: 'How also Antichus the great king of Asia, that came against them in battle having a hundred and twenty elephants, with horsemen, and chariots, and a very great army, was discomfited by them' (1 Maccabees 8:6).

Scipio Africanus was the commander, and he was not the only

general to use elephants. Some time earlier, the Greek Antichus Epiphanes used them to invade Egypt: 'Wherefore he entered into Egypt with a great multitude, with chariots, and elephants, and horsemen, and a great navy' (1 Maccabees 1:17).

And elephants featured in another battle between Antiochus Eupator and Judas Maccabeus. The battlefield was at Bethsura:

> Now when the king heard this, he was angry, and gathered together all his friends, and the captains of his army, and those that had charge of the horse. There came also unto him from other kingdoms, and from isles of the sea, bands of hired soldiers. So that the number of his army was an hundred thousand footmen, and twenty thousand horsemen, and two and thirty elephants exercised in battle . . . And to the end they might provoke the elephants to fight, they shewed them the blood of grapes and mulberries. Moreover they divided the beasts among the armies, and for every elephant they appointed a thousand men, armed with coats of mail, and with helmets of brass on their heads; and beside this, for every beast were ordained five hundred horsemen of the best. These were ready at every occasion: wheresoever the beast was, and whithersoever the beast went, they went also, neither departed they from him. And upon the beasts were there strong towers of wood, which covered every one of them, and were girt fast unto them with devices: there were also upon every one two and thirty strong men, that fought upon them, beside the Indian that ruled him. As for the remnant of the horsemen, they set them on this side and that side at the two parts of the host, giving them signs what to do, and being harnessed all over amidst the ranks. Now when the sun shone upon the shields of gold and brass, the mountains glistered therewith, and shined like lamps of fire . . . Then Judas and his host drew near, and entered into the battle, and

there were slain of the king's army six hundred men. Eleazar also, surnamed Savaran, perceived that one of the beasts, armed with royal harness, was higher than all the rest, and supposing that the king was upon him, put himself in jeopardy, to the end he might deliver his people, and get him a perpetual name: wherefore he ran upon him courageously through the midst of the battle, slaying on the right hand and on the left, so that they were divided from him on both sides. Which done, he crept under the elephant, and thrust him under, and slew him: whereupon the elephant fell down upon him, and there he died.

1 Maccabees 6:28–47

Like elephants, the primates are almost ignored by the Bible writers. Apes are cited twice, both as imported goods for King Solomon: 'the king had at sea a navy of Tharshish with the navy of Hiram: once in three years came the navy of Tharshish, bringing gold, and silver, ivory, and apes, and peacocks' (1 Kings 10:22); 'the king's ships went to Tarshish with the servants of Huram: every three years once came the ships of Tarshish bringing gold, and silver, ivory, and apes, and peacocks' (2 Chronicles 9:21).

The mention of Tarshish (or Tharshish) in these two passages may be confusing, for ancient Tarshish was a Mediterranean port. It's likely the reference is to the sailors of Tarshish, who helped Solomon crew his ships, rather than the place itself.

Solomon commissioned the building of a fleet of ships at Ezion-geber (between today's Elat and Al 'Aqabath) on the Red Sea coast. They were probably crewed by the sailors of King Hiram, whose own ships were based at Tyre, a sea port built on an island, known now as Sur in southern Lebanon, and by experienced seamen from Tarshish, an ancient seaport in southern Spain where Cadiz is today. Solomon's ships were crewed by specialists and they were free of the constraints of the

Mediterranean (there was no Suez Canal in those days). They could enter the Indian Ocean, where the Indian subcontinent and the coast of East Africa would have been accessible.

The imports mentioned in the passage were probably acquired from Ophir, a producer of fine gold. The precise location of Ophir is unknown; in fact, nobody seems to know even which continent it was on. In Genesis 10:29 Ophir is located on the Arabian Peninsula, but by Solomon's time (c 920 BCE) it was a place reached only by sea.

Some scholars place Ophir in East Africa, for the Egyptian pharaohs sent naval expeditions to Punt in Somaliland to obtain monkeys, ivory, frankincense (resin from a tree of the genus *Boswellia* from Arabia and Somalia) and slaves. St Jerome and the Jewish historian Josephus, on the other hand, place Ophir – or Sophir, as they called it – in India. This was most probably Sopara or Surparaka, an ancient port to the north of Bombay on India's west coast.

Ivory and apes could well have come from either place. True apes – chimpanzees and gorillas – together with ivory from African elephants could have come from Africa. If so, another identity for 'apes' could be baboons. Although baboons are not native to the Holy Land, they appear on ancient reliefs. The Egyptians worshipped them, believing that their calls in the morning were prayers to the sun god. Thoth, the Egyptian god of wisdom and scribe of the gods, was portrayed sometimes with an ibis head but also as a seated baboon-headed dog.

However, peacocks and another of Solomon's imports – sandalwood – do not occur naturally in East Africa. They are found on the Indian subcontinent. Ivory from the Asian elephant could also have been obtained from there. Further evidence of a southern Asian origin for these animals can be found in the different words for apes and monkeys. The Hebrew word translated in the AV as 'apes' is *koph* or *qoth*, which is similar to the Sanskrit name for monkey, *kapi*, meaning 'swift and nimble'. It follows that the apes may not have been apes at all, but monkeys. At the time the AV was translated, the word 'ape' was less precise than it is today.

One of the most common monkeys that Solomon's voyagers would have encountered was the rhesus macaque (*Macaca mulatto*), which is native to India and other southern Asian countries. This monkey is a tree-dweller that lives on the forest edge and is often found on the outskirts of towns and villages. It feeds on fruit, leaves and the occasional insect and other small animals. Other contenders are the lion-tailed macaque (*M. silenus*) and the bonnet macaque (*M. radiata*) of southern India, and the togue macaque (*M. sinica*) of Sri Lanka. Unidentified long-tailed monkeys resembling macaques can be seen on Assyrian reliefs and painted on Egyptian tombs, and they must have been imported, as no monkey or ape occurs naturally in the Holy Land.

The population of monkeys closest to the Holy Land inhabits the mountain forests of North Africa. Here we find the Barbary macaque (*M. sylvanus*), also known as the 'Barbary ape'. It scrapes a living in forests where the temperature can plummet to below zero and snow is on the ground in winter. However, the mountains of northern Algeria and Morocco are on the opposite shore of the Mediterranean to Tarshish. So, could the Barbary ape be the 'ape' that was delivered by the Tarshish fleet? Its home base was the ancient port of Tartessus, a Phoenician colony on the coast of southern Spain, which was also a centre for smelting ores.

The AV translators would have been familiar with monkeys and apes, for they were brought to England and trained to perform at court. Their ability to copy human activities and behaviour gave rise to the verb 'to ape'. At that time, and for many years afterwards, our nearest relatives in the animal kingdom were considered not only to be the embodiment of extreme ugliness, but also to have a vengeful disposition, to be lustful and to cheat and swindle. They became emblematic of humankind's more dubious side. It was something with which Charles Darwin had to come to terms two hundred years later, when he revealed that we are descended from apes.

7

ALL THE BIRDS OF THE AIR

The Bible lands are remarkably rich in bird life, with nearly four hundred species having been identified from Palestine alone, compared to just over four hundred species in the entire British Isles, an area ten times bigger. They also occur in large numbers, and populations would have been even larger in biblical times, so it would have been difficult for the scripture writers to have missed them. They saw hawks and eagles soar overhead by day, were fearful of the call of an owl at night, were woken up by the crow of the cock at dawn, and they were aware of the seasonal to and fro of passage-migrants in spring and autumn – in fact, the Bible contains our oldest description of bird migration.

It comes as no surprise, then, to find that birds feature strongly in the Bible, with more than three hundred references, and they were present right at the beginning of Creation. Birds, according to the Good Book, were created on the fifth day.

> And God created great whales, and every living creature that moveth, which the waters brought forth abundantly, after their kind, and every winged fowl after his kind: and God saw that it was good.
>
> Genesis 1:21

The word 'fowl', or *oph* in Hebrew, meaning 'flier with feathers', was the first attempt at bird classification. It set birds aside from other beasts and men: 'the fishes of the sea, and the fowls of the heaven, and the beasts of the field, and all creeping things that creep upon the earth, and all the men that are upon the face of the earth' (Ezekiel 38:20).

In reality, of course, the fifth day when 'fowl' were created was not a 'day' in our 24-hour sense, and it happened some 150 million years ago. Birds evolved as a separate animal group during the Jurassic period, when a creature resembling *Archaeopteryx* – a feathered bird-like animal with wings, a beak with teeth, perching feet and a reptile's tail – attempted to escape its reptilian ancestry and fly. Since that significant moment in geological history, birds have evolved into all manner of shapes and sizes and have filled almost every available ecological niche on the planet, bar the bottom of the deepest oceans.

RAVEN

The first modern species to get a mention in the Bible is the raven. It was the bird that Noah first released to search for land as the waters of the Great Flood began to subside:

> And it came to pass at the end of forty days, that Noah opened the window of the ark which he had made: And he sent forth a raven, which went forth to and fro, until the waters were dried up from off the earth.

> Genesis 8:6–7

As a carrion-eating opportunist, it must have found plenty of floating carcases to keep it busy, for though it returned to the ark, it used the vessel only as a perch and did not go right back inside to Noah. Understandably, Noah was not impressed and, according to Hebrew legend, he cursed the bird. Nevertheless, other seafarers valued ravens. The bird was thought to be able to smell out land and was taken on voyages of exploration around the world.

Legend has it that the raven's failure to return to the Ark and the dove's return with the olive branch – the symbol of hope – led to the two birds corning to represent opposite ends of the moral spectrum. The white dove became the emblem of peace and hope, while the black raven came to symbolise evil. Indeed, the raven became known as the devil's bird, and was regarded as a creature that brought bad luck. Large numbers were seen when Alexander entered Babylon in 330 BCE, for instance, and this was considered a portent of his death.

In *Othello* Shakespeare picked up on the superstition, especially the belief that a raven can smell a dying person from the stench wafting from a chimney; it will flap around the windows, looking for the corpse on which it can scavenge.

> O it comes o'er my memory
> As doth the raven, o'er the infected house,
> Boding to all.
>
> *Othello*, IV.i

Legend also holds that the raven is neglectful of its young and so God had to make special provision. During the first three days after hatching, the chicks are supposedly abandoned. God then causes maggots to spring from their parents' droppings so that they have food until their feathers turn black and their parents recognise and care for them. A variation on this story (minus the maggots) is told by Bartholomew:

> The raven beholdeth the mouth of her birds when they yawn. But she giveth them no meat ere she know and see the likeness of her own blackness, and of her own colour and feathers; and when they begin to wax black,

then afterward she feedeth them with all her might and strength. Raven's birds be fed with dew of heaven all the time that they have no black feathers.

It is thought that this story of deficiency in parental care may have originated with one of the psalmists: 'He giveth to the beast his food, and to the young ravens which cry' (Psalms 147:9).

Other legends tell how the raven once walked like other birds, but it had a strong desire to step out as gracefully as the dove. It tried to imitate the dove but failed miserably, almost breaking the bones in its leg during the attempt. The other birds mocked it, but when it reverted to walking like a raven it found that it had forgotten, and now it walks very clumsily, taking short hops. The raven was a parable for the dissatisfied, an indication of how a person unhappy with their lot might well lose what they had in the first place if they coveted that which belongs to others.

Although nowadays its plumage is jet-black, legend has it that the raven was once white. The stories vary. Hebrew folklore has it that the bird's failure to return to the Ark caused God to change its colour. Another – a Greek legend – tells how Apollo sent the raven to a spring to fetch water. Next to the spring grew a fig tree, and when the bird visited, the fruit was ready to eat. The raven stayed and gorged itself, but how could it explain away its delay? It had a brainwave. It grabbed a water snake that was basking in the sun, and took it back to Apollo, telling the god that the snake had drunk the spring dry. Apollo, quite understandably, failed to believe the bird and he changed its plumage from white to black. Not only that, but he also condemned the raven to continuous spasms of thirst, and that's why the raven calls not with a melodious song but an unimpressive squawk.

The raven certainly made an impression on the minds of the mythmakers. Carvings of ravens have been found on Assyrian and Egyptian monuments, and the Romans regarded ravens as omens. In Scandinavian myth the raven is the sacred bird of Odin, and in Arthurian legend King Arthur lives on in the guise of a raven (the Cornish chough in some accounts), so people who believe in him will avoid killing the bird for fear of slaying the warrior king.

In the seventeenth century the AV translators would have been influenced by the way naturalists gave the raven magical powers. In his *Of the Virtues of Animals*, Albertus Magnus wrote of the raven:

> If a raven's eggs be boiled and put again in the nest, straightway the raven goes to a certain island in the Red Sea where Aldoricus or Alodrius is buried, and brings a stone with which it toucheth its eggs and immediately they become raw as they were before. It is wonderful that the boiled eggs should be revived. Now, if that stone be set in a ring with a laurel leaf under it, and a man bound in chains of a closed gate be touched, straightway the bound shall be loosened and the gate opened. And if that stone be put in the ear, it gives understanding of all birds. This stone is of diverse colours, and causes all anger to be forgotten.

And when a raven kills a mythical chameleon, it is able to neutralise the creature's poison by eating laurel leaves.

The raven also had supposed medicinal uses. Raven broth was prepared by burning a bird and mashing the dried body and bones to powder. This was added to a suitable liquid and drunk, in the belief that it would be good for gout. This kind of supernatural hogwash was the pseudoscientific background to the AV. Nonetheless, unlike some other birds, the raven comes through as an undisputed translation. The Hebrew word for the bird is *oreb*, from the root meaning 'to be black', a feature cited in Solomon's description of the 'beloved': 'His head is as the most fine gold, his locks are bushy, and black as a raven' (Song of Solomon 5:11).

The bird, however, was unlikely to have been the raven (*Corvus corax*) that we see in the North, but more probably the brown-necked raven (*C. ruficollis*) that is more common in the Bible lands. In flight, it can be recognised by its wedge-shaped tail and square ends to its wings, and it will soar to great heights like a bird of prey. It nests on rocky crags, and will hunt for small mammals. The brown-necked raven is also a scavenger, taking advantage of dead lambs and sheep placentas at lambing time. Tristram describes how he had seen ravens on more than one occasion attacking newly born kids. It also has a reputation for pecking out their eyes, and the eyes of any weak or sick animal: 'The eye that mocketh at his father, and despiseth to obey his mother, the ravens of the valley shall pick it out' (Proverbs 30:17).

The ravens could, in fact, be one of several species common in the Holy Land. Beside the common and brown-necked ravens, there is the fan-tailed raven (*C. rhipidurus*) found also in northeast Africa, Arabia and Syria, the hooded crow (*C. corone comix*) of eastern Europe, the jackdaw (*C. monedula*) and the Alpine chough (*Pyrrhocorax graculus*). Tristram encountered the smaller brown-necked raven:

> They are present everywhere to eye and ear, and the odours that float around remind us of their use. The discordant jabber of their evening sittings round the temple area is deafening. The caw of the Rook and the chatter of the Jackdaw unite in attempting to drown the hoarse croak of the old Raven, but clear above the tumult rings out the more musical call-note of hundreds of lesser species. We used to watch this great colony as, every morning at day-break, they passed in long lines over our tents to the northward; the rooks in solid phalanx leading the way, and the ravens in loose order bringing up the rear, far out of shot. Before retiring for the night, popular assemblies of the most uproarious character were held in the trees of Mount Olivet and the

Kedron, and not until after sunset did they withdraw in silence, mingled indiscriminately, to their roosting-places in the sanctuary.

Altogether there are eleven references to the raven in the Bible, ten of which are in the Old Testament. It is one of the entries on the unclean list: 'Every raven after his kind' (Leviticus 11:15). Not only the raven itself is not to be eaten, but also all the other members of the corvid family, such as crows, rooks and jackdaws, which are all numerous in the Middle East. Moses probably included them on his hit list because he recognised that they are all mainly carrion-eaters. Ravens (along with a whole host of wretched birds mentioned later) also turn up in the desolated environment of Edom, the land between the Dead and Red Seas that is the driest region in Israel and which is known today as the Negev: 'the raven shall dwell in it: and he shall stretch out upon it the line of confusion, and the stones of emptiness' (Isaiah 34:11). Tristram's expedition in the 1860s found ravens in the most desolate of places:

> Even at the south end of the Dead Sea, where the ancient fortress of Masada overlooks a waterless, lifeless wilderness of salthills, the three species of Raven were to be found; and during our sojourn under Jebel Usdum, the salt mountain, we constantly saw the great ravens perched on the salt cliffs; though what, save a love of desolation, could have brought them there, it were hard to guess.

Ravens often nest and roost in ravines – inaccessible sheer-sided valleys and gorges that are common in the Holy Land. In such wilderness areas its food is scarce, and so it must fly great distances constantly searching. It is also, however, an image used as a sign of God's goodness and his provision of care: 'Who provideth for the raven his food? When his young ones cry unto God, they wander for lack of meat' (Job 38:41); 'Consider the ravens: for they neither sow nor reap; which neither have storehouse nor barn; and God feedeth them: how much more are ye better than the fowls?' (Luke 12:24).

Food may be difficult to find, but it was the raven that brought food to the prophet Elijah at the brook called Cherith:

> And it shall be, that thou shalt drink of the brook; and I have commanded the ravens to feed thee there. So he went and did according unto the word of the Lord: for he went and dwelt by the brook Cherith, that is before Jordan. And the ravens brought him bread and flesh in the morning, and bread and flesh in the evening; and he drank of the brook.
>
> 1 Kings 17:4–6

Some commentators have suggested that Elijah plundered carrion from the raven's nest, but others contend that the text mentions nothing of bird catching and nest robbing, but rather acknowledges a supernatural provider.

DOVES AND PIGEONS

Noah gave up on the raven, no matter how uproarious it might be, and his next pioneer was the dove. This bird is the second bird species to appear in the Bible and it is also the most frequently mentioned. It appears more than fifty times – 31 as dove and 11 as pigeon in the AV. Its first outing is a flight from the Ark:

> Also he sent forth a dove from him, to see if the waters were abated from off the face of the ground; But the dove found no rest for the sole of her foot, and she returned unto him into the ark, for the waters were on the face of the whole earth: then he put forth his hand,

and took her, and pulled her in unto him into the ark. And he stayed yet other seven days; and again he sent forth the dove out of the ark; and the dove came in to him in the evening; and, lo, in her mouth was an olive leaf pluckt off: so Noah knew that the waters were abated from off the earth. And he stayed yet other seven days; and sent forth the dove; which returned not again unto him any more.

Genesis 8:8–12

Not long after the dove was venerated for its valiant excursion over uncharted waters, however, it was for the chop: the dove's second appearance in the Bible is in a sacrifice by Abraham: 'Take me an heifer of three years old, and a she goat of three years old, and a ram of three years old, and a turtledove, and a young pigeon' (Genesis 15:9).

It became a tough (and in some cases short) life for doves. According to Moses, the dove or pigeon was the only bird that could be offered up in a religious ceremony. It was readily available and an acceptable sacrificial substitute for people who could not afford a kid or lamb. Indeed, it was the custom for a mother to sacrifice a lamb and a pigeon not long after the birth of her child, but if she was poor she could sacrifice two pigeons:

> And when the days of her purifying are fulfilled, for a son, or for a daughter, she shall bring a lamb of the first year for a burnt offering, and a young pigeon, or a turtledove, for a sin offering, unto the door of the tabernacle of the congregation, unto the priest: Who shall offer it before the Lord, and make an atonement for her; and she shall be cleansed from the issue of her blood. This is the law for her that hath born a male or female. And if she be not able to bring a lamb, then she shall bring two turtles, or two young pigeons; the one for the

burnt offering, and the other for the sin offering: and the priest shall make an atonement for her, and she shall be clean.

Leviticus 12:6–8

Mary the mother of Jesus was poor and she could afford only pigeons: 'And to offer a sacrifice according to that which is said in the law of the Lord, A pair of turtledoves, or two young pigeons' (Luke 2:24). Pigeons were used so extensively in sacrifice that pigeon sellers had their stalls stockpiled with ample birds at the temple. It was this trading that annoyed Jesus so much: 'And [He] said unto them that sold doves, Take these things hence; make not my Father's house an house of merchandise' (John 2:16).

Other mentions of doves in the New Testament include the time Jesus was baptised in the Jordan by John: 'And Jesus, when he was baptized, went up straightway out of the water: and, lo, the heavens were opened unto him, and he saw the Spirit of God descending like a dove, and lighting upon him' (Matthew 3:16). And there was the time when Jesus's disciples were sent out into the world: 'Behold, I send you forth as sheep in the midst of wolves: be ye therefore wise as serpents, and harmless as doves' (Matthew 10:16).

The Old Testament recognises some of the dove's many attributes, such as its ability to fly great distances: 'And I said, Oh that I had wings like a dove! for then would I fly away, and be at rest' (Psalms 55:6). The metallic lustre of its plumage also drew admiring remarks: 'Though ye have lien among the pots, yet shall ye be as the wings of a dove covered with silver, and her feathers with yellow gold' (Psalms 68:13).

This suggestion that the dove was beautiful extended especially to the eyes: 'Behold, thou art fair, my love; behold, thou art fair; thou hast doves' eyes'; 'O my dove, thou art in clefts of the rock, in the secret places of the stairs, let me see thy countenance, let me hear thy voice; for sweet is thy voice, and thy countenance is comely'(Song of Solomon 1:15, 2:14). While it may have represented stupidity for Hosea – 'Ephraim also is like a silly dove without heart' (Hosea 7:11) – it was more usually a symbol of purity.

Solomon wrote eloquently of the dove's 'sweet voice', but Hezekiah thought it was more morose, and Isaiah seemed to get carried away entirely: 'Like a crane or a swallow, so did I chatter: I did mourn as a dove' (Isaiah 38:14); 'We roar all like bears, and mourn sore like doves' (Isaiah 59:11); 'Huzzab shall be led away captive, she shall be brought up, and her maids shall lead her as with the voice of doves, tapering upon their breasts' (Nahum 2:7).

The pigeons and doves that were (and still are) present in the Holy Land were many. There was the *Columba* group that included the wood pigeon (*C. palumbus*), the stock dove (*C. oenas*) and the rock dove (*C. livia*), and the *Streptopelia* group, featuring the turtle dove (*Streptopelia turtur*), the laughing or Egyptian palm dove (*S. senegalensis aegyptiaca*) and the collared dove (*S. decaocto*).

Of all the birds mentioned in ancient records, the dove or pigeon was probably one of the first to be domesticated. Indeed, before Solomon introduced peacocks and other game birds from India there is no evidence of any other bird being domesticated in the region. It became popular and was reared widely. Tristram, for example, tells how the village sheikh in Syria in the 1860s would have a separate dovecot built of mud or brick in which were placed earthen pots, each containing a pair of doves. Poorer people reared birds in their houses: 'In the village of Carmel there is a row of small square pigeon-holes formed in the wall just under the roof opposite the door, each of which has a pair of tenants, who fly in and out over the heads of the family through the common door.'

At that time, according to Tristram, there were more pigeon fanciers in Syria than in England. The dovecots were alluded to in a passage describing the return of God's people from distant lands: 'Who are these that fly as a cloud, and as the doves to their windows?' (Isaiah 60:8).

To this day, flocks of pigeons 'fly as a cloud' in many cities around the world. Both pigeons and doves have the rock dove as their common ancestor, a bird that nests in the wild in rocky cliffs and ravines – another characteristic mentioned by the scripture writers: 'O ye that dwell in Moab, leave the cities, and dwell in the rock, and be like the dove that maketh her nest in the sides of the hole's mouth' (Jeremiah 48:28); 'they that escape of them shall escape, and shall be on the mountains like doves of the valleys, all of them mourning, every one for his iniquity' (Ezekiel 7:16).

The doves and pigeons are so numerous in these valleys that several places have been named after them. Wady Hamam, for example, is the 'ravine of pigeons'. Tristram visited the place:

> One of the most remarkable of these [gorges] is the Wady Hamam, leading from the Plain of Gennesaret at the south-west, where are the famed robbers' caves, inhabited by thousands of rock-doves, whose swift flight and roosting-places far in the fissures render them secure from the attacks of the many hawks that share the caverns with them. They likewise swarm in the ravine of the Kelt by Jericho, in the sides of the Mount of Temptation [Quarantania], and in the Kedron. Above all, they people the recesses of the cliffs which shut in the Arnon and the Zerka in the land of Moab. as thev did in the time of Jeremiah.

In ancient times, the dove was on the standards of the Assyrians and the Babylonians, not as in modern times a representation of peace but to celebrate the goddess Semiramis, who reigned for 42 years and then handed over to her son. Semiramis flew to heaven in the shape of a dove. The bird was also an emblem of Israel, and over Solomon's throne was a dove with its foot resting on a hawk, a symbol of a time when all the warring nations will succumb to the influence of Israel.

Of the *Streptopelia* doves, the collared dove is resident all year round where there are trees, such as close to the streams feeding into the Dead Sea. The palm dove is also a permanent resident and more widely distributed throughout the region. In Egypt it is found in palm trees, but where these are absent it will swarm among thorn or jujube trees. The turtle dove is not a resident but a migrant, a point noticed by Solomon: 'For, lo, the winter is past, the rain is over and gone; The flowers appear on the earth; the time of the singing of birds is come, and the voice of the turtle is heard in our land' (Song of Solomon 2:11–12).

Solomon had noticed that songbirds only sing in springtime and that this was the time that the turtle dove arrived from faraway lands. Tristram observed them, too.

> Search the glades and valleys even by sultry Jordan, at the end of March, and not a Turtle-dove is to be seen. Return in the second week in April, and the clouds of doves are feeding on the clovers of the plain. They stock every tree and thicket. At every step they flutter up from the herbage in front – they perch on every tree and bush – they overspread the whole face of the land.

The bird would have been known to the writers of the AV. It was observed in southern England and written about in the most complimentary way by Bartholomew in the early sixteenth century: 'if he loseth his mate, he seeketh not the company of any other, but goeth alone, and hath mind of the fellowship that is lost . . . He cometh in Springtime and warneth of novelty of time with groaning voice.'

The turtle dove is but one of a multitude of birds passing through the region each spring and autumn, for the Holy Land is a crossroads for bird migrants travelling between Eurasia, Africa and the Middle East.

CRANES

Every spring and autumn the skies are filled with birds on their way north or south, and nothing is more spectacular than a flight of noisy cranes. The Bible writers could not have failed to notice them: 'Like a crane or a swallow, so did I chatter: I did mourn as a dove: mine eyes fail with looking upward' (Isaiah 38:14). They also noticed that the birds pass by on migration with incredible regularity: 'the turtle and the crane and the swallow observe their time of coming' (Jeremiah 8:7).

The crane of the Bible is *aqur* or *agur* in Hebrew, and in the texts quoted above the AV translators inadvertently transposed the names of the crane (*aqur*) and swallow (*sis*) from the original, but it does not affect the meaning. The crane in question is the common crane (*Grus grus*), the largest flying bird in the Holy Land. Large numbers overwinter in northern Israel, and still more pass through the region in September en route to the Nile Valley in Sudan. They travel in V- or V-V-formation at speeds of 44km/h (27mph) over land and 67km/h (42mph) over the sea and at heights up to 5,000m (16,400ft). Tristram describes how cranes visited the cultivated areas in spring in the 1860s, and flocks roosted in winter to the south of Beersheba:

> The clouds of these enormous birds, four feet high, and many eight feet from wing to wing, quite darkened the sky towards evening. Their roosting place was marked like some resort of sea-fowl – a gently sloping isolated knoll, where no ambush was possible, and where they could keep a good look out on all sides. Their whooping and trumpeting enlivened the watches of the night, and till dawn we could hear the flocks passing overhead on their way to their quarters close by.

Tristram's associate, the Reverend F W Holland, provided a graphic account of the spring migration through the Sinai, and an example of the predilection of cleric naturalists at the time to catch or even kill anything they encountered:

> On March 22, when about twelve miles south of Tor, we saw an immense flock of cranes crossing the Red Sea from Africa. The line appeared to stretch across the whole breadth of the sea. Five days afterwards we found a solitary one amongst the mountains, which did not attempt to fly, but stalked majestically on before our camels, quite regardless of a few revolver bullets whizzing close past him. At last an Arab boy gave chase, and, running him into a bush, soon caught him, and returned in triumph, holding him up by the tips of his wings. When released, he stalked on as unconcernedly as before, but when on the point of being caught again, the strange bird suddenly took wing, and after wheeling round several times, flew away over the mountains. On April 13, three days south of Beersheba, in the desert of Tyh, another large flock of more than 2000 cranes passed over our heads, going north as the others. In the beginning of May I saw several smaller flocks crossing the same desert from Akabah to Suez. There were also a few birds stalking about the head of the Gulf of Akabah.

A less frequent visitor to the region is the demoiselle crane (*Anthopoides virgo*), which often travels at high altitude and at night, and is rarely seen over the Levant, Sinai or Egypt, even though it travels to and from wintering sites due south in Sudan and breeding sites to the west of the River Volga and the Caspian Sea.

STORK

Another tall and imposing bird migrant that passes through the Holy Land is the white stork (*Ciconia ciconia*). The Hebrew word is *chasidah*, meaning 'the pious one' or 'kindness', an attribute recognised by the Romans, too. They also considered the bird pious and gave it the name *pia avis*. Storks had a reputation of looking after their offspring particularly well, and it was thought that the young repaid the sacrifice of their parents by looking after them in old age. The stork was said to be an example to all humanity, though Bartholomew records that the male can exact a stiff penalty for infidelity: 'While the female liveth, the male keepeth truly to her in nest. And if the male espy, in any wise, that the female hath broken spousehead, she shall no more dwell with him, but he beateth and striketh her with his bill, and slayeth her, if he may.'

In the Bible the stork is included on the unclean list: 'And the stork, the heron after her kind, and the lapwing, and the bat' (Leviticus 11:19). Nevertheless, the prophets admired the bird's striking appearance, especially its large and impressive wings: 'Then lifted I up mine eyes, and looked, and, behold, there came out two women, and the wind was in their wings; for they had wings like the wings of a stork: and they lifted up the ephah between the earth and the heaven' (Zechariah 5:9). As with the crane, its migration in and out of the region was recognised: 'Yea, the stork in heaven knoweth her appointed time' (Jeremiah 8:7).

Tristram felt that this passage from the Bible was particularly poignant, for he was able to witness the passage of birds on their spring migration:

> There is peculiar force in the words 'the stork in the heaven', for, unlike most other emigrants, the Stork voyages by day at great height in the air, and the vast flocks cannot but attract the notice of the least observant. The multitudes which arrive, and the suddenness with which these huge birds distribute themselves over the whole face of the land, is in Palestine truly startling. In winter not one is to be seen. On the 24th of March 1864, vast flocks suddenly appeared, steadily travelling northward, and leaving large detachments on every

plain and hill. From that period until about the 4th of May, they kept possession of the whole land, except where the ground was utterly barren, abounding especially in any marshy plains. They did not congregate like rooks; but, like sheep or cattle scattered over a wide pasture, they systematically quartered every acre of the country probably until they had cleared it of all the snakes, lizards, and frogs they could find, when either scarcity or the increasing heat of the summer, reminded them of their northern homes, and they proceeded as suddenly as they had arrived, leaving behind them only a pair here and there at the established nesting-places. They were equally abundant on both sides of the Jordan. On Mount Nebo they so covered the range, that at first, and until we had examined them through our telescopes, we took them for vast flocks of Moabite sheep pasturing.

When they return to their breeding areas, storks tend to go back to exactly the same nest that they have used before; not only that, but successive generations use the same nest. A psalmist noticed how storks build their platform-like nests high in trees or on buildings: 'Where the birds make their nests: as for the stork, the fir trees are her house' (Psalms 104:17).

Today in Europe, storks tend to nest on the tops of buildings, sometimes on special platforms supplied by the house owners.

Storks are welcomed as the harbingers of spring and good luck. In the Holy Land in the 1860s, Tristram described how the stork would set up home close to its food supply, particularly in marshland areas. It nested on houses or on ruins, but in the absence of any would take to the trees, as the psalmist described:

But where neither houses nor ruins occur, it selects any trees tall and strong enough to provide a firm platform for its huge nest, and for this none are more convenient than the fir tree . . . and doubtless in the days of the psalmist, when trees were more plentiful and towns were scarce, this habit was more noticeable . . . The instinct of the Stork is to occupy the highest and most isolated platform it can select for security.

In Hebrew legend Moses was reputed to have taught the people of Ethiopia how to attack and conquer a city that is guarded by serpents. He told them to train young storks to fly and hunt like hawks, then starve them for a minimum of three days before releasing them upon the city. The storks will then kill all the serpents and the city will fall.

The stork Moses would have been familiar with was probably the white stork, but there is another species present in the region, namely the black stork (*Ciconia nigra*), which differs not only in colour but also in behaviour. The black stork prefers wilderness desert areas, shunning the company of people; it lives in flocks, and nests in the trees of secluded forests. Tristram watched it fishing beside the Dead Sea, at places where freshwater streams entered the salt lake. Here the fish were poisoned and debilitated, and the stork simply picked off the casualties.

HERON

Another 'giant' among birds is the heron. Several species are found in Bible lands, and this was recognised by their inclusion in the unclean list in Leviticus 11:19 as 'the heron after her kind'. The expression 'after her kind' takes in the many species of herons present in the region, as well as their smaller relatives the egrets and bitterns. They range in size from the goliath heron (*Ardea goliath*) standing 1.2m (4ft) tall, to the diminutive little bittern (*Ixobruchus minutus*) at just 36cm (14in) high. The most common species to be encountered, however, are the common grey heron (*A. cinerea*), the purple heron (*A. purpurea*), the black-crowned night heron (*Nycticorax nycticorax*), the squacco heron (*Ardeola ralloides*), the great egret (*Egretta alba*) and lastly the little egret (*Egretta garzetta*).

They frequent marshlands and riverbanks, where they feed on fish, reptiles and amphibians, particularly frogs. Tristram saw several of the above species fishing by the Sea of Galilee, where he thought the heron might have been a more appropriate addition to Raphael's famous cartoon drawing than the crane, which is rarely seen there.

The Hebrew word is *anafa* or *anaphah*, meaning 'the wrathful one', and therefore quite the opposite of the stork. Like the ostrich, the heron was thought to neglect its offspring. In AV times, it was the principal target of falconers, and it was considered a cowardly bird because it flew high to avoid being caught by a hawk. Edward III was served a dish of heron to mark his cowardice after he failed to invade France.

BITTERN

Closely related to the heron is the bittern, a secretive bird that was adopted by the AV translators for the identity of *kippod*, a bird that occupies desolate places: 'I will also make it a possession for the bittern, and pools of water: and I will sweep it with the besom of destruction, saith the Lord of hosts' (Isaiah 14:23).

> And he will stretch out his hand against the north, and destroy Assyria; and will make Nineveh a desolation, and dry like a wilderness. And flocks shall lie down in the midst of her, all the beasts of the nations: both the cormorant and the bittern shall lodge in the upper lintels of it; their voice shall sing in the windows; desolation shall be in the thresholds: for he shall uncover the cedar work.
>
> Zephaniah 2:13–14

The bittern was probably chosen for this role on account of its evocative booming voice, what Pliny described as a 'bellow like oxen'. It was thus given the name *Taurus*, and medieval writers called it *botaurus*, from which 'bittern' is derived. In fact, on account of its voice it has received all manner of names: in 1544 it was 'miredromble', followed in later years by 'botley-bump', 'bog-bull', 'stake-driver' and 'thunder-pumper'. At dusk its low-frequency call emanates from the marshes but it is so diffuse that it is almost impossible to locate the bird producing it. This is made all the more difficult because the bittern is so well camouflaged. About the size and shape of a small heron, it is able to stretch out its long, thin neck vertically and merge in with its background of tall reeds; it is almost invisible. It remains hidden among the reeds for most of the day, emerging at dusk. Aristotle recalls its name as *oknos*, meaning 'an idle disposition', probably a reference to the way it hides in the swamp by day and will not flee until it is almost stepped upon.

Some modern translators have dropped the bittern in favour of the owl. Others felt *kippod* was similar to the Arabic name for hedgehog and porcupine – *kunfod* – and have suggested these creatures for the desolate places, but it is Tristram's view that they do not 'meet any of the requirements of the sacred text'. He feels that the bittern would have been the choice of the prophets. Besides, hedgehogs and porcupines are least likely to be found in proximity to 'pools of water', and Nineveh would have been close to the reedy marshes of the Tigris (at least in those days before the marshes were drained). It was the call of the bittern, he contends, that would have drifted eerily through the ruins: 'Its strange booming note, disturbing the stillness of the night, gives an idea of desolation which nothing but the wail of the hyena can equal.' Curiously, it was once believed that the bittern made its call by thrusting its bill into a reed. An alternative explanation was that it pushed it into mud and water. It actually makes its call with the aid of a specialised oesophagus. The bittern is one of the heron tribe, but unlike many of its relatives it is a solitary bird. Its main food is frogs, but it will also go for worms, voles and the young of other birds.

CORMORANT

The other bird mentioned in the desolation texts in the AV is the cormorant. The Hebrew word is *qath*, but many commentators believe that its true identity is either the pelican or a species of owl. Pelicans, though, are more likely to be at the coast or close to a lake or major river, so it has been suggested that the bird in the context of bleak and ruined cities is more likely to be an owl.

The cormorant itself is more likely a translation of the Hebrew word *shalak*, meaning 'plunging', one of the birds on the unclean list: 'And these are they which ye shall have in abomination among fowls . . . the little owl, and the cormorant, and the great owl' (Leviticus 11:13–17). That said, it is odd that it should be listed alongside owls. Gannets and terns, as plunging birds, have also been offered as identities for *shalak*, but authors such as Tristram have favoured the cormorant. There are at least three species to be found in the region – the common cormorant (*Phalacrocorax carbo*), which is a widespread winter visitor, a Mediterranean subspecies of the shag (*P. aristotelis desmarestii*) and the pygmy cormorant (*Halietor pygmeus*), an occasional visitor. In the 1860s, for example, Tristram spotted the pygmy species on the rivers Kishon, which runs into the Mediterranean to the north of Haifa, and Litany in Lebanon. Common cormorants were also seen on the Sea of Galilee as well as at the coast.

In the Mediterranean cormorants and shags are mainly birds of the coast, lakes and major rivers. They nest on rocky ledges and sea caves, often close to the high tide line, but will roost in trees lining rivers. They are diving birds with webbed feet placed to the rear of the body. They swim low in the water and dive frequently to chase fish underwater. Cormorants usually stay below water for about a minute, feeding on flatfish on the bottom in shallow water, but they will dive down to depths in excess of 37m (120ft). Shags usually submerge for three to four minutes, diving to midwater depths. Both species disperse the air trapped in their feathers and replace it with water before diving, so when they return to the shore after a fishing expedition they are waterlogged. They stand on a rock, pier or buoy with their wings outstretched and drying in the sun.

Both species have dark plumage, and consequently artists and poets have used these birds as representations of evil. In 1667, for instance, Milton's *Paradise Lost* depicted Satan as a cormorant sitting atop the Tree of Life scheming to bring about the downfall of Adam and Eve. Likewise, a painting by Andrea Mantegna bearing the title *The Agony in the Garden* has two egrets in a brook and rabbits playing in the foreground, but more sinister is a cormorant as a dark shape in a withered tree behind Jesus praying in the Garden of Gethsemane. Maybe the cormorant is a suitable candidate for desolation after all.

PELICAN

Today, the cormorant is classified scientifically with the pelican (Order: Pelecaniformes), another bird that features in the Bible. Its lugubrious manner, long bill and voluminous throat pouch have earned it a place as one of the most frequently used animal caricatures from the wild, and it has attracted the attention of writers and mythmakers down the centuries. At the time the AV was translated, for instance, the pelican was a symbol of adolescent wickedness, on account of the myth that its growing chicks would rebel against their parents and even strike them. None other than Shakespeare's *The Tragedy of King Lear* (1605–06) refers to the story: 'Twas this flesh begot those pelican daughters' (*The Tragedy of King Lear*, III.iv)

This was probably taken from the legend, mentioned in Bartholomew's *De Proprietatibus Rerum* of 1535, that told of how some fledgling pelicans struck their parents in the face, and in return the mother pelican struck and killed them. Then she slashed into her breast with her bill and shed blood onto her offspring; the fledglings came back to life. In another myth a snake kills the chicks and again the mother sheds her blood and restores them to life. The tale suggests that even when we have rejected Christ's teachings, He will raise us from the dead to eternal life.

As a consequence, the pelican was considered a pious bird. In heraldry it is described as 'a pelican in her piety, vulning herself'. The sixteenth-century printer Richard Jugge used the pelican as his printer's mark.

In the Bible, however, the pelican faces the same indignity as the cormorant and is included on the unclean list: 'And the swan, and the pelican, and the geir eagle' (Leviticus 11:18). The Hebrew word here is *kaath*, meaning to 'disgorge' or 'vomit', a reference to the way in which parent pelicans provide food for their young. The birds regurgitate food to their chicks, but why the pelican should be singled out in this way is a bit of a mystery, as many birds do it. It might refer to the way in which pelican parents frequently regurgitate small quantities of liquid, predigested fish to young chicks. As the youngsters grow, they are offered more solids gradually until they take whole fish from the parent's gullet (not from the pouch).

Two species are present in the Holy Land – the eastern white pelican (*Pelecanus onocrotalus*) and the Dalmatian pelican (*P. crispus*). Another species of white pelican, *P. roseus*, is found in the Persian Gulf, and yet another – the pink-backed pelican (*P. rufescens*) – is an occasional tropical visitor. Both white and Dalmatian pelicans can be recognised by the way in which they sometimes feed cooperatively. Birds line up in a semi-circle and drive fish into the shallows, where they scoop them up with a rapid dip of the bill into the water.

The pelican – whichever the species – is a big bird. The Dalmatian pelican is the biggest, though the white pelican has the greater wingspan of up to 3.6m (12ft). Both species frequent low-lying, shallow, warm freshwater habitats, especially deltas and wetlands. At one time – up to the 1930s – they bred in Iraq and Kuwait, but they have not been doing so in recent years. The closest breeding area to the Holy Land is now in Turkey, but large numbers still overwinter in Egypt. Most are seen as migrants over Syria and Israel in spring and autumn. White pelicans fly in large flocks on their passage between summer breeding grounds around the shores of the Black Sea and wintering sites in East Africa. They soar in thermals like storks or in V-shaped formations at high altitudes.

Like the cormorant, the pelican has also been roped in for desolation duties in the AV: 'I am like a pelican of the wilderness: I am like an owl of the desert' (Psalms 102:6). The words 'pelican of the wilderness' have puzzled modern translators, so they have opted for expressions such as 'a wild bird in the desert', 'desert owl', or 'vulture of the wilderness'. One version even went for 'melancholy pelican'. However, it is just in fact possible that the seventeenth-century translators were right in the first place, for the ancient scripture writers were good observers. When the conditions are right, the pink-backed pelican may abandon its aquatic habitat and head for the desert. Here it feeds not on fish but on locust swarms.

SWAN

Grouped with the pelican in the unclean list (Leviticus 11:18) in the AV is the swan. The Hebrew word is *tinshemeth*, but earlier translations, such as the Septuagint, prefer the sacred ibis (*Threskiornis aethiopicus*) or the purple swamp hen (gallinule) (*Porphyrio porphyrio*), and later ones have opted for anything from the little owl (*Athena noctua*) to the moorhen (*Gallinula chloropus*). One thing they all agree on is that it is not 'swan'.

For the AV translators, however, the swan must have been an attractive candidate. In folklore it was thought that swans sang a sad song just before they died, hence the expression ' swan song'.

It must have been an ancient belief, for Pliny is at pains to refute the claim: 'Some say that Swans sing lamentably just before their death; but untruly, I suppose, for my experience with several has showed the contrary.'

This didn't stop the poets, however, from using the image frequently. Coleridge used the story in one of his epigrams when he had a go at some of his fellow writers: 'Swans sing before they die; 'twere no bad thing/Did certain persons die before they sing' ('On a Volunteer Singer').

Another belief is that cygnets hatch out during a thunderstorm. In fact, swans appear in all sorts of legends. There are the swan-maidens who can change into swans using a cloak made of swan's feathers. There is Fionnuala, daughter of the Irish King Lir, who was transformed into a swan by Lir's second wife Aoife. In Greek mythology Nemesis took the form of a swan when escaping from Zeus. He dropped an egg from which came Helen. And then there was Leda, who was wooed by Zeus, also in the form of a swan.

Strong though the imagery is, the reality is that swans were, and are still, rare visitors to the Holy Lands. Wayward mute swans (*Cygnus olor*) sometimes reach as far south as Egypt, Jordan and Iraq in winter. They are from populations that breed in the summer from the Ukraine to Kazakhstan. Bewick's swan (*C. columbianus bewickii*) occasionally appears in Israel and Iraq – Tristram saw one at the Pools of Solomon in the 1860s – and the whooper swan (*C. cygnus*) has straggled to Egypt and the Persian Gulf. They could have been occasional visitors when Moses proclaimed his list, but they were not at all common even then.

Like other commentators, Tristram favours either sacred ibis or the purple gallinule for the 'swan's' true identity. The ibis featured strongly in Egyptian myth. The sacred ibis of Thoth was the god of learning, science and art, and was preserved in mummy form and depicted on tombs and monuments. It is less common today than in Moses' time, and although it was once found in the papyrus thickets on the lower reaches of the Nile, now one must travel to the upper reaches to find any. The purple gallinule is a large water hen, related to the moorhen and coot, and is more common locally. Both birds are omnivorous feeders, probing the mud for crustaceans, molluscs and worms, a diet that would establish them firmly as 'unclean'.

LAPWING

Like the 'swan', the lapwing (*Vanellus vanellus*) has probably also been misidentified. It is listed with the unclean birds: 'And the stork, the heron after her kind, and the lapwing, and the bat' (Leviticus 11:19).

The Hebrew word is *dukipath*, translated as 'lapwing' in the AV. The seventeenth-century translators would certainly have known it as 'unclean', especially if they had read Bartholomew's description: 'The Lapwing eateth man's dirt; for it is a bird most filthy and unclean, and it is copped on the head and dwelleth always in graves or dirt.'

The word 'copped' means 'crested', but Bartholomew was not the only one to condemn this unfortunate bird. Legend has it that the lapwing ridiculed Christ on the cross and was condemned to the desolation of the wilderness, where it will cry despondently until the end of time. Its recognisable call – 'pewit' – is often heard in estuaries and salt marshes around the British Isles, and at certain times of the year large flocks can be seen flying untidily across fields. The birds are recognised by their black-and-white plumage and the loud flapping of the wings that gives the bird its common English name. However, it is probably not the *dukipath* of the Bible.

The most likely candidate for this bird is the hoopoe (*Upupa epops*), another very conspicuous bird in the Mediterranean region with what one might consider 'unclean' habits. Hoopoes like to probe camel and horse dung for grubs and rubbish tips for worms, and they do not keep their nests clean – they are usually fouled by droppings. The hoopoe is easily spotted on account of the long, black-tipped, erectile crest on its head, the pale pinkish-brown body plumage, and the brightly barred black-and-white feathers of the wings and tail. It was probably less well known to the AV translators, for it is thought that in those days it rarely reached British shores. Nowadays, with changes in global climate, it is a more frequent visitor to northern lands.

Like most wildlife in the Bible lands, the hoopoe appears in Hebrew legend – it carried the invitation from Solomon to the Queen of Sheba, shielded Solomon in the desert (for which it received its crest), and brought Solomon the *shamir* – a stone, insect or worm (depending on which version of the legend you read) that enabled him to give shape to the stonework of the temple without using tools: 'And the house, when it was in building, was built of stone made ready before it was brought thither: so that there was neither hammer nor axe nor any tool of iron heard in the house' (1 Kings 6:7).

In ancient Egypt it was considered sacred, and in more recent times the Arabs called it the 'Doctor Bird' on account of its supposed medicinal properties. Its head, according to Tristram, was an important ingredient in witchcraft potions. It was also credited with the ability to listen to whispers, betray people's secrets and find hidden water supplies. Today, the hoopoe is considered a common resident in the region.

CUCKOO

The hoopoe's common English name is onomatopoeic. It repeats its call much like a cuckoo, another Bible bird. There are two species that frequent the Bible lands in summer – the common European cuckoo (*Cuculus canorus*), which we see in Britain, and the greater spotted cuckoo (*Clamator glandarius*). The cuckoo in the AV is a translation from the Hebrew word *shachaph*, from the root word meaning 'lean' or 'slender', and is included in the list of unclean birds: 'And the owl, and the night hawk, and the cuckow, and the hawk after his kind' (Leviticus 11:16).

The cuckoo is a brood parasite – the female deposits her eggs in the nests of other birds and then relies on the host mother to bring them up. It has always been an important bird in the folklore of many countries for it is generally considered a bird that brings good fortune, and the AV translators would have known it much as we do today, though there were a few odd notions with which they would have been acquainted. *Hortus Sanitatis* (*Garden of Health*), whose author is unknown but which was thought to have been compiled by Jacob Meydenbach and printed in Mainz in 1491, offered the following: 'They have their own time of coming and are born upon the wings of kites, because of their short and small flight, lest they be tired in the long tracts of air and die. From their spittle, grasshoppers are produced.'

The folk interest exists to this day. In the UK each year, for example, *The Times* carries reports of hearing the first cuckoos, the first signs that spring has arrived. Many strange beliefs have attached to the bird. It is said that on hearing a cuckoo, any wish you make will come true, and that your state of health at that moment is the way you will stay for the rest of the year. If you are a young man or woman, the number of times the cuckoo calls (one call for each year) tells when you will marry. For married couples, the number indicates the arrival of the next child, and it tells old people how long they have before they die. When a young man hears the cuckoo call, he must look inside his shoe for a hair. Its colour will indicate the colour of the hair of the girl he will marry.

It is unlucky to hear a cuckoo while in bed, but lucky to hear it out of doors, especially when standing on grass or if you have money in your pocket. On hearing the bird, you must take the money out and spit on it, and then you will never fall on hard times. If the call is heard from your right, you will have good luck, but the reverse is true if it is heard from your left, particularly if you happen to be looking at the floor.

It is bad luck if you hear a cuckoo before 6 April, but especially beneficial if you hear it on 28 April, for the following twelve months will be prosperous. Hearing the cuckoo after August, by which time the bird should have flown south, is considered extremely unlucky.

Some Bible commentators, however, are unconvinced that *shachaph* is the cuckoo, preferring petrel or shearwater as the true identity – especially the Manx shearwater (*Puffinus puffinus*), which is seen skimming along Mediterranean coasts in long lines containing many hundreds of birds. Several species of shearwater are found along the shores of the eastern Mediterranean, and their reliance on fish as food would immediately rank them as 'unclean'. Their dark and sombre plumage, according to Tristram, has meant that Muslims believe them to be 'tenanted by the souls of the condemned'.

Others look to the gull family for a reliable identity for *shachaph*. Several species are present on coasts and around the Sea of Galilee, including the great black-headed gull *Larus ichthyaetus*, and Audouin's gull (*L. audounii*), as well as the more widely distributed herring gull (*L. argentatus*), great black-backed gull (*L. marinus*), common gull (*L. canus*), slender-billed gull (*Larus genei*) and black-headed gull (*L. ridibundus*).

SPARROW

Another identity crisis looms over the sparrow. It was common in biblical times and was seen in familiar sparrow haunts: 'Yea, the sparrow hath found an house' (Psalms 84:3).

Hebrew legend has it that a gold statuette of a sparrow perched on Solomon's throne. Through some ingenious mechanism Solomon could stamp his foot and cause the bird to chirp. The AV translators, however, would not have recognised the sparrow as an appropriate regal accompaniment if they had considered Bartholomew's observations: 'The sparrow is an unsteadfast bird with voice and jangling, and is a full hot bird and lecherous, and the flesh of them oft taken in meat exciteth to carnal lust.'

But the sparrow of the Bible may not have been the familiar house sparrow *Passer domesticus*, though it is common in the region. There are several other sparrow species present, such as the Spanish sparrow (*P. hispaniolensis*), the Dead Sea sparrow (*P. moabiticus*), the rock sparrow (*Petronia petronia*) and the pale rock sparrow (*P. brachydactyla*). In the Jordan Valley Tristram noted that the thorn trees bore so many nests of Spanish sparrows that their weight bent the branches.

One reference to the sparrow in the Bible sees the bird behaving in a very unsparrow-like way: 'I watch, and am as a sparrow alone upon the house top' (Psalms 102:7). House sparrows are gregarious, and are seen usually in noisy, chattering flocks. The Hebrew word is *tzippor*, meaning 'to chirp', and the forty references to it in the Bible are thought to refer not specifically to sparrows but in a more general sense to small perching birds (passerines) – what ornithologists refer to technically as 'small brown jobs'. However, the solitary bird in the psalm must have been something other than a sparrow, and it has led Tristram and many commentators since to suggest the blue rock thrush (*Monticola solitarius*) as the 'sparrow's' true identity. As its scientific name suggests, it is a solitary bird that finds a prominent perch, such as the roof of a house, and sits there alone for some time. It is a common bird in towns in the Holy Land, and is found throughout the Mediterranean.

As for the other Bible references to *tzippor*, they could be to almost any small bird, with mention of their characteristics and where they roost or nest. Including the temple: 'Yea, the sparrow hath found an house, and the swallow a nest for herself, where she may lay her young, even thine altars' (Psalms 84:3).

The biblical writers also noticed how these birds would abandon their nests if disturbed: 'As a bird that wandereth from her nest, so is a man that wandereth from his place' (Proverbs 27:8).

Whichever bird it turns out to be, it was considered 'clean'.

Small birds would have been trapped, killed and eaten in biblical times just as they are today, and there is a reference to their trade in the New Testament:

> Are not two sparrows sold for a farthing? and one of them shall not fall on the ground without your Father. But the very hairs on your head are all numbered. Fear ye not therefore, ye are of more value than sparrows.
>
> Matthew 10:29–31

Another reference shows that the 'buy two get one free' incentives seen at supermarkets today had their origins thousands of years ago: 'Are not five sparrows sold for two farthings' (Luke 12:6).

The practice of trapping birds is also mentioned in the Bible: 'Surely in vain the net is spread in the sight of any bird' (Proverbs 1:17). But even in those ancient times, it seems there was sensitivity for conservation:

> If a bird's nest chance to be before thee in the way in any tree, or on the ground, whether they be young ones, or eggs, and the dam sitting upon the young, or upon the eggs, thou shalt not take the dam with the young.
>
> Deuteronomy 22:6

And there was and still is a lot to conserve, including an enormous diversity of bird species in the region: larks, pipits and chats are common in hill country and wilderness; small birds that would be at home in Britain occur on the maritime plains to the north; while in the Jordan Valley the avian fauna is more akin to that in India. It is a veritable crossroads of bird life.

SWALLOW

Often mentioned in the same passage as the sparrow is the swallow. There are two Hebrew words translated as 'swallow' in the AV. The word *deror*, meaning 'bird of freedom', is thought to refer to the familiar, migrating swallow: 'Yea, the sparrow hath found a house, and the swallow a nest for herself (Psalm 84:3); 'As the bird by wandering, as the swallow by flying, so the curse causeless shall not come' (Proverbs 26:2).

The second word – *agur* – is a little more complicated, however. It seems the AV translators have got their words muddled up again, and confused the two Hebrew words *agur* and *sis*. Take the following two passages: 'Like a crane (*sis*) or a swallow (*agur*), so did I chatter' (Isaiah 38:14); 'Yea, the stork in heaven knoweth her appointed times, and the turtle and the crane (*sis*), and the swallow (*agur*) observe the time of their coming' (Jeremiah 8:7).

In both passages the crane and swallow have somehow been switched (*see also* Crane). The word *agur* actually refers to the crane, while *sis* or *sus* refers to a swallow, or more accurately the swift. Knowing this makes more sense of the first of the verses above, for swifts rather than swallows are known for their screaming calls that are repeated constantly when flying and catching the 'aerial plankton' on which they feed.

As well as the barn swallow (*Hirundo rustled*) and common swift (*Apus apus*), other members of the swallow tribe in the Holy Lands include the red-rumped swallow (*H. daurica*) and crag martin (*H. [Ptyonoprogne] rupestris*), while representing the swifts are also the Alpine swift (*A. melba*) and the house swift (*A. affinis*). In the time that Tristram travelled the Holy Land, the house swift was known to him as the Galileean swift and it caught his eye, mainly on account of its nest:

> It resides all the year in the Jordan Valley, where alone it is found, living in large communities, and has a pleasing note, a gentle melodious wail, different from the harsh scream of other swifts. Its nests are very

peculiar, being composed generally of straw and feathers agglutinated together by the birds' saliva, like those of the Edible Swallow of Eastern Asia. They are without any lining, attached to the underside of an over-hanging rock.

It was Tristram's view also that included in the term 'swallow' were other birds, such as the bee-eaters (*Merops* spp.), of which three species occur in the region. They are swallow-like in their movements, though they have much more striking and colourful plumage.

As with many birds, the swallow turns up in fanciful stories. In folklore swallows are another of those creatures that can do magical things with stones. They were thought to search the seashore for stones that could restore sight, a mystical attribute to which Longfellow alluded in his *Evangeline*: 'Seeking with eager eyes that wondrous stone which the swallow/Brings from the shore of the sea to restore the sight of her/fledgings'.

QUAIL

Swallows and swifts aside, one of the great migration stories in the Bible involves a quite different bird – the quail (*Coturnix coturnix*). The quail is the smallest of the game birds and the only one that migrates. It is a secretive creature, active by night rather than by day. It is still a passage migrant in the Bible lands, flying across the nightscape in spring and autumn, and touching down to rest on southern coasts, where they are caught in nets for city markets. There was one notable touchdown in the Bible. It was the occasion when the children of Israel were able to take full advantage of birds migrating through the region; in fact, it saved their lives. They were starving in the desert when flocks of exhausted quail suddenly appeared: 'And it came to pass, that at even the quails came up, and covered the camp' (Exodus 16:13).

And there went forth a wind from the Lord, and brought quails from the sea, and let them fall by the camp, as it were a day's journey on this side, and as it were a day's journey on the other side, round about the camp, and as it were two cubits high upon the face of the earth. And the people stood up all that day and all that night, and all the next day, and they gathered the quails: he that gathered least gathered ten homers: and they spread them all abroad for themselves round about the camp.

Numbers 11:31–32

The quails were on migration, the two cubits high not referring to the pile of birds, but to the height at which quail fly above the ground. They must have put down in the desert to rest. At one time they travelled through the Middle East in enormous flocks. Pliny mentions how they would land on a small boat in the Mediterranean in such numbers that they could sink it:

As touching quails, they always come before the cranes depart. Their manner of flying is in troops; but not without some danger of the sailors, when they approach near to land. For oftentimes they settle in great numbers on their sails, and there perch, which they do evermore in the night, and with their poise, bear down barks and small vessels, and finally sink them.

Pliny records that these birds fly at night, which is why usually no one sees them. The Hebrew word is *slav* or *selav*, similar to the Arabic word *salwa* from the root 'to be fat', and it occurs in several other Bible references referring to the same event: 'He rained flesh also upon them as dust, and feathered fowls like as the sand of the sea: And he let it fall in the midst of their camp'; 'The people asked, and he brought quails, and satisfied them with the bread of heaven' (Psalms 78:27 and 105:40). This phenomenon of large numbers of birds on the move occurred until quite recently. In the nineteenth century, for example, 160,000 quail were taken on the island of Capri, off Naples.

The Bible relates that the children of Israel collected too many birds. What were they going to do with all this quail meat?

> And while the flesh was yet between their teeth, ere it was chewed, the wrath of the Lord was kindled against the people . . . with a very great plague. And he called the name of that place Kibroth-hattaavah: because there they buried the people that lusted.
>
> Numbers 11:33–34

Could this have been a serious salmonella outbreak? Maybe, but Tristram was definitely impressed with the timing of the biblical story:

> The period when they were brought to the camp of Israel was in spring, when on their northward migration from Africa. According to their well-known instinct, they would follow up the coast of the Red Sea till they came to its bifurcation by the Sinaitic Peninsula, and then, with a favouring wind, would cross at the narrow part, resting near the shore before proceeding. Accordingly we read that the wind brought them up from the sea, and that, keeping close to the ground, they fell, thick as rain, about the camp in the month of April, according to our calculation. Thus, the miracle consisted in the supply being brought to the tents of Israel by the special guidance of the Lord, in exact harmony with the known habits of the bird.

PARTRIDGE

Another game bird – the partridge – occurs only twice in the Bible. In Hebrew it is *kore*, meaning 'caller', and probably refers to one of three species – the rock partridge (*Alectoris graeca*) and the chukar partridge (*A. chukar*), which are common in the region, or the smaller sand partridge (*Ammoperdix heyi*) of the desert. All species are inhabitants of rocky areas, rather than the cultivated fields occupied by partridges in Britain. The first mention is made as David complains to Saul about his treatment of him: 'the king of Israel is come out to seek a flea, as when one doth hunt a partridge in the mountains' (1 Samuel 26:20).

Here the reference is to the method used to hunt down partridges. The bird was chased continuously but when it tired, sticks were thrown along the ground to bring it down. Unlike the partridge of the British 'shoot', desert partridges prefer to escape by running rather than flying.

The second mention has generated considerable ornithological debate as to its origin: 'As the partridge sitteth on eggs, and hatcheth them not; so he that getteth riches, and not by right, shall leave them in the midst of his days, and at his end shall be a fool' (Jeremiah 17:11).

Some observers have thought that the partridge steals the eggs of other birds, and they do not hatch. There is another belief in the area that the hen partridge lays two eggs, in separate nests. One egg is hatched by the hen in her nest and the other egg by the cock in his. He could be said to be gaining from an egg he did not lay. The reality is probably quite different.

Desert partridges, according to Tristram, lay an enormous number of eggs in their nest. He once discovered a nest containing 26 eggs, but he thought that few of these eggs would be hatched because people tended to collect them. The nests are easily found and plundered, so a hen would not hatch out all her eggs for this reason: 'We had in one spring in Palestine about 800 eggs of the Greek Partridge brought to our camp, and were in the habit of using those that were fresh for omelettes daily. They were doubtless collected of old for the same purpose.'

There was, however, another explanation. In his *Memoirs of a Jewish Zoologist*, Dr Israel Ahrani mentions that he once came across a desert partridge nest containing thirty eggs. The large number, he thought, was the result of two hens laying close together. One drove off the other and tried in vain to incubate all the eggs herself. She would have moved the eggs around, and so none would have been protected sufficiently from the sun to develop properly. She then abandoned the nest and none of the clutch made it to hatching. The original moral outlined in the AV seems to be borne out by field observations – a person who obtains something illegally will not gain from it.

THE COCKEREL

The Bible's most famous domestic bird is probably the cock – the male chicken. In fact, a cockerel is a male chicken that is less than one year old; after that it becomes a 'rooster'. In the New Testament the cockerel is probably best known for marking Peter's denial of Jesus, an event that Jesus predicts: 'And Jesus saith to him, Verily I say unto thee, That this day, even in this night, before the cock crow twice, thou shalt deny me thrice' (Mark 14:30).

We usually think of the cock crowing only at dawn, but there was a tradition that at the time of the Passover (around about Easter time) the first cockcrow was at 2.30 a.m. or thereabouts, and the second at 5.00 a.m. So Peter's denials must have been in the early hours of the morning, before dawn. Cockcrow has always been significant in folklore, for it warns away evil spirits. The sound welcomes the dawn, so evil spirits are aware that it is time to return to the underworld. Therefore, if the cock crows as you set off to work, your day will be a good one, but if it crows at dusk the weather the following day will be bad. And if it crows during the night, there will be a death in the family. Shakespeare seems to have been unaware of this danger, for in *Hamlet* the cockerel is said to crow from Christmas Eve until Christmas morning to ward off evil spirits. Cockcrow was so punctual that the Roman legions were thought to change their guard when the cock crowed.

Roman generals had a unique way of predicting the outcome of battles, known as the *oraculum ex tripudio*, and the key ingredient was chickens. The fowl were observed when given food and their behaviour was crucial. If they ate quickly it was a good omen, but if they dallied it was a bad sign. If they failed to eat at all, the likely outcome was a disaster. Generals were known to starve their hens before feeding them, in order to try to assure victory in battle. One tale from the Punic War (264–241 BCE) tells of consul Claudius Pulcher losing his cool when his hens would not perform before the Battle of Drepana (249 BCE), and throwing them in the sea. He was defeated.

The colour of the cockerel is significant. A white bird is considered to be lucky, whereas a black cock is thought to be in league with the devil. Its power in days gone by was considerable. As recently as the nineteenth century, a cockerel was buried in the foundations of a church to repel evil spirits.

In the Bible the cockerel was also the bird that was supposed to have announced the birth of Christ, and it will herald the 'Day of Judgement', when all cocks – both living birds and those made of metal or wood – will start to crow, and they will make such a noise that they will wake the dead as well as the living.

The cock's part in the birth of Christ gave rise to a folk story. It tells how all the animals in Palestine received news that a great event was about to take place. A bright star was to be the signal, so all the creatures stared up at the sky and looked for it; all, that is, except the cock. He thought he would rely on the others to do all the watching. One morning he arose as usual and crowed, but to his amazement his world was empty. Then, in the distance, he saw the other creatures returning. They were very happy and talked exuberantly about the special mother and child they had seen in a stable near by. They had been so overawed by the sight of the star that they had forgotten to wake up the cock. Late though he was, the cock decided to take a look for himself. He turned up at the stable just as the shepherds arrived, so he tried to sneak in with them. Just then, an angel challenged him and stopped him going in. He was asked why he had not been with the others who had followed the star. The cock admitted that he had been asleep, so the angel denied him entry and set a curse on him. The angel said, 'When He is denied thrice by one of His followers, it will be your voice by which all the people of the world shall hear of it.' The cock was mortified, and streams of tears fell from his eyes. The angel took pity and made another pronouncement: 'One day in the distant future, Jesus will return to Earth, and the star will be in the heavens again. Keep watch for it, and your song will announce its arrival to the world.' Ever since that day, the cock watches the sky, and he practises his crowing, waiting for the day when the star reappears.

The cock and other related word forms, such as 'hen' and 'chicken' appear many times in the Bible, but all in the New Testament. When Jesus was berating the scribes and Pharisees, for example, he used the chicken looking after her brood as a symbol of God's concern for His impenitent people.

> O Jerusalem, Jerusalem, thou that killest the prophets, and stonest them which are sent unto thee, how often would I have gathered thy children together, even as a hen gathereth her chickens under her wings, and ye would not!

> Matthew 23:37

There is only one mention of chicken-like creatures as 'fatted fowls' in the Old Testament, and it comes in the list of delicacies enjoyed by Solomon. Exactly what these 'fatted fowls' were is unknown, and they have been variously described as geese, swans or even guinea fowl that Solomon could have imported from Africa. On the other hand, as Solomon acquired peacocks from the East he might well have brought the domestic version of the jungle fowl – the chicken – too.

PEACOCK

The peacock was imported from Tarshish, which in this context is likely to have been on the Malabar coast of India or in Sri Lanka: 'once in three years came the navy of Tharshish, bringing gold, and silver, ivory, and apes, and peacocks' (1 Kings 10:22).

The Hebrew word is *tuk* or *tuki*, which was derived from the Tamil word *tokei*. Peafowl are native to the subcontinent, but the splendid plumage of the male so impressed the rich and famous that today the species is found all over the world. The AV's translators would have believed that its flesh was impossible to cook. The Romans, however, considered peafowl a great delicacy and reared them not for their feathers but for the table. Alexander the Great, on the other hand, found them of such great beauty that he forbade his army from killing them.

One other reference to the peacock in the Bible is another misidentification: 'Gavest thou the goodly wings unto the peacocks? or wings and feathers unto the ostrich?' (Job 39:13). Mention here of the peacock is thought to be erroneous. The Hebrew word is *renanim*, which modern translators have agreed should be rendered as 'ostrich'.

OSTRICH

The African ostrich is the world's largest living bird, and the subspecies that lived in the Middle East was the Asian ostrich (*Struthio camelus syriacus*). It was found in the Syrian and Arabian deserts, and was present in Palestine, both on the coastal plain and in the Negev.

The ostrich is well adapted for life in arid environments. It is flightless, but has powerful legs that enable it to power along at

50km/h (30mph) or kick out at predators, disembowelling them in a blink of the eye. It has long eyelashes to keep out wind-blown sand, and the long neck enables it to see for long distances across the flat terrain that it inhabits. Although no good for flying, floppy wings can be used as stabilisers when running at high speed, or flapped enthusiastically in courtship or distraction displays. On the wings two shaft-like feathers, like porcupine quills, help in defence. The bird also has a bladder, like a mammal, that collects uric acid.

Curiously, though, the Bible describes a bird with a bad reputation. The ostrich was considered a cruel mother. In one of his poems about the destruction of Jerusalem in 586 BCE, Jeremiah singles out the ostrich for criticism: 'the daughter of my people is become cruel, like the ostriches in the wilderness' (Lamentations 4:3). Job explains, perhaps, why the ostrich should be pilloried in this way:

> Gavest thou the goodly wings unto the peacocks? or wings and feathers unto the ostrich? Which leaveth her eggs in the earth, and warmeth them in dust, And forgetteth that the foot may crush them, or that the wild beast may break them. She is hardened against her young ones, as though they were not hers.

> Job 39:13–16

The truth of the matter is that some of the eggs are not in fact hers, for the male ostrich has several partners and they all deposit their eggs in the same nest. During the breeding season, he makes a number of shallow scrapes on the ground and one hen, known as the 'major' hen with whom he has a loose affinity, chooses one and deposits about a dozen eggs in it. Then a bevy of 'minor' hens – maybe six or more – lay their eggs in the same nest and they leave, playing no further role in the rearing of the young. All the eggs are incubated and guarded by the male and major hen, the female in her drab brown camouflage on duty during the day and the flamboyant black-and-white male at night. The major hen tries to ensure that her eggs are at the centre of the nest, for if egg thieves, such as the Egyptian vulture (*Neophron percnopterus*), are about they are more likely to steal eggs from the edge of the nest than from the centre. And if there are too many eggs for her to cover, she will even roll some into a ring around the nest, and it is these that will be pillaged rather than her own.

The idea that the ostrich runs away from its nest, neglecting its eggs, stems from its response to predators, such as hyenas and jackals, which approach too closely. It explodes into a distraction display, flapping its loose-feathered wings and running erratically. Continuing Job's meditation, we can see that the bird's description in the Bible could be based on field observations: 'What time she lifteth up herself on high, she scorneth the horse and his rider' (Job 39:18). This also refers to the extraordinary turn of speed that the ostrich possesses. Its long, muscular legs enable it to outrun Greek cavalry horses, according to the ancient Greek historian Xenophon, and nowadays it can still outpace four-wheel-drive, off-road vehicles.

The ostrich also appears in the Bible as one of the animals that represents desolation. It is thought that this was on account of what was considered its doleful voice. The ostrich is the only bird that makes a sound that has been described as a 'deep roar'. It achieves this by forcing air down its gullet rather than its windpipe. The sphincter at the entrance to the stomach is closed, so its neck balloons out. When the pressure is released, the ostrich gives a great belch, which can be heard from several kilometres away.

Job used the sound of the ostrich to represent misery and despair on several occasions, though there seems to be some confusion with the owl in translations. In the AV the owl's voice is mentioned, whereas in modern versions, such as the Good News

Bible, it is that of the ostrich. In Job 30:28–31, for example, the AV reads: 'I went mourning without the sun . . . I am a brother to dragons, and a companion to owls.' More recent translations have: 'I go about in gloom, without any sunshine . . . My voice is as sad and lonely as the cries of a jackal or an ostrich.' Similarly, in Isaiah's prediction of the fall of Babylon, the AV states: 'But wild beasts of the desert shall lie there; and their houses shall be full of doleful creatures; and owls shall dwell there, and satyrs shall dance there' (Isaiah 13:21). The Good News Bible has both owls and ostriches: 'It will be a place where desert animals live and where owls make their nests. Ostriches will live there, and wild goats will prance through the ruins.'

Later in Isaiah, the animals are put back in their normal wilderness environment. First in the AV: 'The beast of the field shall honour me, the dragons and the owls: because I give waters in the wilderness, and rivers in the desert, to give drink to my people, my chosen' (Isaiah 43:20). And then in the Good News Bible: 'Even the wild animals will honour me; jackals and ostriches will praise me when I make rivers flow in the desert to give water to my chosen people.'

Two other things for which the ostrich is known are its ability to eat just about anything, and the way in which it buries its head in the sand. Alas, neither of these widely held beliefs is true, but it didn't stop Shakespeare from perpetuating one of the myths in Jack Cade's conversation with Iden: 'I'll make thee eat iron like an ostrich, and swallow my sword like a great pin, ere thou and I part' (*King Henry VI, Part 2*, IV.x).

One translation of the *Physiologus* in 1924 by James Carlill reveals that some of the ancient writers had even more bizarre beliefs: 'It is also related of him that he swallows even glowing iron and fiery coals; and all these do good to his stomach, for his nature is very cold.'

As for burying its head in the sand so that it could not see and therefore not be seen, we have Pliny to thank for the error: 'The veriest fools they be of all others – for as high as the rest of their body is, yet if they thrust their head and neck once into any shrub or bush and get it hidden they think they are safe enough and that no man seeth them.'

In reality, the ostrich feeds with its beak down on the ground, so it appears as if its head is in the sand. In this position it is indeed vulnerable to attack, but it frequently raises its head and neck to look about. The Hebrew word for ostrich is *ya'anah*, meaning 'greediness', which probably describes the varied and seemingly indiscriminate diet. The ostrich, however, is a highly selective gatherer of sparsely scattered high-quality foods. It picks up shoots, leaves, flowers and seeds.

When Europeans first saw the ostrich they were bemused, for it looked like neither bird nor beast, but rather a combination of the two. Sir Thomas Browne – apparently a believer in the iron-swallowing trick himself – called it *Struthiocamelus*, meaning 'sparrow camel'.

The wonderful plume-like feathers of the male ostrich have attracted the attention of admirers since early times. The ancient Egyptians used them as a symbol of justice because they are symmetrical. Ostrich brains were a delicacy, too. Desert chieftains incorporated ostrich feathers as part of their royal vestments. In the early twentieth century, the feather adorned the hats of upper-class ladies, and today the plumes appear in heraldry. The Prince of Wales has three white ostrich plumes on his standard.

Since time immemorial people have collected ostrich eggs. One egg can provide an entire meal for a small family. Lawrence of Arabia tells how his men would obtain a complete meal out of an ostrich egg while in the desert during the First World War. It could well be that Job was referring to an ostrich egg when he wrote: 'Can that which is unsavoury be eaten without salt? or is there any taste in the white of an egg?' (Job 6:6).

The ostrich itself is on the unclean list, though it only appears in modern translations and not in the AV. Why it should be included is a mystery as it is a vegetarian, with nothing unpleasant in its diet to taint its flesh.

Nevertheless, ostriches were hunted like all large creatures and since the 1930s few have been seen in the region. In 1948 two were killed near the junction of the Saudi Arabia, Iraq and Jordan borders, and in 1966 a female (probably the last of its kind) was swept into the Dead Sea by a flash flood near A-Safi. Today, ostriches from Africa have been reintroduced to the Hai-Bar Reserve.

BIRDS OF PREY

The reserve is also home to the most regal of birds – the birds of prey. These would have been the species most immediately visible to the writers of the Bible. Birds of prey would have congregated over camps and villages, and perched on city walls waiting to steal food. Meat prepared for the table or for sacrifice would have been their targets, as well as any pigeons being reared, young livestock and even small children.

Tristram recognises fifteen Hebrew words related to raptors: *ayit*, 'fowls'; *peres*, 'ossifrage'; *nesher*, 'eagle'; *racham*, 'gier eagle'; *dayah*, 'vulture'; *asniyeh*, 'osprey'; *raah*, 'glede'; *ayah*, 'kite'; *netz*, 'hawk'; *tachmas*, 'night-hawk'; *bath-hay a'anah*, 'owl'; *yanshooph*, 'great owl'; *cos*, 'little owl'; *kippoz*, 'Scop's owl'; and *lilith*, 'screech owl'. Let's look at them one by one.

The Hebrew word *ayit*, meaning 'to attack violently', refers very much to the behaviour of birds of prey. The word occurs three times in the Bible: 'And when the fowls came down upon the carcases, Abram drove them away' (Genesis 15:11); 'There is a path which no fowl knoweth' (Job 28:7); 'They shall be left together unto the fowls of the mountains, and to the beasts of the earth: and the fowls shall summer upon them, and all the beasts of the earth shall winter upon them' (Isaiah 18:6).

The first passage draws attention to the well-known fact that vultures and, indeed, eagles, will see a carcase from a distance and gather over it. Tristram observed this:

> These birds detect their food by sight, not by scent. If an animal falls by night, it is not attacked till daylight, unless by jackals and hyaenas; but if it be slaughtered after sunrise, though the human eye may scan the firmament for a vulture in vain, within five minutes a speck will appear overhead, and, wheeling and circling in a rapid downward flight, a huge griffon will pounce on the carcase. In a few minutes a second and a third will dart down; another and another follows – griffons, Egyptian vultures, eagles, kites, buzzards, and ravens, till the air is darkened with the crowd.

Tristram had realised something that has only been scientifically proved in very recent times: the griffon vulture espies the quarry first, and its neighbours in the sky then watch it drop down to earth. Others, in turn, watch them, and still others watch them, until birds from many kilometres away flock to stake their claim to a share of the food.

Tristram's second bird of prey is the ossifrage, which comes from the Latin *ossifragus*, meaning 'bone breaker'. In Hebrew the word is *peres*, which also means 'breaker'. At one time the word in English referred to the osprey (*Pandion haliaetus*), a fish-eating eagle, but in the Bible the bird the translators had in mind was undoubtedly the lammergeier or bearded vulture (*Gypaetus barbatus*). It is included with the eagle and osprey in the unclean list: 'And these are they which ye shall have in abomination among fowls; they shall not be eaten, they are an abomination: the eagle, and the ossifrage, and the ospray' (Leviticus 11:13).

The lammergeier acquired its name of 'bone breaker' from its habit of carrying bones into the air and dropping them from a great height on to rocks or hard ground in order to break them. The bones are from freshly killed mammals, reptiles and birds.

After eating the meat, a bird might tackle the bones, and it will eat quite long ones. These are swallowed whole; sometimes one end is being digested in the stomach while the other is still protruding from the mouth. Very large bones are carried in its talons to a height of about 80m (260ft) and then dropped on to a flat rock, usually a favourite bone-breaking spot. The bird might repeat this up to twenty times before it is successful and the bone breaks open to expose the marrow. Tortoises may be treated the same way. It was said that an oracle predicted that 'a blow from heaven' would kill the Greek dramatist Aeschylus; what actually happened was that a lammergeier dropped a tortoise on him, thinking his bald head was a rock! The lammergeier also takes weak, sick or injured animals, and is credited with pushing lambs and young goats off cliff tops. Tristram suggests that even people climbing rocks and cliffs were in danger from the birds, though their preferred fare is carrion or reptiles:

> I have repeatedly watched a pair of Lammer-Geiers, who had an eyrie close to our camp, pass and repass in front of our tents for hours at a time, invariably dropping something upon a smooth ledge of rock hard by. For several days we imagined that these were sticks they were carrying to their nest; for prompt as we were in endeavouring to be first at the spot, the birds swooped down like lightning and seized their quarry again. At length we caught a serpent, writhing and dislocated, which we had taken for a stick, and found that our imagined stones were tortoises, which had to be dropped perhaps a dozen times before the shell was sufficiently shattered.

The lammergeier once occupied mountainous areas all around the Mediterranean, but it is now extremely rare. The main reason for its decline was that carcases laced with strychnine were put out to control wolves and foxes. The reduced wolf population, however, also meant that there would be less carrion. In the Holy Land only a few pairs are known to nest in the Negev, and a few visiting birds are seen sometimes in the Sinai.

The third bird of prey is translated in the AV as 'eagle'. The Hebrew word is *nesher*, meaning 'to tear with the beak'. It is similar to the Arabic *nissr*, which refers not to an eagle but to the griffon vulture (*Gyps fulvus*). It occurs in ancient times as the Nisroch or griffon-headed god of the Assyrians: 'And it came to pass, as he was worshipping in the house of Nisroch his god, that Adrammelech and Sharezer his sons smote him with a sword' (2 Kings 19:37). It also appeared on the Assyrian standard:

> Their horses are also swifter than the leopards, and are more fierce than the evening wolves: and their horsemen shall spread themselves, and their horsemen shall come from far; and they shall fly as the eagle that hasteth to eat.
>
> Habakkuk 1:8

The identity of *nesher* as a vulture is confirmed in Micah: 'Make thee bald, and poll thee for thy delicate children; enlarge thy baldness as the eagle' (Micah 1:16).

The griffon vulture has its neck covered with short down, a feature not seen in any eagle. There are also many references to the bird eating prey that is already dead, a scavenging habit shared with eagles but more usually associated with vultures: 'The eye that mocketh at his father, and despiseth to obey his mother, the ravens of the valley shall pick it out, and the young eagles shall eat it' (Proverbs 30:17); 'For wheresoever the carcase is, there will the eagles be gathered together' (Matthew 24:28).

And there are the griffon vulture's behaviour and nesting habits in high gorges and cliff tops, which the prophets Job and Jeremiah accurately describe:

Doth the eagle mount up at thy command, and make her nest on high? She dwelleth and abideth on the rock, upon the crag of the rock, and the strong place. From thence she seeketh the prey, and her eyes behold far off. Her young ones also suck up blood: and where the slain are, there is she.

Job 39:27–30

Tristram found that griffon vultures were present in Palestine throughout the year. An especially large population that he observed inhabited the Wady Hamam and Wady Leimum: 'In either of these sublime gorges the reverberating echoes of a single rifle would bring forth griffons by the hundred from their recesses. I counted on one occasion, 120 thus roused, and then gave up the reckoning in despair.'

The cliffs in these sites rise to a height of about 240m (800ft), and the limestone is honeycombed by caves, caverns and arches. Tristram watched the undisputed owners of this rugged place:

> The griffons were in the habit of soaring high, and sweeping the horizon about daybreak; then in about two hours they would return, and either betake themselves to the duties of incubation, or perch motionless in long rows on the most conspicuous ledges and points of the precipices until the evening.; they would then take a little airy exercise before retiring to rest.

Tristram was amazed at their capacity for fasting. In excess of 500 vultures would scavenge in these areas, and there would not have been enough food to go round. Wolves and jackals attended first any horse or cow that died in the vicinity, so the vultures got barely a look in. Understandably, when they did find a food source they gorged avidly, and this was followed by long periods of abstinence.

The griffon vulture is a widely distributed bird of prey, found from Spain in the western Mediterranean all the way to India in the east and South Africa in the south. It is a big bird with a wingspan of 2.4m (8ft) or more. It was common in biblical times, and until the end of nineteenth century it was so numerous that it was virtually impossible to look up into the sky anywhere in the Holy Land without spotting several of them soaring high in the sky.

In Bible times, black vultures (*Aegypius monachus*) were resident on the eastern side of the Arbel Cliffs, but today they are no more than passing migrants.

The fourth of Tristram's list of birds of prey – the gier eagle - receives just a couple of mentions in the Bible. It is included on the unclean list: 'And the swan, and the pelican, and the gier eagle' (Leviticus 11:18). Modern versions tend to avoid assigning the gier eagle to any particular species, favouring all-embracing terms such as eagles, hawks, falcons, buzzards and vultures, but maybe we can be a little more precise. The Hebrew word is *racham*, from the root meaning 'parental affection' or 'love', and it is generally thought by ornithologists to refer to the Egyptian vulture or Pharaoh's chicken (*Neophron percnopterus*) because mated pairs are often seen together throughout the year, and they form long-term partnerships.

The Egyptian vulture is smaller and less robust than the larger vultures. It has a wingspan of 1.55–1.8m (5–6ft) when full grown, and is recognised by its mainly white plumage and bare face that becomes a livid orange-yellow at breeding time. It is found both in hot lowlands and cool mountains, including desert fringes and mountains surrounded by desert. It is migratory, with birds – sometimes in the company of other raptors or cranes – passing through the Levant in spring and autumn. It is still widespread in Turkey, but populations in Syria, Israel and Egypt have been in decline.

The name 'Pharaoh's chicken' comes from the bird's

propensity for gathering around campsites and at rubbish tips, where it can resemble a dirty white hen (*Gallus*). It also follows the plough, and tracks the seasonal movements of domestic stock. The bird's small size and lack of any need to soar high on thermals like other vultures means that it can quickly take advantage of any feeding opportunity.

The Pharaoh's chicken eats just about anything, from scavenged human waste to live insects. Its small bill can tackle only soft tissues, but it will break into eggs, including those of pelicans, which it breaks by dropping them from a height, and of ostriches, which it cracks by dropping rocks on them.

Today, the word 'gier' or 'gyr' is reserved for birds such as the gyr falcon (*Falco rusticolus*) and the lammergeier (*Gypaetus barbatus*). The root is probably the German word *gier*, meaning 'greedy'. German naturalists call the gyr falcon *gierfalke*. The lammergeier's name comes from the German *lammer*, meaning 'lamb', and *geier*, meaning 'vulture', a reference to its propensity for snatching lambs from fields, though this has never been proven. In German, the word *geier* means 'vulture', so the seventeenth-century English gier eagle translates literally as 'vulture eagle'.

Next comes the Hebrew word *dayah*, translated as vulture in the AV, but more probably referring to a kite, or other smaller bird of prey, such as a buzzard. The Arabic word *h'dayah* is very similar, and refers specifically to the black kite (*Milvus migrans*). It turns up in the unclean list: 'And the vulture, and the kite after his kind' (Leviticus 11:14). The bird is recognised by Isaiah to be exceptionally gregarious throughout the year, except winter: 'there shall the vultures also be gathered, every one with her mate' (Isaiah 34:15).

According to Tristram, the kite returns to the Holy Land at the beginning of March, when it is often found in close proximity to a village:

It does not appear to attack the poultry, among whom it may often be seen feeding on garbage. It is very sociable; and the slaughter of a sheep near the tents will soon attract a large party of black kites, which swoop down regardless of man and guns, and enjoy a noisy scramble for the refuse, chasing each other in a laughable fashion, and sometimes enabling the wily Raven to steal off with the coveted morsel during their contention.

A subspecies, the Egyptian kite (*Milvus migrans aegyptius*), has lighter coloured plumage and a white rather than black bill, and is also present in the region. In Bible times, kites would have been found near towns and villages, where they would pick over the scraps on refuse tips.

The sixth raptor is the osprey – *asniyeh* in Hebrew. The osprey or fish eagle (*Pandion haliaetus*) is one of the medium-size raptors with a maximum wingspan of 1.7m (5.6ft) wings. It is included in the Bible in the list of unclean birds: 'But these are they of which ye shall not eat: the eagle, and the ossifrage, and the ospray' (Deuteronomy 14:12).

The adult bird is relatively easy to recognise by its mainly white head and white underparts, but when it glides its wings are held at an angle so it can be mistaken for a large gull. It feeds mainly on fish, which it catches by first hovering over the sea in order to spot its target accurately and then plunging down and seizing it in its talons. Small, sharp protuberances on the feet, known as 'spicules', prevent the slippery fish from escaping. The bird then carries the prey torpedo-fashion, with the head facing forwards to reduce drag.

Although we read 'ospray' in the AV, again this does not necessarily mean that the osprey is the correct identification. The precise naming of birds of prey by both writers and translators, as we have seen, was often inaccurate. The word *asniyeh* could refer also to the slightly larger and more powerful short-toed eagle

(*Circaetus gallicus*), with a maximum wingspan of 1.95m (6.4ft). It is found throughout southern Europe and is one of the more abundant eagles to be seen in the Holy Land today. In fact, it is easy to misidentify the two birds, for the short-toed eagle also has a pale underside. It differs in feeding behaviour from the osprey, however, for it prefers reptiles, especially snakes. It nests in Sinai, and large numbers pass through the region on their spring and autumn migrations. Tristram clearly found it impressive:

> I do not know a more magnificent-looking bird, as it sits with its great flat head bent down on its shoulders, its huge yellow eyes glaring about, and the bright spotting of its breast and abdomen as distinct as that of a missel-thrush. It is very noisy, and always betrays the neighbourhood of its nest by the loud harsh scream with which the male and female pursue each other, rising into the air and making short circling flights, after which they suddenly drop down, one to the nest, the other to a neighbouring post of observation. They will often dash down from the cliffs to the fields below, sweep for a few minutes like a harrier, and then, seizing a snake, sit down and occupy some minutes in killing the reptile, after which they carry the prize away in their claws, not, like most other eagles, devouring it on the spot.

Other eagles that also might be categorised as *asniyeh* include the golden eagle (*Aquila chrysaetos*), which although uncommon is found in mountainous areas in Palestine; the more frequently seen imperial eagle (*Aquila heliaca*), recognised by its dark plumage and white shoulders; and four more raptors that are present in the region but are uncommon – the tawny eagle (*A. rapax*), the greater spotted eagle (*A. clanga*), the Bonelli's eagle (*Hieraaetus fasciatus*) and the smaller booted eagle (*H. pennatus*). All will eat carrion when nothing else is available, but most times they kill their own food.

One intriguing reference to eagles in the Bible concerns the way they look after their young: 'As an eagle stirreth up her nest, fluttereth over her young, spreadeth abroad her wings, taketh them, beareth them on her wings' (Deuteronomy 32:11). This refers to the way early observers thought the mother eagle deliberately 'stirred up' her nest to encourage her fledglings to learn to fly, and how she would take them on her back and tip them off so they had to fly. She was always there ready to swoop below and catch them on her back if she felt they would not make it, however. This behaviour has not been seen by modern bird watchers, but it was a neat way of describing God's caring – the way He stirs things up to make you more self-reliant, but He is always there to save you if you fall. It was a sentiment conveyed to Moses: 'I bare you on eagles' wings, and brought you unto myself' (Exodus 19:4).

Eagles also stimulated the mythmakers. There is a Hebrew legend that tells how Solomon came across a great building for which he could not find the door. Perched near by was an old eagle, who was 700 years old. Solomon asked if he knew the whereabouts of the door, but the eagle was not sure. He suggested that he ask his elder brother, an even older eagle about 900 years old. Solomon duly asked the older eagle if he knew how to find the door, but he shook his head and pointed Solomon in the direction of his even older brother who was 1,300 years old. Solomon found this even older eagle and asked the same question. The eagle cocked his head to one side, as if in thought, and said he remembered his father mentioning a door on the west side of the building. Solomon went to look and, lo and behold, there was a door there, all rusted up and covered in the dust of ages. On it, though, was a metal plate with an inscription: 'We, the residents of this palace, lived in luxury for many years; then came famine, and we ground pearls into flour instead of wheat – but it was no good, and so, just before we died, we donated this place to the eagles.'

The next Hebrew word for a bird of prey is *raah*, which was translated in the AV as 'glede' and appears in the unclean list in Deuteronomy but not in the parallel passage in Leviticus: 'And the glede, and the kite, and the vulture after his kind' (Deuteronomy 14:13).

'Glede' in Old English refers to keenness of eyesight and in Ireland and northern English counties referred to buzzards, of which there are three species present in the Holy Land, including subspecies of the common buzzard (*Buteo buteo*) and the long-legged buzzard (*B. rufinus*). Some commentators have included some of the falcons in this term, too. Several species live in the region, including the peregrine (*Falco peregrinus*), lanner falcon (*F. biartnicus*) and sakk'r falcons (*F. cherrug*). Peregrines are found in more westerly habitats; sakk'r falcons are mainly in the east of the Jordan, particularly near Gilead; but by far the most numerous are lanner falcons that nest on cliffs in valleys on both sides of the Jordan, from the Dead Sea to Mount Hermon.

The eighth bird of prey is *ayah*, which has been translated in the AV as 'vulture'. It turns up in the unclean lists in Leviticus and Deuteronomy, and appears in Job 28:7: 'There is a path which no fowl knoweth, and which the vulture's eye hath not seen.' The vulture's eye on this occasion is thought more likely to be that of another species of kite – the red kite (*Milvus milvus*), which is common in winter but scarce in the lowlands during summer because it nests in the mountains. Tristram found it breeding on Mt Carmel, near Nablous, and in the hills of northern Galilee. The reference in Job to its keen eyesight was confirmed in Tristram's field notes: 'In wet and stormy weather the kites gather like rooks, and sit motionless for hours on a wall or in a clump of trees, so long as the moisture in the atmosphere renders their keen sight useless.'

Its prey is caught on the ground and includes voles, rats, mice, frogs and the young of game birds. The red kite can be recognised by its pointed wings and a long, deeply forked tail.

Some commentators have considered the merlin (*Falco colum-*

barius) another contender for the identity of *ayah*, from its Arabic name *yuyu*, an onomatopaeic word that describes its call, but this species is only a very rare winter visitor to Syria and Egypt.

The next raptor name is *netz*, a generic term for small birds of prey, such as hawks: 'Doth the hawk fly by thy wisdom, and stretch her wings toward the south?' (Job 39:26).

The passage refers either to the migration patterns of small raptors or the belief that they can fly towards the sun without being dazzled. The ancients believed eagles, hawks and kites had this power. The birds in question probably included the kestrel (*Falco tinnunculus*), lesser kestrel (*F. naumanni*), hobby (*F. subbuteo*), Eleonora's falcon (*F. eleonorae*) black-shouldered kite (*Elanus caeruleus*), red-footed falcon (*F. vespertinus*), shikra (*Accipiter badius*) and the sparrowhawk (*A. nisus*) and Levant sparrowhawk (*A. brevipes*). Some are residents, others migrants.

The kestrel is widely distributed, its nests often found in ruined buildings, ten or twenty pairs breeding in the same ruin. It is also one of the few birds that other birds of prey will allow as neighbours. The common kestrel is present all year round, unlike the lesser kestrel, which is a spring and summer visitor. The two differ in that the common kestrel has white claws while those of the lesser kestrel are black.

The hawks are esteemed for their fast flight and keen eyesight, and would have been known to the AV translators from their prowess in falconry. This was probably the most intensely followed sport in the seventeenth century, and there was even a hierarchy of ownership – emperors could fly eagles, kings had gyr falcons, earls were allowed peregrines, goshawks were flown by yeomanry, priests had sparrowhawks, and knaves or servants were allowed kestrels.

The tenth bird of prey is *tachmas* or *tahmes*, which has been translated in the AV as 'night-hawk'. It is included only in the list of unclean birds, and its identity has been hotly debated. The AV translators probably considered the bird to be the nightjar or goatsucker, of which three species occur in the Bible lands, including the secretive European nightjar (*Caprimulgus europaeus*). It is known for its eerie call and ghostly wing beats, and like most nocturnal creatures it has its own share of associated myth and legend. It was thought, for example, that the nightjar stole milk from the udders of goats, a belief that was held as far back as Aristotle's time.

Some commentators, however, consider *tachmas* to be a type of owl, the last great group of birds in the Bible. Owls have come to represent the darker side of Bible stories. There are fifteen references associated with ruins, desolation and dragons, and one mention on the unclean list: 'And the owl, and the night hawk, and the cuckow, and the hawk after his kind, And the little owl, and the cormorant, and the great owl' (Leviticus 11:16–17).

The grouping of the birds on the unclean list is rather strange, with no hint of modern classification, and there is the equally curious distinguishing of 'owl', 'little owl' and 'great owl'. Elsewhere in the AV, another type is mentioned – the 'screech owl' – in the same passage as a 'great owl':

> The wild beasts of the desert shall also meet with the wild beasts of the island, and the satyr shall cry to his fellow; the screech owl shall also rest there, and find for herself a place of rest. There shall the great owl make her nest, and lay, and hatch, and gather under her shadow.
>
> Isaiah 34: 14–15

Clearly, the seventeenth-century translators found it difficult to interpret the thirteen or so Hebrew words for owl, and even the experts cannot agree, so they opted for three sizes – small, medium and large. Some modern translators plump simply for the word 'owls', with no sizes mentioned at all. However, naturalists have tried to work out which species could be represented.

The 'owl' in Leviticus 11:16 is not thought to be an owl at all. In Hebrew the word is *bath-hay a anah*, meaning 'daughters of greed', and is more appropriately associated with the ostrich.

The *yanshooph* or 'great owl' in Leviticus 11:17 and Deuteronomy 14:16, and 'owl' in Isaiah 34:11 is thought to be the Egyptian eagle owl (*Bubo bubo ascalaphus* – a subspecies of the familiar eagle owl of Europe), which inhabits the semi-deserts of North Africa. It is a big and powerful bird, larger than any other owl in the region. It feeds on a diversity of prey, including more than 100 known species of mammals and 140 species of birds. It will even take other predatory birds, such as eagles and buzzards, and one individual was once seen carrying a full-grown fox.

Outside the breeding season it leads a solitary life, though the male and female may share territory but not roost together. The bond, however, lasts for life. Call bouts may start before sunset and continue for an hour or more. It is seen in ruins in Egypt and elsewhere in the Holy Land. Tristram described its call: 'Its cry is a loud, prolonged, and very powerful hoot. I know nothing which more vividly brought to my mind the sense of desolation and loneliness than the re-echoing hoot of two or three of these great owls as I stood at midnight among the ruined temples of Baalbek.'

Another subspecies, *Bubo bubo aharonii*, inhabits the desert regions of Israel. Curiously, the Septuagint and Vulgate translate *yanshooph* as 'ibis'.

The 'great owl' in Isaiah 34:15 is not actually 'great'. It is *kippoz* in Hebrew, an onomatopaeic rendering for Scop's owl, one of the smaller owls. There are several species occurring in Bible lands, including the African Scop's owl (*Otus senegalensis*) and collared Scop's owl (*O. bakkamoena*). Tristram relates that it is 'Very common among ruins, caves, and old walls of towns . . . It is a migrant, returning to Palestine in spring.'

Some modern translations of Isaiah 34:15 do not include an owl at all, but something quite different. The English Revised Version has 'arrowsnake' from a nineteenth-century translation by

Wilhelm Gesenius that suggests that the snake is so-called because of the spring by which it propels itself. The American Standard Revised Version has 'dart-snake'.

The 'little owl' in Leviticus 13:17 is *cos* in Hebrew. Its English common name has not changed and it refers to the subspecies (*Athene noctua lilith*), which is by far the commonest owl in the region. The Arabs refer to the bird as 'the mother of ruins'. The Bible, similarly, notes: 'I am like a pelican of the wilderness: I am like an owl of the desert' (Psalms 102:6). The word also translates as 'cup', the inference being that owls have cup-shaped eyes.

Several 'medium-size' owls are present in the region, including the long-eared owl (*Asio otus*), short-eared owl (*A. flammeus*) and barn owl (*Tyto alba*), but whatever the species, since ancient times it has gained for itself a sinister image. It is a bird that is out and about when most others are at their roost. It has a large head, with enormous eyes that point forwards – a feature often associated with demons and goblins – and it presents to us an altogether strange and sombre face. It hoots, screams and screeches in the darkness. It flies on silent wings, an adaptation of its plumage that enables it to locate prey by listening for the noise it makes when running through the undergrowth. And it can turn its head in such as way that it looks as if it might twist off. All in all, it was considered to be a creepy creature. Shakespeare used this to invoke an atmosphere of terror:

> Now the wasted brands do glow,
> Whilst the scritch-owl, scritching loud,
> Puts the wretch that lies in woe,
> In remembrance of a shroud.
> Now it is the time of night,
> That the graves all gaping wide,
> Every one lets forth his sprite,
> In the church-way paths to glide.

> *A Midsummer Night's Dream*, V.ii

Chaucer, Spenser, Ben Jonson, Milton and Coleridge, to name but a few, have all employed similar images.

Finally, the word for 'screech owl', *lilith*, comes from the root word in Hebrew signifying 'night' and may signify the North African subspecies of the tawny owl (*Strix aluco mauretanica*). It is common across North Africa, including Egypt and is also found in Syria and Israel.

In the early seventeenth century, when Shakespeare was writing his later plays and the AV was translated, owls were held to be very spooky indeed. It was thought that they lived in graves during daylight hours, but if they should be abroad by day and are seen flying in a town or city, that place is surely in danger of imminent destruction. Shakespeare referred to this belief in *Julius Caesar*: 'And yesterday the bird of night did sit, even at noonday upon the market place, howling and shrieking' (*Julius Caesar*, I. iii). Such was the strength of this belief that there was a time when the city of Rome had to undergo a lustration (ritual cleansing) because an owl flew into the city during the day. This was satirised by Samuel Butler in his poem in three parts published between 1663 and 1678 with the title *Hudibras*:

> The Roman senate, when within
> The city walls an owl was seen,
> Did cause their clergy with lustrations
> (Our synod calls humiliations)
> The round-fac'd prodigy t'avert
> From doing town and country hurt.

This association with destruction features strongly in the Bible. In the Old Testament, for example, Isaiah uses owls to create a picture of the destruction of Babylon: 'But wild beasts of the desert shall lie there; and their houses shall be full of doleful creatures; and owls shall dwell there, and satyrs shall dance there' (Isaiah 13:21).

Modern translators, incidentally, translate 'doleful creatures' as ostriches rather than owls. However, Isaiah calls upon owls again with more death and destruction at Edom:

> But the cormorant and the bittern shall possess it; the owl also and the raven shall dwell in it . . . And thorns shall come up in her palaces, nettles and brambles in the fortresses thereof: and it shall be an habitation of dragons, and a court for owls.

Isaiah 34:11 and 13–14

Much of the later belief that owls are directly linked with destruction was the fault of the Romans and the Etruscans. The Romans made decisions on the basis of what their gods would say, and to talk to the gods they needed augurs – religious officials who could foretell the future from omens. Roman-style augury came from the Etruscans, and they were of the firm opinion that owls were evil.

The Greeks, on the other hand, thought that owls were symbols of wisdom, an attribute celebrated nowadays in children's stories. In Athens there were so many owls that the expression 'taking owls to Athens' had a similar meaning to 'carrying coals to Newcastle'. The owl was the bird of Pallas Athene (Minerva), and it appeared on Athenian coins, the head of Pallas Athene on one side and an owl on the other. The coins were called 'owls'.

As with many creatures that have been afforded supernatural qualities, the owl figures in pharmacopoeia. According to Albertus Magnus, dogs will not bark at a person if he has an owl heart tucked under his armpit. If the heart is hung above the bed while sleeping it helps restore memory, and owl fat serves as a love potion. Owl eggs, according to the Romans, are a cure for drunkenness, while others prescribe them for baldness. A broth of owl eggs is supposed to relieve whooping cough. The preparation of an owl as a cure for gout was somewhat more elaborate: 'Take an owl, pull off her feathers, salt her well for a week, then put her in a pot and stop it close, and put her into an oven, that she may be brought into a mummy.' The dried carcase was then ground down to a powder, mixed with boar's grease, and applied to the 'grieved place'. Pliny has another owl recipe: 'The feet of a schriche Owle burnt together with the herb Plumbago is very good against serpents.'

Finally, the reason why the owl flies at night is explained in a French folk tale. One day, the wren brought down fire from heaven, but it scorched its plumage. All the other birds, except one, got together and donated a feather each to replace the lost plumage. The exception was the owl. She said she needed all her feathers to keep warm. As a consequence, the owl was excluded from flying during the warmth of the day, and condemned to suffer the perpetual cold of night.

EVERY THING THAT CREEPETH UPON THE EARTH

In the Authorised Version (AV) reptiles, amphibians and insects – and no doubt spiders, scorpions and other invertebrates with legs – were considered 'creeping things that creep upon the earth'. By the same token we might consider snakes, legless lizards and worms to be 'slithering things'. One slithering thing that injects fear whenever and wherever it appears is the snake.

SNAKE

Snakes are mentioned often in the AV, though the identity of individual species is not always clear. Take the adder, for example. The AV translators would have been familiar with the European adder or viper (*Vipera berus*) as the only naturally occurring venomous snake in the British Isles, and a species common throughout Europe and Asia, but not present in the Bible lands. The word 'adder' comes from the Anglo-Saxon *noedre* or *naedre*, meaning 'snake' or 'serpent'. This became 'an aedre' in the Middle English period and then 'adder'. Consequently, 'adder' seems to have been the ambiguous term used to describe at least four different species of dangerous snakes mentioned in the Bible.

The first reference involves Dan, the fifth son of Jacob. It was said that his tribe would use stealth, like a snake, rather than open force to increase its territory: 'Dan shall be a serpent by the way, an adder in the path, that biteth the horse heels, so that his rider shall fall backward' (Genesis 49:17). Snakes that fit this scenario are probably horned vipers (*Cerastes* spp.) and *Pseudocerastes* spp. Canon Tristram described how such a snake hid in the impression in the sand made by a camel's foot and shot out suddenly to bite passing animals. In reality, horned vipers do not hijack larger animals deliberately, but may be forced to strike in defence if disturbed. More usually they bury themselves in the sand, with just the eyes, nostrils and the tiny 'horns' on the head visible and then wait for their prey – mice, lizards or other small creatures – to pass within striking distance.

In Hebrew the word used in the passage for serpent is *nachash*, while the adder is *shephiphon*, meaning 'creeping'. This is thought to refer to the desert horned viper (*Cerastes cerastes*). It has a thick, short body that grows to a maximum length of 75cm (30in) and a long, spike-like horn above each eye. In the Sinai the Persian horned viper (*Pseudocerastes persicus*) closely resembles the desert horned viper, but its horns are small scales rather than spikes. A second reference in Proverbs imaginatively likens a hangover to being bitten by an 'adder': 'Look not thou upon the wine when it is red, when it giveth his colour in the cup, when it moveth itself aright. At the last it biteth like a serpent, and stingeth like an adder' (Proverbs 23:31–2).

The adder mentioned here is *tsiphoni* or *tsepha* in Hebrew, meaning 'hissing'. 'Cockatrice' is offered as a margin note in the AV, which suggests a pretty serious snake indeed. One that fits the bill is Ottoman's viper (*Vipera xanthina*), a heavy-bodied species that, according to snake expert Tony Phelps, is 'of a nervous disposition and quick to strike'. It grows to 1m (3.3ft) long and is considered 'a potentially very dangerous snake'.

Other vipers present in the region include the more vividly marked Palestine viper (*V. palaestinae*), which is found often close to houses, and the robust blunt-nosed viper or kufi (*V. lebetina*), another bold and dangerous species that can grow up to 1.2m (4ft) in length. The third biblical reference to a venomous 'adder' is in a Psalm of David: 'They have sharpened their tongues like a serpent; adders' poison is under their lips' (Psalm 140:3). The snake in this passage is *akshub* or *ashuv* in Hebrew, meaning 'coiling' or 'lying in wait'. When the words of the psalm are repeated in the New Testament by St Paul, the AV translators have used the Greek *aspis:* "Their throat is an open sepulchre; with their tongues they have used deceit; the poison of asps is under their lips' (Romans 3:13).

The asp or *pethen*, meaning 'twisting' in Hebrew, is identified as the Egyptian cobra (*Naja haje*). Both terms – adder and asp – have been used in the AV. In Psalms 'adder' appears again, but the references are probably to the cobra (the serpent here is *nachash*): 'Their poison is like the poison of a serpent: they are like the deaf adder that stoppeth her ear; which will not hearken to the voice of charmers, charming never so wisely' (Psalms 58:4–5); 'Thou shalt tread upon the lion and adder: the young lion and the dragon shalt thou trample under feet' (Psalms 91:13).

Cobras, more than any other species of snake, are more usually associated with snake charmers, but their name was not known in Britain until 1668. There were, however, some observations recorded by Bartholomew, who published his *Bartholomeus De Proprietatibus Rerum* in 1535. It picks up on the Bible reference to a snake charmer's asp that 'stoppeth her ear':

> The adder aspis, when she is charmed by the enchanter
> to come out of her den by charms and conjurations, for
> she hath no will to come out, layeth her one ear on the
> ground, and stoppeth that other with the tail, and so she
> heareth not the voice of the charming, nor cometh out to
> him that charmeth, nor is obedient to his saying.

This would be strange behaviour indeed, though there may be a little truth in it – not in the 'tail trick' but in the 'ear to the ground' routine. Snakes have neither external ears nor eardrums but they appear to have good hearing. They mainly pick up low-frequency sounds that travel through the ground, warning them of the approach of potential predators, and burrowing snakes can hear the scraping sounds made by their prey. The sounds or vibrations are detected by the bones of the lower jaw and then transmitted to the ear via a delicate bony rod (the stapes), but new research indicates that the snake's ear could be sensitive to airborne sounds, too, the lung playing a part in their transmission. It was once assumed that it was the movements made by the snake charmer and his flute that mesmerise the snake rather than the music he plays, but it turns out that the music itself could be persuasive as well.

The asp is most well known for the fatal bite it delivered to Cleopatra. It was a known instrument of suicide in ancient Egypt, though a 2.5m (8ft) long Egyptian cobra does not fit Shakespeare's description of the 'pretty worm of Nilus that kills and pains not'. Cleopatra was reputed to have taken the snake from a basket and goaded it to bite her on the arm and breast.

A more likely candidate is one of the horned vipers, particularly the sand viper or horned asp (*Cerastes cornutus*). An alternative is a baby asp, or perhaps one of the smaller stiletto snakes (Family: Atractaspidinae), known as the burrowing asps or mole vipers. These snakes are no more than 60cm (24in) long but they have disproportionately lengthy fangs that deliver venom containing not only the usual nerve and blood system poisons but also a series of unique amino acid peptides, known as sarafotoxins, which constrict the victim's blood vessels. No other snakes have venom containing these peptides. Stiletto snakes strike with little provocation and deliver venom that can cause temporary unconsciousness and even death in people who suffer from a weak heart. They are difficult to restrain safely when handled because of particularly flexible neck vertebrae. They are found throughout Africa with two species (*Atractaspis engaddensis* and *A. microlepi-dota*) living in Egypt, Arabia and Israel. Could one of these snakes rather than the cobra have been the asp that killed Cleopatra? Curiously, the stiletto snake has a 'tail trick': when disturbed, it raises the end of its tail and wriggles it in a way that mimics a moving head. Could this have been what Bartholomew observed?

Whatever its true identity, the asp was important to the ancient Egyptians, and the AV translators must have known it, for respected naturalists such as Topsell were writing about it at the time. In 1607 his *The History of Four-Footed Beasts and Serpents and the Theatre of Insects* included the following:

> In Egypt, so great is the reverence they bear to Asps that if any in the house have need to rise in the night time out of their beds, they first of all give the sign by knacking of the fingers, lest they harm the Asp, and so provoke it against them; at the hearing whereof all the Asps get them to their holes and lodgings, till the person stirring be again in his bed.

In the Bible the asp appears several times. In Job the asp is translated from the Hebrew word *pethen* and the viper from *epheh:* 'Yet his meat in his bowels is turned, it is the gall of asps within him . . . He shall suck the poison of asps: the viper's tongue shall slay him' (Job 20:14 and 16).

In Deuteronomy 32:33 *pethen* is used again: 'Their wine is the poison of dragons, and the cruel venom of asps', and it makes another appearance in Isaiah 11:8: 'And the sucking child shall play on the hole of the asp, and the weaned child shall put his hand on the cockatrice' den.'

In AV times, the word 'viper', from the Hebrew *ephem* or *epheh*, meaning 'to hiss', would have been used to describe any venomous snake. A reference to its flicking tongue was used as an image suggesting death, as in Job 20:16 above prophesying the fate that the wicked man brings upon himself.

In reality, the tongue of a poisonous snake is harmless. It is merely a sense organ used for 'tasting' the air. When it flicks out, odour molecules adhere to its surface, particularly on the forked tips. Inside the roof of the mouth is a pit known as the Jacobson's organ, which analyses the sample brought in by the tongue. This chemo-reception system is so sensitive that it can detect the faintest trail left behind by prey. The dangerous parts are the fangs.

In venomous snakes the fangs can be rear- or front-mounted. The burrowing asps, for example, have rear-mounted fangs. Vipers have a pair of enlarged, front-mounted fangs that can be swivelled out for action and can pivot independently. To help them work effectively, the mouth can be opened extremely wide so the fangs can be brought down forcibly on the prey – and all in a split second. When not in use they are folded back along the upper jaw.

There are several species of viper in the Bible lands and they were clearly held in great respect: "The burden of the beasts of the south: into the land of trouble and anguish, from whence come the young and old lion, the viper and fiery flying serpent' (Isaiah 30:6); 'They hatch cockatrice' eggs, and weave the spider's web: he that eateth of their eggs dieth, and that which is crushed breaketh out into a viper' (Isaiah 59:5).

In the second passage modern versions of the Old Testament have either 'snake' or 'sand viper' as the translation. In the New Testament the viper is used again as a figure of speech: 'But when he saw many of the Pharisees and Sadducees come to his baptism, he said unto them, O generation of vipers, who had warned you to flee from the wrath to come?' (Matthew 3:7). Here Matthew reported how Jesus likened authorities to vipers. It was a metaphor He used several times: 'O generation of vipers, how can ye, being evil, speak good things?'; 'Ye serpents, ye generation of vipers, how can ye escape the damnation of hell?' (Matthew 12:34 and 23:33).

A further reference to vipers is found later on in the New

Testament, in an account of St Paul being bitten by a snake when he was on the island of Malta, known in AV times as Melita. 'And when Paul had gathered a bundle of sticks, and laid them on the fire, there came a viper out of the heat, and fastened on his hand' (Acts 28:3).

Which species of snake this could have been is difficult to determine, as no vipers exist on Malta today. The adder or common viper, though the world's most widespread species of poisonous snake, is not present in southern Italy and therefore was unlikely to have been on Malta. The aspic viper (*V. aspis*) or the long-nosed or sand viper (*V. ammodytes*) are better candidates. The aspic viper, for example, is found on mainland Italy and islands, such as Elba and Montescristo, so there is a vague possibility that it could once have been present on Malta.

Today, there are four species of snake to be spotted on the island. The black whip snake (*Coluber viridiflavus carbonarius*) is common and active by day. The Algerian whip snake (*C. florulentus algirus*) is a relatively new introduction, as is the cat snake (*Telescopus fallax*). The cat snake is a venomous species. It has fangs that hinge at the back of the mouth, but it could not have been the snake that bit St Paul because it is a recent introduction. It was brought to the island along with firewood shipments during the First World War.

The most likely candidate for St Paul's 'viper' is Malta's fourth species, the indigenous lm (3.3ft) long leopard snake (*Elaphe situal leopardina*), which is also found on Gozo and Comino. It is not venomous but it is a hefty snake and can give quite a bite if disturbed. It would also explain why St Paul miraculously survived the attack.

In the Bible lands as a whole, snakes or serpents are not especially abundant, though there are several species commonly encountered, some harmless, others less so. The most common is the 1.5m (5ft) long coin snake (*C. mummifer*). The Arabs know it as *aqd-ul-jauz*, meaning 'string of walnuts', on account of the series of dark, diamond-shaped patches on its back. It is not venomous but it is very fast and aggressive, and is one of the few snakes that will stand and fight rather than slink away. It often finds its prey, such as mice, in old stone walls. It catches and wraps it body around its victim, and squeezes the life out of it in the manner of the large constricting snakes.

In the same genus is another common snake, the smaller Balkan whip snake (*C. [gemonensis] laurenti*). Its close relative the red-headed whip snake (*C. dahlii*) and the equally harmless dice snake (*Natrix tessallatus*) are often found lying in pools and streams. Another harmless species is the blind worm snake (*Typhlops vermicularis*). This extremely slender, subterranean species of dry, open habitats feeds on invertebrates, especially ants and their larvae. The spotted or javelin sand boa (*Eryx jaculus*), which as its name suggests is found in sandy areas, is mainly nocturnal, and hunts for lizards and rodents that it kills by constriction. The black-headed snake (*Oligodon melanocephalu*) is recognised by the conspicuous black top to its head.

Other relatively common snakes that are harmless include four species of dwarf racer snakes (*Eirenis* spp.).

The venomous snakes include the 2m (6.6ft) long *Coelopeltis monspessulana*. In Arabic it is known as *al-chayat ul-barshat*, and is recognised by its reddish topside and paler belly. The much smaller *Micrelaps mulleri* is no more than 45cm (18in) long. The Sind sand snake *Psammophis schokari* is known as *an-nashshab* in Arabic, meaning 'the arrow'. This slender, 'polished' snake grows to about 1.2m (4ft) long and its rather stiff appearance has given rise to many improbable tales. It is supposed, for instance, to be able to leap and shoot through the air for more than 30m (100ft) and imbed itself in a tree like a rifle bullet. All these snakes could be termed 'mildly dangerous', but the 80cm (30in) long small-toothed or carpet viper (*Echis coloratus*) is in a different league altogether. It strikes without provocation, delivers a powerful venom, and is considered by some authorities to be one of the world's most dangerous snakes. Snake bites attributed to other species are often as not due to this species.

LIZARD

There is a creature living in the region that looks like a snake but is not one. The scheltopusik is often mistaken for a venomous snake when in fact it is not a snake at all but a limbless lizard (*Ophiosaurus apus*). Lizards and other reptiles, such as chameleons and tortoises, are mentioned in the Bible, and some species that are attributed other identities in the AV, such as the ferret, mole, spider and snail, may not be mammals, arachnids or molluscs but reptiles. Whatever they are, they appear on the unclean list:

> There also shall be unclean unto you among the creeping things that creep upon the earth; the weasel, and the mouse, and the tortoise after his kind, And the ferret, and the chameleon, and the lizard, and the snail, and the mole. These are unclean to you among all that creep; whosoever doth touch them, when they be dead, shall be unclean until the even.

> Leviticus 11:29–31

The Hebrew word for 'lizard' is *letaah*, but whether it refers to a particular species is impossible to tell, for there are many in the Holy Land, every district and landscape with its own species or subspecies. The most common is the rough-tailed agama (*Agama stellio*), which basks on rocks, scuttles about on rocks and walls and hides in caves and crevices. The green lizard (*Lacerta viridis*) and common wall lizard (*L. laevis*) of southern Europe are also widespread. They run about in the fallen leaves and brushwood feeding on beetles, locusts and worms.

Tristram describes the skink (*Plestiodon auratus*) as 'one of the largest and most beautiful lizards in Palestine'. At the time of his visits, it was found close to the Dead Sea and was easily recognised by its yellowish body with red and orange spots. He also mentions the 60cm (24in) long glass snake (*Pseudopus pallasii*) as a common species of legless lizard in Syria.

The Hebrew word *coach* or *koach* has been translated in the AV as 'chameleon', though the root word that gives rise to *coach* signifies 'strength' or 'power', not words usually associated with the delicate chameleon. Several commentators opt instead for a large monitor lizard as the true identity, in particular the desert monitor (*Varanus griseus*) known also as the 'land-crocodile' in the Revised Authorised Version of the Bible and *Waran-el-hard* by the Arabs. This 1.2m (4ft) long monster is found in Palestine and Egypt, where it feasts on smaller lizards, desert rodents and eggs. The Nile monitor (*V. niloticus*), known to the Arabs as *Waran-el-bahr*, is also found in the region, mainly in Egypt. This giant, which can reach 2m (6ft) in length, is distinguished from the desert monitor by a high keel along the length of its tail and spots on its skin. It has a penchant for crocodiles' eggs, and will risk the wrath of gigantic female Nile crocodiles in order to steal their brood. It was revered by the ancient Egyptians and appeared frequently on their ornaments and tombs.

The chameleon itself is probably the correct identity for the 'mole', fifth on the unclean list in the AV. In Greek it is the 'earth-lion', from *chamai*, meaning 'earth', and *leon*, meaning 'lion'. The Hebrew word is *tinshemeth*, meaning 'breathe', and might well be linked to the ancient belief that the chameleon lived on air because it has such enormous lungs. There's even a reference in Shakespeare's *Hamlet*. When Hamlet is asked how he is feeling, he replies: 'Excellent i'faith. Of the chameleon's dish. I eat the air, promise-crammed' (*Hamlet*, III.ii).

At the time of the AV, the creature was attributed with all sorts of strange abilities. Topsell noted them down:

> If the chameleon at any time see a serpent taking the air,
> and sunning himself under some green tree, and settleth

himself directly over the serpent, then out of his mouth
he casteth a thread like a spider, and at the end whereof
hangeth a drop of poison as bright as any pearl, which
lighting upon the serpent killeth it immediately.

The chameleon, of course, does not attack serpents in this way and
it is not venomous. Topsell's reference is actually to its
extraordinarily long tongue that can shoot out to a length longer
than its body in order to catch insects before they can escape. The
'poisonous pearl' is the sticky tip.

The chameleon is mainly a tree dweller, and although not
helpless on the ground it is distinctly uncomfortable there. Its eyes
are on turrets, and can move independently. In this way the
chameleon can not only watch its target – an insect or a spider –
but also be aware of danger approaching from behind. Its ability
to change colour is legendary, but the reason given for the colour
changes is often flawed. The colour change reflects the
chameleon's mood rather than its background. It will turn black
with rage.

Tristram also draws attention to words that have been translated
as 'snail' in the AV. The Hebrew word mentioned in Leviticus is
chomet, meaning 'to lie low', which is thought to describe a lizard
and not a mollusc. The French scholar and pastor Samuel Bochart,
who in 1663 wrote *A Book in Two Parts Concerning the Animals of the
Holy Scripture*, goes a step further and argues that as *chometon*
signifies 'sand', *chomet* must be a sand lizard – the *chaluca* of the
Arabs. Sand lizards or sandfish are skinks (*Scincus* spp.), and as
their common name suggests they are inhabitants of the driest
places, such as the wilderness areas of Judaea, the Jordan Valley and
the Sinai Peninsula. Their distinguishing feature is the ability to
burrow rapidly into the sand, as if swimming. They were once
considered a delicacy in North Africa. One species that has been put
forward for its identity is the cylindrical skink (*Chalcides lineatus*). It
is one of the sandfish that is found in deserts and semi-deserts

from the western Mediterranean to the east of Pakistan.

Another anomaly is the mention of 'ferret'. The Hebrew word is *anakah*, which means 'that which sighs or groans' – hardly a description of a ferret. The Greek translation has 'shrew-mouse' and elsewhere it has been dubbed 'hedgehog', but Tristram suggests that it must be a reptile from its place in the Mosaic clean or unclean list in Leviticus 11. The Hebrew description of the sound produced by this creature makes it more likely that it is a vocal lizard, such as a gecko, and modern translations opt for this interpretation.

There are several species of geckos found in the Holy Land, including the fan-footed gecko (*Ptyodactylus hasselquistii*) and another gecko known only by its scientific name – *Ptyodactylus lobatus*. They are lizards most frequently found in houses and ruins, where they run up and down walls and across ceilings. The gecko does this with special lamellate pads on its feet that enable it to grip even the smallest irregularity and run over apparently smooth surfaces. It can move in almost complete silence and it does so by night. Geckos vary in colour from red through brown to blue, but all have white spots on their back and flanks. They can vibrate their broad tongue against the roof of the mouth to create a rapid clucking sound, which has given them their onomatopoeic common name – 'gecko'. The ancients thought they were poisonous and feared them. They thought that if a gecko crawled over the skin, ulcerous sores would appear. In Hebrew folklore the lizard was believed to have supernatural properties. It was a deterrent against scorpions and its dried skin can be found in old apothecaries.

The Hebrew word *smamit* has also been associated with the gecko but it was translated by the AV writers as 'spider': 'The spider taketh hold with her hands, and is in kings' palaces' (Proverbs 30:28).

More recent translations, however, substitute 'lizard' for 'spider', and the special mention of the creature as frequenting palaces seems to suggest the gecko rather than the common-or-garden spider.

Looking at other reptiles mentioned in the Bible, even the tortoise may not be what it seems. The Hebrew word is *tzab*, but it is not clear to the scholars which animal is intended. Some believe it to be a lizard and not a tortoise. Bochart, for example, thought the *tzab* to be the same as the Arab *dhabb*, a large, 60cm (24in) long spiny-tailed lizard that inhabits the deserts of North Africa and Arabia, but is also found occasionally in Palestine. There are several species present in the region, including the ornate dab lizard (*Uromastix ornatus*) and the Arabian thorny-tailed lizard (*U. spinipes*). These species are recognised by the green tint to their scales and their powerful tails, covered in prickly scales. They are found hiding in rock crevices or burrowing under the sand, and they feed chiefly on beetles.

The tortoise itself was once common in the Holy Land. Several species are still present, including the well-known Mediterranean spur-thighed tortoise (*Testudo graeca*), often kept as pets in the UK. They are active in summer and hibernate in shallow holes under roots or rocks in winter. They feed on vegetation, including grasses, vetches, mallows and dandelions, and have a regular daily routine. The tortoise expert Andy Highfield recorded the daily schedule of a Turkish subspecies. A tortoise will emerge from its overnight scrape (burrow) between 8.30 a.m. and 9.30 a.m. and, depending on the weather, it will then bask for an hour. It stretches its legs, head and neck and props itself up against a rock in order to expose as much of its body to the sun as possible. It will then forage until about 7 p.m., with a break at midday if it is hot. At about 8 p.m. it returns to its scrape and beds down for the night.

An aquatic relative – the Caspian terrapin (*Mauremys caspica*) of rivers, marshes and lakes, such as Lake Huleh or the Waters of Merom in northeast Israel – is carnivorous, feeding on fish, frogs and aquatic invertebrates. The terrapin differs from its land-based cousin in having a flatter carapace and a longer tail and neck.

SNAIL

Another reference to the 'snail' in the AV is *shavluv* or *shablul* in Hebrew and on this occasion it is thought that the true identity really is 'snail', in particular one of the *Helix* species that includes the common garden snail (*H. aspersa*) and the edible Roman snail (*H. pomatia*). The creature is called on by one of the psalmists: 'As a snail which melteth, let every one of them pass away' (Psalms 58:8). This passage seems to refer to the trail of mucous slime left on the ground behind a moving snail, as if the creature is slowly disintegrating into slime and leaving part of itself behind, which of course is biologically incorrect. In Hebrew folklore, however, on the one hand it signifies that the snail is losing its vigour, but on the other hand the slime is considered a cure for boils. It is seen as an example of how something so lowly can actually have a useful purpose.

Another example is the *Murex* sea snail, from which the important royal dye Tyrian purple was extracted. Each animal was said to yield just a single pure drop. The rest of the shellfish was crushed to produce an inferior version of the dye. The colour was the insignia of royalty or high office.

Pliny describes how at first the juice is white but on exposure to air it becomes a yellow-pus-like yellow, then green and then gradually redder until it reaches a deep red-purple. Wool was steeped in it before being spun or woven. Tyre was an ancient production centre, and middens of crushed shellfish were found outside the city similar to the Mons Testaceus of Rome and the kitchen-middens of Denmark. Cloth prepared in Tyre fetched high prices in Rome. By CE 301 a pound of Tyrian dyed wool cost about 50,000 denarii – that is, the equivalent of a baker's wages for a thousand days.

In Rome itself the restriction on the wearing of robes dyed with Tyrian purple was rigorous. The emperor, two censors and triumphant generals were permitted to wear togas and cloaks dyed completely purple. Consuls and praetors were allowed only a purple edging. And the manufacture of royal purple was very restricted in the Empire; it was a capital offence to produce the stuff other than at the imperial dye works.

In the Holy Land there was also a blue dye from snails, known as *tekhelet* in Hebrew. The Lord brought it up in a conversation with Moses:

> Speak unto the children of Israel, and bid them that they make them fringes in the borders of their garments throughout their generations, and that they put upon the fringe of the borders a ribband of blue: And it shall be unto you for a fringe, that ye may look upon it, and remember all the commandments of the Lord, and do them.

Numbers 15:38–39

Over time, the method of extraction of these dyes was lost – *tekhelet* by CE 760 and Tyrian purple by 1453, when the Byzantine imperial purple works disappeared after Constantinople fell. The snail link was rediscovered in 1856, when the French zoologist Felix Henri de Lacaze-Duthiers saw a fisherman drawing a yellow pattern on his shirt using a shellfish, knowing that it would turn red eventually. Today, extracts from these gastropod-snails have been analysed and three have been identified as the main sources of the two dyes – *Trunculariopsis trunculus, Murex (Bolinus) brandaris* and *Thais haemastoma*. The raw dye is found in the hypobranchial gland in the animal's mantle. The gland is a tiny 'chemical factory' and two key pigments are present – indigo or indigotin and a brominated derivative, 6,6'-dibromoindigo. The brominated compound is thought to be Tyrian purple and a combination of the two produces *tekhelet*. The colour of the pigments varies from species to species and even between sexes in the same species. The male rock murex (*T. trunculus*), for example, yields indigo and the female the brominated purple.

Other marine molluscs give us 'onycha', one of the ingredients in the holy perfume of the tabernacle: 'And the Lord said unto Moses, Take unto thee sweet spices, stacte, and onycha, and galbanum; these sweet spices with pure frankincense: of each shall there be a like weight' (Exodus 30:34).

The onycha here is the horny operculum cover that is attached to the foot of shellfish. It is the cover that protects them when they retreat into their shell. In Bible times, it was collected from shellfish known as conches (*Strombus* spp.), mainly the larger species living in the Red Sea. These chunky gastropod shellfish reside in shallow sand and often use the operculum to make leaping movements like a pole-vaulter. When the horny material is burned, it has a strong pungent smell, and it is still used like frankincense in some places.

Pearls – another product of molluscs – are mentioned once in the Old Testament and several times in the New. They were highly prized in Bible times, even more so than precious stones: 'the kingdom of heaven is like unto a merchant man, seeking goodly pearls' (Matthew 13:45). They were worn as a component of jewellery even then: 'And the woman was arrayed in purple and scarlet colour, and decked with gold and precious stones and pearls' (Revelation 17:4).

Pearls are also a common Eastern metaphor for valued sayings or well-chosen words, so a short moralising poem is known as a 'string of pearls'. It was used memorably by Jesus in his Sermon on the Mount when warning his listeners against passing on the message of the Kingdom to Gentiles: 'Give not that which is holy unto the dogs, neither cast ye your pearls before swine, lest they trample them under their feet, and turn again and rend you' (Matthew 7:6).

The pearls of Bible times, like the pearls of today, come from bivalve molluscs, such as oysters and mussels. Each pearl starts as a piece of grit that slips between the animal's two shells. The animal secretes a substance around the irritant, which gradually hardens and forms the pearl. In the Old Testament, however, the single reference to 'pearls' is another suspect translation. The AV translates the Hebrew word *gabish* in the following passage as 'pearls': 'No mention shall be made of coral, or of pearls: for the price of wisdom is above rubies' (Job 28:18).

Modern commentators have replaced 'pearls' with 'crystal' as the word is used elsewhere to mean 'ice'. In the same passage there is also mention of coral (Class: Anthozoa), another material highly prized in biblical times. At the time, it was much more difficult to collect and so was much more valuable than it is today. Coral jewellery, beads, charms and seals have been found in ancient Egyptian tombs. The Hebrew word is *ramoth*, meaning 'that which grows high' like a tree, and there is a second mention in the Old Testament: 'Syria was thy merchant by reason of the multitude of the wares of thy making: they occupied in thy fairs with emeralds, purple, and broidered work, and fine linen, and coral, and agate' (Ezekiel 27:16).

The best corals were probably from the Red Sea and Persian Gulf, and were brought to Tyre by the Syrians. The material they brought was produced by myriads of tiny sea anemone-like creatures that live together and secrete a massive calcareous skeleton. The shape of the coral depends on the species – some are the shape of brains, others are like stags' horns or fans. Today, the trade in corals is so great that some species are in danger of disappearing altogether.

In ancient times, the red or precious coral (*Corallium rubrum*) was valued, and it could be an alternative identity for the 'rubies' mentioned in Job 28:18. The Hebrew word is *peninim*, from the root 'to divide up' or 'to separate', and it occurs in several passages: 'Her Nazarites were purer than snow, they were whiter than milk, they were more ruddy in body than rubies, their polishing was of sapphire' (Lamentations 4:7).

Red coral is found in the Mediterranean and Adriatic Seas and differs from the reef-building corals in having a soft body with numerous red spicules that fuse together to form a strong central axis coloured bright red. Nowadays, it is scarce because of overfishing, but can still be found on the roofs of submarine grottoes and in rock crevices at depths down to 50m (165ft). It was (and still is) used in the manufacture of jewellery.

WORM
Further up zoology's taxonomic tree are the worms, and they are well represented in the AV, albeit erroneously in some cases. One 'worm' that comes in for special mention is the leech, and the horse leech in particular. There is only one reference: 'The horse-leach hath two daughters, crying, Give, give' (Proverbs 30:15).

This curious piece of text about the insatiable devouring of the poor probably refers either to the mythical vampire or to the real-life leech (Class: Hirudinea), and the insatiable appetite for blood they both have. The Hebrew word is *aiuka* or *aluqah*, which translates simply as 'leech'. The same word in Arabic translates as 'ghoul', a creature that behaves in a similar way to a vampire, while the Arabic word for leech is *alaqah* from the root *aliq*, meaning 'to cling'. A marginal note in the Revised Authorised Version suggests 'vampire' as an alternative translation.

Leeches are related to earthworms. They can live in water (including the sea) or on land, where some are external parasites, others carnivorous predators. The parasites survive by sucking the blood of other animals, usually vertebrates. They have large suction discs at either end of the worm-like body, and the front one has a mouth with large jaws at its centre. With this the leech can pierce its host's skin and extract blood, a form of feeding known as 'sanguivory'. It keeps the blood flowing and avoids detection by secreting anticoagulants (hirudin), an anaesthetic, a spreading factor (hyaluronidase), a vasodilator (like histamine), antibiotics and mucus from salivary glands behind the mouth. Of necessity, it feeds irregularly and has adaptations for storing food for long periods.

Many species of leech are endemic to the Holy Land, and some species will parasitise horses when they come to drink at ponds or streams. In his *Natural History of the Bible*, published in 1880, Tristram describes how they attach themselves to the nostrils, tongue and palate and are very difficult to remove. Today, leeches are less common because many wetland areas have been drained or water courses diverted for agriculture. Fish farms, however, are providing a new habitat.

The seventeenth-century translators of the AV would have known the 'horse leech'. By the mid-sixteenth century the term was used to describe a voracious person. Shakespeare provided Pistol with the words in *Henry V*: 'Let us to France, like horse leeches, my boys/To suck, to suck, the very blood to suck!' (*Henry V*, II.iii).

And in a Renaissance debate on the nature of women in 1615, Joseph Swetman published a tirade against women in his long-titled work *The Arraignment of Lewd, idle, froward, and unconstant women. Or the vanity of them, choose you whether. With a commendation of wise, virtuous, and honest women. Pleasant for married Men, profitable for young Men, and hurtful to none:* 'They will play the horse-leach to suck away thy wealth, but in the winter of thy misery shee will flie away from thee.'

There is, however, a slight biological problem with all these references. The so-called 'horse leech' (*Haemopsis* spp.), which can be up to 30cm (12in) long when fully extended, is not a bloodsucking parasite. It is an amphibious predator and scavenger, feeding every few days on worms and other leeches, slugs and snails, frogs' eggs and tadpoles. It does not 'suck away' the blood of horses.

More problems arise when we consider the generalised term 'worm' in the AV. The worm is used as a symbol of what Tristram described as the 'gnawing pain of eternal punishment'. 'And they shall go forth, and look upon the carcases of the men that have transgressed against me: for their worm shall not die, neither shall their fire be quenched; and they shall be an abhorring unto all flesh' (Isaiah 66:24); 'Where their worm dieth not, and the fire is not quenched' (Mark 9:44).

Mention here of carcases, however, conjures up an image not of worms but of maggots or blowfly larvae (Family: Diptera). This might also refer to the way in which piles of garbage and offal were piled up outside cities in biblical times, and although the fires were kept burning to keep the heaps in check, they were crawling with maggots. Worms or maggots were also implicated in the deaths of Herod Agrippa and Antiochus Epiphanus. Whether they were the cause is not clear: 'And immediately the angel of the Lord smote him [Herod], because he gave not God the glory: and he was eaten of worms, and gave up the ghost' (Acts 12:23); 'So that the worms rose up out of the body of this wicked man [Antiochus], and whiles he lived in sorrow and pain, his flesh fell away, and the filthiness of his smell was noisome to all his army' (2 Maccabees 9:9).

In the case of Antiochus, his demise might well have been something quite different. He had just fallen off his chariot and must have been badly injured. Bacteria could well have infected his wounds and the resulting gangrene, which became infested with maggots, caused his flesh to fall away. Eventually he must have died of septicaemia or blood poisoning.

Maggots also seem a likely candidate for the identity of other 'worms'. Two Hebrew words *tole'ah* and *rimmah* that have been translated in the AV as 'worm' appear together in several passages and seem to be interchangeable. In Exodus we read of how the children of Israel were offered manna, but they were only to take their fill and not store any until the following day because it would putrefy (though preparing manna on the day before the Sabbath and holding it over was permitted):

And Moses said, Let no man leave of it till the morning. Notwithstanding they hearkened not unto Moses; but some of them left of it until the morning, and it bred worms [*tola'im*], and stank . . . And he said unto them . . . Tomorrow is the rest of the holy sabbath unto the Lord: bake that which ye will bake to day, and seethe that ye will seethe; and that which remaineth over lay up for you to be kept until the morning. And they laid it up till the morning, as Moses bade: and it did not stink, neither was there any worm [*rimmah*] therein.

Exodus 16:19–20 and 23–24

It is curious that the same 'worm' has two different Hebrew words in one passage. Likewise in these verses: 'How much less man, that is a worm [*rimmah*]? and the son of man, which is a worm [*tole'ah*]?' (Job 25:6); 'Thy pomp is brought down to the grave, and the noise of thy viols: the worm [*rimmah*] is spread under thee, and the worms [*tola'im*] cover thee' (Isaiah 14:11).

Tristram believes that the two words do refer to different creatures. He suggests that *tole'ah* refers to caterpillar-like pests: 'Thou shalt plant vineyards, and dress them, but shalt neither drink of the wine, nor gather the grapes; for the worm shall eat them' (Deuteronomy 28:39); 'But God prepared a worm when the morning rose the next day, and it smote the gourd that it withered' (Jonah 4:7).

He proposes that *rimmah* is used for maggot-like creatures that feed on dead bodies: 'My flesh is clothed with worms and clods of dust; my skin is broken, and become loathsome'; 'I have said to corruption, Thou art my father: to the worm, Thou art my mother, and my sister' (Job 7:5 and 17:14).

Worms that we would understand as the familiar earthworms (*Lumbricus* spp.) seem to be hard to come by in the Bible, even though there are several species present in the soils of the Holy Land. Just one passage has worms behaving almost as worms should: 'They shall lick the dust like a serpent, they shall move out of their holes like worms of the earth' (Micah 7:17).

MOTHS

Another Hebrew word that was translated in the AV as 'worm' is *sas*. It occurs just once and clearly denotes the caterpillar or larval stage of the clothes moth: 'For the moth shall eat them up like a garment, and the worm shall eat them like wool' (Isaiah 51:8).

The clothes moth (*Tineloa* spp.) was an especially serious pest in Bible times. Wool was expensive in man-hours to collect, spin and weave and so a wool garment would have been a treasured possession, like Joseph's multicoloured coat. If it were destroyed prematurely, it would have been something of a disaster; consequently, the references to moths in the Bible are associated with destruction. Another Hebrew word is *ash*, and there is no doubt at all in the minds of scholars that this also refers specifically to the clothes moth, of which there are several species in the region: 'And he, as a rotten thing, consumeth, as a garment that is moth eaten' (Job 13:28).

The destructive phase of the house moth is not the adult but the larvae or caterpillar. As some point in mankind's distant past, the caterpillar switched from living in and feeding upon pieces of wool collected by birds to line their nests, to collections of wool that had been made into clothes, and a pest was born. A fragile tube of self-spun silk and wool fragments protects the caterpillar itself, a feature alluded to perhaps when Job compared the frailty of a man's house to a moth's larval tube: 'He buildeth his house as a moth'; 'How much less in them that dwell in houses of clay, whose foundation is in the dust, which are crushed before the moth?' (Job 27:18 and 4:19).

There has been much debate about what is meant here. The hoarding of large numbers of garments was a sign of wealth in those times and one reading could be that a basket of woollen clothes that has been left and has become infested with moths might be eaten from the inside. When the clothes are picked up, they are so moth-eaten that they simply crumble into dust. It was an image utilised by Jesus in a warning in the New Testament:

'Lay not up for yourselves treasure upon the earth, where moth and rust doth corrupt, and where thieves break through and steal' (Matthew 6:19).

References to the clothes moth are the only mentions of moths in the Bible, though many species of moths and butterflies live in the Holy Land. Most are similar to or the same as species that frequent southeast Europe, and they are joined by migrants from northeast Africa.

LOCUST AND GRASSHOPPER

While moth larvae were clearly a household problem, it is the group of insects that include locusts, grasshoppers and crickets (Order: Orthoptera) that has made the biggest impact on people in the Holy Land, and this is reflected in the number of references to these creatures in the Bible. In the AV there are nine references to grasshoppers and 56 to locusts, though in Hebrew there are several words for grasshoppers and locusts (and various stages in their life histories) and in some cases the translated English words could be interchangeable. Some names in the AV are not used today.

There are many species living in the region, and most are strictly vegetarian. They have mouthparts that can slice rapidly through vegetation, and large numbers can devastate crops as a result. They are highly mobile – some just hop, using their long back legs; others fly, and still others hop when they are young and fly when adult.

Taking the Hebrew words one by one, we come first to *arbeh*, meaning 'to multiply', an appropriate description of one of the plagues of Egypt: 'and when it was morning, the east wind brought the locusts' (Exodus 10:13). In fact, most references involving the word *arbeh* are either to the devastation of crops or the power to multiply and gather together in huge numbers: 'Thou shalt carry much seed out into the field, and shalt gather but little in; for the locust shall consume it' (Deuteronomy 28:38);

'If there be in the land famine, if there be pestilence, blasting, mildew, locust' (1 Kings 8:37); 'make thyself many as the locusts' (Nahum 3:15). The locusts in these passages must have been a migratory species, probably either the migratory locust (*Locusta migratoria*) or the desert locust (*Schistocerca gregaria*).

Locusts do not always swarm in large numbers. They spend most of their life as relatively harmless grasshoppers, but as soon as conditions are right their numbers can increase rapidly and enormously. When temperature and humidity are favourable, there is an abrupt change in behaviour. The normally solitary grasshoppers produce a chemical known as 'locustine' that is deposited as a dark pigment in the insect's cuticle. It is passed on to the hatching nymphs, known as 'hoppers' because they have yet to develop their adult wings and, like any self-respecting grasshopper or cricket to which they are related, literally hop to get about. The chemical makes them darker than their non-swarming cousins, and it causes them to come together into large, unusually active groups. Males produce a pheromone (chemical messenger like a hormone) that hastens the maturation process and synchronises the swarm to mate and lay their eggs at the same time. And when all this happens, you have a plague on your hands. Swarms have even reached Britain. On one occasion in the summer of 1748, migratory locusts invaded England, stripping trees bare near Bristol, and in Shropshire and Staffordshire so that they looked as they do at Christmas.

In the AV the word *arbeh* has also been translated as 'grasshopper'. This occurs in four passages: 'they [Midianites] came as grasshoppers for multitude' (Judges 6:5); 'And the Midianites and the Amalekites and all the children of the east lay along in the valley like grasshoppers for multitude' (Judges 7:12); 'Canst thou make him afraid as a grasshopper' (Job 39:20); 'they are more than the grasshoppers, and are innumerable' (Jeremiah 46:23).

A second Hebrew word is *chasil*, meaning 'consumer', which the AV has translated as 'caterpillar'. It is mentioned along with the locust in Solomon's prayer at the dedication of his extraordinary temple, by the prophet Joel, and by the psalmists: 'He gave also their increase unto the caterpiller [sic]' (Psalms 78:46). Modern translations, however, seem to agree that it refers to a development stage of the locust, though locusts actually do not have a caterpillar stage. They start out as 'hoppers'.

Locusts are insects that have a reproduction system known as 'incomplete metamorphosis'. They do not have the 'egg-to-larva (caterpillar)-to-pupa (chrysalis)-to-adult' system as do beetles and butterflies, but instead have a more primitive series of steps that involve only nymphs. The nymphs – like miniature adults – hatch from the eggs, eat and grow, casting off their hard 'skin' or cuticle periodically to enable their bodies to expand and therefore progress towards adult size. Although they cannot fly, young locust nymphs or 'hoppers' can, like their grown-up relatives, gather together in immense numbers and are similarly insatiable. Links with the locust are thought to be evident in some passages: 'He spake, and the locusts came, and caterpillers [sic], and that without number, And did eat up all the herbs in their land, and devoured the fruit of their ground' (Psalms 105:34–35); 'And your spoil shall be gathered like the gathering of the caterpiller [sic]: as the running to and fro of locusts shall he run upon them' (Isaiah 33:4).

But were these references to locust nymphs or could they actually have been to caterpillars? From time to time, the caterpillars of moths or butterflies do get out of hand and gather together in plague proportions. One of the most devastating caterpillar pests is the African armyworm (*Spodoptera exampta*), the caterpillar of a noctuid moth that attacks the leaves and stems of cereals and other plants with disastrous consequences for farmers. The adult moths can travel 100km (60 miles) in a night, spreading devastation far and wide, an outbreak covering 100 sq km (39 sq miles) or more. Two of the biggest outbreaks in recent years, for example, were a plague of armyworms (*Pseudaletia unipuncta*) that devastated Tanzania in October 1999 and another that invaded Zimbabwe in February 2003, when field after field of millet and maize was destroyed. The number of individuals can be so great that their presence means trains cannot grip their tracks and cars slide off the road. In the USA seasonal population explosions of tens of thousands of armyworms can destroy a lawn in a single night or an entire golf course in a few days. It is a phenomenon that has been observed and reported in North America as far back as 1646.

The reason for the increase in numbers is usually connected with the weather. Winds, for example, might deposit adult moths on a particular area and each female might deposit two thousand eggs. Unusually heavy rains will ensure there is sufficient vegetation to feed the caterpillars that hatch out, feed and grow and a plague – 'more than 100 caterpillars per sq foot' – is born. So there is no reason to rule out 'caterpillars' as the correct translation.

The third Hebrew word is *sal'am*, which is thought to derive from the Chaldee word meaning 'to devour'. In the Talmud (the collection of ancient Jewish writings that forms the basis of Jewish religious law) it is described as a locust with a smooth head so the AV translators have dubbed it 'bald locust'. It is mentioned just once along with the other edible locust-like creatures: 'and the bald locust after his kind' (Leviticus 11:22).

Tristram believes that the smooth head might refer to the towerhead grasshopper (*Truxalis* spp.), which has 'a long, narrow, smooth head, and straight, sword-shaped antennae' and is common in the Holy Land. It is a master of disguise, its striped pattern blending in superbly with vegetation.

A fourth Hebrew word is *chargol*, meaning 'leaper'. The AV translators have translated it as 'beetle' but mention of leaping clearly indicates a locust-like character and not one of the beetles, which tend to be 'crawlers', 'runners' or 'flyers' but rarely if ever 'leapers' – click beetles (Family: Elateridae) being an exception.

It's a pity really, because beetles are obviously very special in the order of things. Of all the groups of insects living on the earth, beetles (Order: Coleoptera) have the largest number of known species – more than 300,000. One of their greatest fans was Charles Darwin. When he travelled the world in HMS *Beagle* between 1831 and 1836, he collected and identified more beetles than any other group of insects. In the same vein, the eminent biologist J B S Haldane was asked what the study of biology taught him about the Creator. He replied, 'I'm not sure, but He seems to be inordinately fond of beetles.' Yet despite so many representatives, beetles get just one mention in the AV Bible:

> Yet these may ye eat of every flying creeping thing that goeth upon all four, which may have legs above their feet, to leap withal upon the earth; Even these of them ye may eat; the locust after his kind, and the bald locust after his kind, and the beetle after his kind, and the grasshopper after his kind.

> Leviticus 11:21–22

Whatever they are, they are edible and 'clean' under Mosaic law, and the grouping of 'beetles' with the other locust-like creatures suggests that *chargol* is not in fact a beetle but a locust or grasshopper, too. The exact identification must remain a mystery. Modern translations tend to ignore them, and the word 'beetle' is dropped altogether.

Our fifth Hebrew word is *chagab*, which has been translated in the AV as both 'locust' and 'grasshopper': 'If I shut up heaven that there be no rain, or if I command the locust to devour the land, or if I send pestilence among my people' (2 Chronicles 7:13); 'And there we saw the giants, the sons of Anak, which come of the giants: and we were in our own sight as grasshoppers, and so we were in their sight' (Numbers 13:33).

The two references to the smallness of this creature seem to indicate one of the less significant locust species, of which there are many in the region, some brightly coloured. In the Talmud *chagab* is used as a collective term for all the locusts and grasshoppers, so it is difficult to pin down the species described in the Bible.

Which brings us to the sixth Hebrew word, *gazam*, meaning 'shearer', from the root 'to cut off', and which is translated in the AV as 'palmerworm'. Firstly, the palmerworm is most likely an insect not a worm, but its identity is uncertain. In North America 'palmerworm' refers to several species of moth larvae, especially the small green caterpillars of the North American moth (*Dichomeris ligulella*), which attack fruit trees and are considered pests, so *gazam* could refer to a similar creature. It is mentioned several times in the AV, including a significant reference in which it is used as an instrument of judgement on people who have gone away from God: 'I have smitten you with blasting and mildew: when your gardens and your vineyards and your fig trees and your olive trees increased, the palmerworm devoured them' (Amos 4:9). Modern translators substitute 'locust' for palmerworm, but the verse in Amos seems to indicate an insect pest with a penchant for fruit trees and bushes, which is common to many moth larvae.

Sixteenth-century naturalists knew the palmerworm from a slightly different perspective. A reference dated 1560 described a hairy, migratory caterpillar that consumed vast quantities of vegetation. Its name came from the palmers or pilgrims from the Holy Land who carried a palm leaf as a sign that they had completed their pilgrimage. Basically, it was a way of showing off. Chaucer mentions palmers in his Prologue to *The Canterbury Tales*: 'And palmers for to seeken strange strandes'.

A seventh Hebrew word is *yelek*, which the AV translates as 'cankerworm'. North American farmers and foresters will know the cankerworm as a small, wingless moth that emerges in the spring (the spring cankerworm, *Paleacrita vernata*) – or the autumn, or fall (the fall cankerworm, *Alsophila pometaria*). It is one reason why English house sparrows are in North America. Cankerworm caterpillars strip the leaves from beech, apple, oak, maple and hickory trees, so sparrows were introduced to control them.

In the Bible, however, the cankerworm could be an altogether different insect. In fact, there is some debate about exactly what it is. It is mentioned several times in the AV. Joel, a little-known prophet of the fifth or fourth century BCE, mentions the cankerworm in his description of an invasion of agricultural pests, which also includes locusts and palmerworms: 'That which the palmerworm hath left hath the locust eaten; and that which the locust hath left hath the cankerworm eaten; and that which the cankerworm hath left hath the caterpiller [*sic*] eaten' (Joel 1:4).

Which means there's not much left! In modern translations the event is interpreted as 'swarm after swarm of locusts' rather than four separate pests. The Hebrew word *ye'lek* is from the root word for 'lick up' or 'devourer', which has been translated as 'a creature that licks up the grass', meaning a pest perhaps. However, *ye'lek* is translated elsewhere in the AV as 'caterpillar': 'He spake, and the locusts came, and caterpillers [*sic*]' (Psalms 105:34); 'Surely I will fill thee with men, as with caterpillers [*sic*]' (Jeremiah 51:14).

Again, modern translations stick with locusts here, as they do in the vision of Nahum, recorded in a poem celebrating the prediction of the fall of the Assyrians at Nineveh, where the different pests are mentioned specifically by the AV writers:

> There shall the fire devour thee; the sword shall cut thee off, it shall eat thee up like the cankerworm: make thyself many as a cankerworm, make thyself many as the locusts. Thou hast multiplied thy merchants above the stars of heaven: the canker-worm spoileth, and flieth

away. Thy crowned are as locusts, and thy captains as
the great grasshoppers, which camp in the hedges on
the cold day, but when the sun ariseth they flee away,
and their place is not known where they are.

Nahum 3:15–17

A good piece of field observation this, and the cankerworm is
clearly described separately from the locust and the grasshopper.
This passage, though, may give us a clue. It states that there are
lots of them; they slice through things like a sword; and eventually
they fly away. Could this refer to the young hoppers again? With
a voracious appetite for any vegetation, they can be just as
devastating as their parents. This is the interpretation agreed on by
most modern Bible translators.

The fact that the creature is called a canker 'worm', however,
might indicate that it should be worm-like if nothing else, so
maybe this points to an insect larva. The caterpillars of butterflies
and moths can be pests – witness the armyworm. Worm-like grubs
of beetles can devastate crops, too, their larvae eating foliage, buds
and flowers and burrowing into roots, and the adults spreading
virulent plant diseases. The phrase 'the canker-worm spoileth'
could refer to the spread of plant diseases.

Also, in some editions, 'the cankerworm spoileth and flieth
away' has been translated as 'the cankerworm putteth off and
fleeth away'. It has been suggested that 'putteth off' refers to the
way the creature pulls back the envelope that covers its wings. If
the latter, the insect would have to be a beetle, for beetles have
their front wings modified as hard elytra that protect the wings
when resting.

The eighth word is *tzelatzlal*, meaning 'tinkler', a reference
perhaps to the way in which many grasshoppers and crickets
communicate with high-pitched sounds that are made by rubbing
body parts together. Grasshoppers, for example, stridulate by

rubbing a back leg against the wing case, while crickets rub their back legs together. Significantly, elsewhere in the Bible the word is linked to cymbals. In the AV *tzelatzlal* is translated as 'locust'. It occurs only once in the Bible: 'All thy trees and fruit of thy land shall the locust consume' (Deuteronomy 28:42). Again, this must refer to a species that congregates in large numbers and can cause serious damage, but its actual identity will have to remain for ever a mystery.

The ninth word is *gob* or *gobaim*, which is interpreted in the AV as 'locust'. There are several references but again the AV translators have hedged their bets and opted for both grasshopper and locust: 'as the running to and fro of locusts shall he run upon them' (Isaiah 33:4); 'behold, he formed grasshoppers in the beginning of the shooting up of the latter growth' (Amos 7:1). There is nothing here that gives away the species involved, or indicates whether it refers to an adult or a nymph.

In Tristram's time, Dr Pusey, author of *The Minos Prophets* (1886), put forward the notion that *ye'lek*, *chasil*, *gazam* and *arbeh* are four distinct species rather than developmental stages of a single species, but more recently the naturalist, Jehuda Feliks, in trying to make sense of the various Hebrew words, has ended up linking them with the various stages. He considers the first-stage nymphs that hatch from the egg to be *ye'lek*, and then the larger pink-coloured nymphs into which they develop and grow to be *chasil*; the short-winged stage is *gazam* and the mature insect is *arbeh*. No doubt the discussions will continue, but the argument about which word is appropriate for what species pales into insignificance when the sheer power of a locust swarm is considered. The prophet Joel compared their arrival to that of an advancing army:

> A day of darkness and of gloominess, a day of clouds and of thick darkness, as the morning spread upon the mountains . . . the land is as the garden of Eden before

them, and behind them a desolate wilderness; yea, and nothing shall escape them. The appearance of them is as the appearance of horses; and as horsemen so shall they run. Like the noise of chariots on the tops of mountains shall they leap, like the noise of a flame of fire that devoureth the stubble, as a strong people set in battle array. Before their face the people shall be much pained: all faces gather blackness. They shall run like mighty men; they shall climb the wall like men of war; and they shall march every one on his ways, and they shall not break their ranks . . . They shall run to and fro in the city; they shall run upon the wall, they shall climb up upon the houses; they shall enter in at the windows like a thief. The earth shall quake before them; the heavens shall tremble: the sun and moon shall be dark, and the stars shall withdraw their shining.

Joel 2:2–10

Tristram had a similar experience in 1864, when he reached the banks of the Jordan at the same time as a swarm of hoppers. However, while farmers were losing their crops, fish in the river were enjoying a feeding bonanza.

On arriving at the banks of the Jordan, the swarms . . . marched steadily up the trees that fringe the river. These they denuded of every strip of foliage, and even of the tender bark, not sparing even the resinous tamarisk. As they stripped the twigs they crept onwards, pushed by the hordes behind, and fell by myriads into the rapid stream. Few out of many escaped to the farther bank, for the scene below was indeed marvellous. The river was full of fish. In serried ranks, with noses up and mouths open, rested just on the surface shoals of the common Jordan fish Scaphiodon capoeta, in quiet anticipation of the feast, which was literally for hours dropping into their mouths. By thousands the locusts disappeared as they fell – even before they had time to touch the water they were seized.

A year later, the Reverend F W Holland, another natural historian cleric, observed another plague of winged adults when he and his party were camped out at the foot of Mt Sinai. It was about 10 a.m. in the morning when the first locusts appeared:

A light breeze from the north-west was blowing and they came up in its face from the south-east, flying steadily against it, many of them at a great height. They soon increased in number, and, as their glazed wings glanced the sun, they had the appearance of a snowstorm. Many settled on the ground, which was soon in many places quite yellow with them, and every blade of grass soon disappeared. For two days the flight passed over our heads undiminished in number.

Disagreeable as it might be as a crop pest, nonetheless the locust appears in the list of creatures that are permissible to eat: 'Even these of them may ye eat; the locust after his kind' (Leviticus 11:22).

Tristram found that many people in the region ate locusts as a matter of course, and this occurs to this day. The Yemenites of Israel, for example, rate locust highly. After being fried in clarified butter, the heads and legs are removed – just like prawns or crayfish – and they are consumed as local gourmet fare. They can even be dried and ground up for flour. I've even eaten them in a sweet toffee. John the Baptist might well have eaten them, too: 'And the same John had his raiment of camel's hair, and a leathern girdle about his loins; and his meat was locusts and wild honey' (Matthew 3:4).

Some commentators have considered that 'locusts' in this passage refers not to the insects but to the locust bean or carob, known also as St John's bread. Interestingly, the locust bean, though housed in a leathery pod, contains a sugary (honey-like) pulp. However, many analysts today believe that part of John's diet in the wilderness really was the insect. Shakespeare praised its taste, though he placed the description in the mouth of a dishonest observer – Iago, who predicted that Othello would tire of Desdemona: 'The food that to him now is as luscious as locusts, shall be to him shortly as acerb as coloquintida' (*Othello*, I.iii).

Coloquintida is a powerful purgative from the bitter yellow fruit of the vine *Citrulus colocynthus*, a plant related to pumpkins and squashes. It has also been suggested that 'locusts' referred to the fruit of the golden shower tree (*Cassia fistula*), which is a mild laxative that tastes like chocolate. Modern commentators, however, claim that when Shakespeare wrote 'locusts' he was aware of the gastronomic ways of the tribes of the Middle East and he meant 'locusts'.

A comparison of the nutritive values of the carob bean and the insect locust is enlightening. Carob flour, it seems, provides 4.5g (0.16oz) of protein per 100g (3.5oz) of meal. This compares with 11.7g (0.4oz) in buckwheat flour and 20.5g (0.7oz) in chickpeas. Likewise it contains just 1.4g (0.05oz) of fat and no vitamins or minerals apart from a little calcium, and provides 180 calories. Analysis of dried preparations of locusts, however, reveals a make-up of 75 per cent protein and 20 per cent fat, together with significant amounts of riboflavin and nicotinic acid (vitamin B2 complex). Locusts are good, wholesome and nutritious food and have been eaten since Neolithic times. They also appear in other historical reports. The Greek playwright Aristophanes referred to locusts as 'four-winged fowl' and Marco Polo describes how the Chinese ate 'brushwood shrimp'.

Locusts were not a poor man's food. In biblical times in Mesopotamia, they appeared on the royal tables of Belshazzar and Asurbanipal. In later years, the ancient Greeks were not averse to nibbling on a locust, though it was not considered a 'royal' food.

In the fourth century BCE, Alex of Thurii described the food of a poor family:

> Yet, alas! Have we
> Nourishment for only three!
> Two must therefore often make
> A scanty meal of barley cake . . .
> And our best and daintiest cheer,
> Throughout the bright half of the year,
> Is but acorns, beans, chick-peas.
> Cabbage, lupins, radishes,
> Onions, wild pears nine or ten,
> And a grasshopper now and then.

In more recent years, the Imperial Government Institute for Nutrition in Japan has recommended them for their food value, and in China they are deep-fried in batter – grasshopper fritters. There is no doubt that locusts are nutritious and plentiful, therefore making them an ideal food source. The Taureg of the Sahara eat them raw, or crush them into a fine powder as flour. Arabs boil them in salted water and then dry them in the sun. In the Far East, Chinese, Japanese and Vietnamese chefs roast or fry them and make them into pancakes, and in the USA some cocktail bars dispense with salted peanuts and potato chips (crisps) and instead provide their clients with canned fried locusts!

FLY

Flies are another group of insects that gather together in plague proportions. The first mention of flies in the AV is as one of the plagues that ravaged Egypt. Indeed, throughout the Bible there are references to the way in which God uses natural events to bring retribution on those who annoy Him, and swarms of flies seem to have been one such weapon. In a slightly different context flies are mentioned in the passage in which the prophet Isaiah predicts the coming of Jesus: 'And it shall come to pass in that day, that the Lord shall hiss for the fly that is in the uttermost part of the rivers of Egypt' (Isaiah 7:18).

The word in this case is *zebub,* which is similar to the Arabic word *dthebab* that is given to any of the larger blood-sucking flies, such as horseflies (Family: Empididae) and gadflies (Family: Tabanidae). Tristram found they were very common in the valley of the Nile and in the hotter parts of the Jordan Valley, where they tormented animals and people alike. He reminds us of how the Phoenicians were so troubled by these flies that they asked for help from one of their idols. His name was Baalzebub, which the Jews changed to Baalzebul, meaning 'Baal of the dunghill', and which we know today as Beelzebub, prince of devils. Another quotation has given us a well-known saying that is in use to this day: 'Dead flies cause the ointment of the apothecary to send forth a stinking savour: so doth a little folly him that is in reputation for wisdom and honour' (Ecclesiastes 10:l). The expression is, of course, 'a fly in the ointment'.

Another fly to receive a mention in the AV is the gnat (*Culex pipiens*), which in reality refers probably to both gnats and mosquitoes (Family: Culicidae). It occurs in the New Testament, on an occasion when Christ is criticising the scribes and Pharisees: 'Ye blind guides, which strain at a gnat, and swallow a camel' (Matthew 23:24).

In later translations, such as the Good News Bible, the words are changed slightly to 'you strain a fly out of your drink'. This refers to the practice of filtering a glass of wine through cloth before it is consumed in order to remove any unclean 'flying, creeping things'. In Arabic there is a similar expression – 'to eat an elephant but to be suffocated by a mosquito'.

In Hebrew folklore the gnat or mosquito is used as a reminder of humankind's humble position in the order of things; after all, God created the mosquito before man. It was also the creature that killed Titus Flavius Vespasianus, destroyer of Jerusalem – a mosquito crawled up his nose and into his brain.

Mosquitoes tend to be found mostly where there is standing water. This is where their larvae and pupae reside, only emerging into the air as flying adults. Female mosquitoes are the troublesome ones, for they are attracted to warm-blooded creatures. They have dart-like mouthparts that can pierce the skin of their victims and draw out blood.

FLEA

Another blood-sucker is the flea. The word is *pa'rosh* in Hebrew, which probably refers to the human flea, a tiny creature that has been assigned the highly appropriate scientific name *Pulex irritans*, though most warm-blooded animals (except monkeys) have their own private kind of fleas and it could refer to any of them. Nowadays, you are more likely to be bitten by a cat flea (*Ctenocephalides felis*) or a dog flea (*C. canis*) than the human flea. It appears just twice in the AV Bible, both references representing something small and insignificant and of little interest to a king: 'After whom is the king of Israel come out? after whom dost thou pursue? after a dead dog, after a flea'; 'Now therefore, let not my blood fall to the earth before the face of the Lord: for the king of Israel is come out to seek a flea, as when one doth hunt a partridge in the mountains' (1 Samuel 24:14 and 26:20).

Fleas must have been common at the time the Bible was written, just as they are today. They have been closely associated with humankind since we hid in caves and picked up the parasites of other animals, such as foxes or badgers, which lived there. They might have transferred to people even though their previous hosts had long gone. Fleas can lie dormant in the chrysalis or pupa stage of their development, the adult only emerging when stimulated by the presence of a warm-blooded individual. This is why a house can become 'alive with fleas' even though it was empty for some time before the new occupants moved in. Tristram discovered a similar fate waiting for humans even in the desert. If his party pitched camp where nomads had previously been, the fleas would break out of their cocoons hidden in the dust and plague the inhabitants.

When they do find a host, fleas suck our blood, using hypodermic mouthparts to pierce the skin. Unfortunately, they leave an irritatingly itchy mark, caused by an injection of saliva containing anticoagulants that ensure the blood does not clot and gum up their mouthparts.

Apart from its blood-sucking habit, the wingless flea's main claim to fame is its ability to jump extraordinary distances, up to 33cm (13in) in one leap, the equivalent of a person jumping over seven soccer pitches. It is behaviour that was recognised in Hebrew legend. In the war with the Ninevites, Judah was said to have jumped over the opposing army like a flea, slaughtering no less than 8,096 soldiers before he had to stop and rest.

SCALE INSECT

Another parasitic insect – a parasite on plants, that is – is responsible for the crimson or scarlet dye mentioned in the Bible, one of many in cloths that draped over the tabernacle. It was found in what was known as the 'crimson-worm', or *tola'ath* in Hebrew – not a worm at all but the scale insect (*Kertnes* [*Coccus*] *ilicus*) that taps into the sap of oak trees, including the Syrian holm-oak (*Quercus coccifera*) of the Middle East. In the Bible the reference is to the colour: 'Come now, and let us reason together, saith the Lord: though your sins be as scarlet, they shall be as white as snow; though they be red like crimson, they shall be as wool' (Isaiah 1:18).

The dye comes from the female insect's body, which contains the pigment carminic acid. The bodies are crushed and subjected to steam or dry heat, but huge numbers of insects are required to produce small quantities of dye, so it is expensive to produce. It was used for the scarlet-red mordant dye for wool, and as a natural food colour; it is also known as cochineal.

A similar scale insect, *Trabutina mannipara*, which sucks the sap of tamarisk bushes and trees in the desert and produces honey dew, could well have been the source of 'sweet manna'. In the warm, dry climate of the Middle East, water contained in the honeydew evaporates and it solidifies into sweet and sticky lumps that resemble cumin seeds. The tiny packages can be collected as they rain down from the tree – the origin, perhaps, of the expression 'manna from heaven'.

ANT

The social insects are represented in the Bible, too. The ant, for instance, is mentioned twice, the Hebrew word being *nemalah* or *nmala*. On both occasions the tiny creature is used as an example of an animal that shows foresight and demonstrates forward planning: 'Go to the ant, thou sluggard; consider her ways, and be wise: Which have no guide, overseer, or ruler, Provideth her meat in the summer, and gathereth her food in the harvest'; 'There be four things which are little upon the earth, but they are exceedingly wise: The ants are a people not strong, yet they prepare their meat in summer' (Proverbs 6:6–8 and 30:24–25).

Solomon and Agur were well informed. Ants can be meat-eaters or plant-eaters or a combination of both, and many species, even predatory ants, take to storing seeds as a dietary supplement during the winter. Their trails, which can extend considerable distances from the nest, can sometimes be seen criss-crossing the threshing-floor and storerooms where they collect seeds. A genus common in the arid lands of Africa and the Middle East is *Atopomyrmex*. Colonies consume about 48 per cent prey, mostly scale insects (Coccidae) and 28 per cent seeds, the rest of the diet being honeydew obtained from white flies or aleurodids (Family: Aleyrodidae) that suck plant sap. Seeds are rich in proteins, and the embryo is sometimes cut out to feed to larvae in spring. Specialist seed-eating ants, such as *Messor structor* of the Mediterranean region, collect unripe green grass seeds in early summer, which are consumed immediately, but later gather the ripe seeds, which are stored first at nest entrances then transferred to special granary chambers.

In the nineteenth century, when it was fashionable to question the substance of the Bible, critics in England would have been familiar with northern European species of ants that do not store grain in winter. They used this to question the authority of the Bible. Solomon knew better, and so did many of the ancient writers. 'The Provident' was the name given to the ant by the early Greek poet Hesiod, who was thought to have lived about 700 BCE. The first-century Roman poet Horace also recognised that the ant was 'not at all ignorant of or unprotected against the future'.

The Bible passage, however, is not quite right. Despite the conviction of Solomon that ants do not have a ruler, in reality they do – the queen, or in some cases many queens. It is she (or they) who controls the colony by a language of pheromones (airborne hormones). She produces pheromones that attract and retain worker ants around her, for example, and if she dies before more queens are produced, the entire colony perishes. Whether she has any influence on when the colony stores food or whether every ant has some built-in switch in its genetic make-up that tells it when to store food is unknown.

BEE

The humble honeybee – *dvora* in Hebrew – together with its nutritious food product honey, features many times in the Bible. People have collected honey since the Stone Age, so honeybees (*Apis mellifera*) were probably one of the earliest insects in which humankind has taken a special interest. Honeybees as such were thought to have originated in tropical Africa and 30 million years ago they were already social insects almost identical to today's honeybees. They spread northwards and eastwards through Europe and Asia, the earliest depiction appearing in south-western Europe. In caves at Bicorp, near Valencia in Spain,

Palaeolithic rock art dated 6,000–7,000 BCE depicts men collecting honey from a high cliff, their heads surrounded by bees.

In the wild, the bees of the Bible would have been more ferocious than the familiar honeybees in our gardens. When disturbed, they were liable to attack in great swarms. Bible writers compared them with the formidable Canaanite nations: 'And the Amorites, which dwelt in that mountain, came out against you, and chased you, as bees do, and destroyed you in Seir, even unto Hormah' (Deuteronomy 1:44).

The Amorites were especially aggressive Canaanites, so if this text is anything to go by, these bees behaved like the 'Africanised' honeybees that have been rampaging through the Americas in recent years, rather than the far gentler European bees. In the Psalms there is another reference to an attack by bees, this time comparing it to being surrounded by enemies but, with the Lord's help, overcoming them: 'They compassed me about like bees; they are quenched as the fire of thorns: for in the name of the Lord I will destroy them' (Psalms 118:12).

The image also featured in Jewish legend. There was the story of a rich man's daughter in the city of Admah who defied the law by giving bread and water to a stranger. She was taken outside the city walls by the townsfolk and smothered with honey. Along came swarms of wild bees and stung her to death. The naturalist Bartholomew reflected not only on their ferocity but also their ability to organise themselves like an army:

> They have an host and a king and move war and battle, and fly and void smoke and wind, and make them hardy and sharp to battle with great noise . . . And no creature is more wreakful nor more fervent to take wreak than is the bee when he is wroth; therefore a multitude of a great host of bees throweth down great hedges when they be compelled to withstand them that destroy their honey.

It was not until 1609 that the naturalist Butler realised that the supposed 'king' is in fact a 'queen', hence the title of his book *Feminine Monarchie*.

However, it is likely that someone somewhere in ancient times realised that bees could be farmed when he or she discovered that a swarm would make its home in any container that resembled a rock crevice or a hollow tree. The transition from honey collector to beekeeper probably happened in many places, but it was the ancient Egyptians who kept the earliest records of apiculture or beekeeping. Bas-reliefs on the walls of tombs dated about 2400 BCE show cylindrical hives, probably made of baked mud and clay, stacked one on top of another. Even today, a cylinder of mulberry withies about 1m (3.3ft) long and 15cm (6in) in diameter and covered with mud or cattle dung is used as a simple beehive to house honeybees. Several cylinders are stacked one on top of the other under some form of simple shelter, to protect the bees from the hot sun. Smoke was used in the past to calm the bees just as it is today, so the beekeepers were able to get to the honeycombs that tended to be built towards the back of the container.

The great majority of the references to bees in the Bible are to honey, rather than to the insects themselves. It is not clear whether the honey was from wild nests or from managed hives, but however it was harvested it was clearly an enjoyable food: 'And I am come down to deliver them out of the hand of the Egyptians, and to bring them up out of that land unto a good land and a large, unto a land flowing with milk and honey' (Exodus 3:8); 'More to be desired are they than gold, yea, than much fine gold: sweeter also than honey and the honeycomb' (Psalms 19:10).

There was, though, a warning that you can always have too much of a good thing: 'It is not good to eat much honey: so for men to search their own glory is not glory' (Proverbs 25:27).

The source of all those bees and their honey has a strange biblical explanation. It is found in the story of Samson. When Samson was on the way to Timnath to take a Philistine wife, he killed a lion with his bare hands, but when he returned to the spot he was in for a surprise (Judges 14:8): 'he turned aside to see the carcase of a lion: and, behold, there was a swarm of bees and honey in the carcase of the lion.' The only bee known to enter carcases is a species of stingless bee, *Trigona hypogea*. It has large mandibles and slices its way into dead bodies – a large swarm can strip down the carcase of a small mammal in a few days – but it occurs only in Latin America and it does not live in the carcase, so it is likely that the insects that invaded Samson's lion were of another species.

It is quite possible that the sun-dried, leathery carcase of a large animal, such as a dead ox, would be the only suitable living space in the desert and therefore might attract a swarm of bees to make its home there. But the chances of this happening would be slim, and the story seems to smack of the supernatural anyway. Other similar tales come to mind – geese hatching from goose barnacles, rags and wheat turning into mice, and so on.

The notion that bees appear spontaneously from animal carcases is not confined to the Bible or ancient Hebrew folklore. In Greek mythology Aristaeus – the god of animal husbandry and the patron of beekeeping – discovered the trick. At the time, he was pursuing Eurydice, with whom he had fallen in love, but as she tried to escape from him she trod on a poisonous snake and died from its bite. The Dryads, female spirits who preside over woods and forests, took revenge for her death and killed all Aristaeus's bees. He confided in his mother Cyrene, and she suggested that he consult Proteus, seer and son of Poseidon. In the first book of *Fasti*, the Roman poet Ovid continues the story: '"Kill a heifer and bury its carcase in the earth. The buried heifer will give the thing thou seekest of me." The shepherd did his bidding: swarms of bees hive out of the putrid beef: one life snuffed out brought to birth a thousand.'

Dated about 250 BCE, the earliest reference after the early Hebrew texts to bees emanating from dead bulls was by

Antigonos of Karystos. Democritus, a Greek philosopher and beekeeper, who lived to be 109, endorsed the myth. He proposed that an ox be killed and placed for 32 days in a room with all its openings blocked. When it was opened up, he predicted, bees would be found clustered round the horns and bones. He added that the 'king bee' was made from decaying bull brains. Down the ages, the myth must have changed gradually into recognised 'fact', for in the fourteenth century it was mentioned first by Thomas de Camtimpré in his *Liber de Natura Rerum* and then by one of Germany's first natural history writers, Konrad von Megenberg. The idea persisted for many years. The English dramatist Ben Jonson included it in *The Alchemist* (1610): 'Art can beget bees, hornets, beetles wasps,/Out of the carcases and dung of creatures;/Yea, scorpions of an herb, being rightly placed'.

It continued well into the seventeenth century, with references in G B della Forta's *Natural Magick* (1658) and Samuel Harclib's *Reformed Commonwealth of Bees* (1655). While Porta merely reiterated what the ancient writers had told, Harclib seemed to be still of the belief that bees really did emerge spontaneously from a cattle carcase 'as practised', according to Harclib, 'by that great husbandman, old Mr. Carew of Anthony in Cornwall'.

Many scholars have tried to figure out the basis of the belief that bees emanate from cattle carcases or, in Samson's story, a lion carcase, and the most attractive suggestion to date proposes that the event is in some way linked to ancient myths and the celestial calendar. In short, the constellation Taurus (the Bull) is in the ascendant at the time that bees swarm in the spring, and the constellation Leo (the lion) rises when the time comes to harvest the honey. Virgil draws attention to the fact that bees do well when Taurus is visible. What is more, these two constellations were known in Mesopotamia as long ago as 4000 BCE. Illustrations on a Sumerian shell goblet dated to about 3000 BCE show a fight between the lion and the bull. It represents the springtime killing of the bull by the lion. It could well be that both bee stories –

Samson's lion carcase in the Bible and Aristaeus's ox carcase in Greek mythology – have their roots somewhere in the way that ancient farmers and beekeepers would have pegged their year to events in the heavens.

However, by the end of the seventeenth century more credible discoveries were being made. In 1684, for example, English beekeeper John Martin recognised that bees make wax rather than collect it. Ironically, at the time naturalists were beginning to understand more about bees, refined sugar was replacing honey as a sweetener.

Honey was the only sweetener available to the ancient Egyptians, as sugar cane had not arrived from the East. Sugar cane was recognised as a sweetener by the South Sea Islanders. It was brought to India and thence to the West when the Persians overran the Indian subcontinent. They described it as 'the reed that gives honey without bees'. In ancient times, however, it was honey and not sugar that was used to sweeten cakes and bread and the Egyptians were one of the first civilisations to ferment honey with grain to produce beer, possibly the first intoxicating drink. The insect was considered so important that the pharaohs who reigned between 3000 BCE and 350 BCE had the bee as their royal emblem. It retained its importance down the centuries, for the honeybee was likened to the godly and came to symbolise royalty. The French emperor Napoleon Bonaparte, for example, had bees on his flag.

Honey from bees was also used to heal wounds, burns and cuts. It was used as a salve, either pure or mixed with fat. Its sugar content is so high that bacteria cannot live in it, and because of its consistency honey prevents air, irritants and dirt entering wounds. These antibacterial properties were recognised by none other than the Greek physician Hippocrates, the father of medicine: 'Honey and pollen cause warmth, clean sores and ulcers, soften hard ulcers of lips, heal carbuncles and running sores.'

Since then, there have been claims that applying a honey ointment can help eye problems, such as conjunctivitis, styes, swellings and cataracts. When taken orally, it is thought to help the immune system to fight infection, and it is often used in home remedies, such as a mix of honey and lemon, for the relief of coughs, colds and 'flu. In general, honey can be considered good for you. It contains the natural sugars fructose and glucose, calcium, potassium, iron, copper, manganese, magnesium, sulphur, zinc, amino acids, antioxidants, traces of various enzymes and a collection of vitamins, including A, B1, B2, B6, C, E and K.

Another medicinal substance produced by bees that has featured in pharmacopoeia down the ages is a substance known as propolis, from the Greek word meaning 'before the city'. It is a mixture of wax and plant resins that the bees collect from buds and plant wounds, and it is used to line the entrance of the hive (where it is a kind of door mat on which the returning foragers must wipe their feet to prevent dirt and disease entering the hive), patch cracks, seal drafts and fill the gaps between the combs and the hive walls. Its efficacy as a medicine depends on which plants the bees have visited, but most samples of propolis tested so far have had some antibiotic properties.

The Egyptians also used honey and beeswax as ingredients in embalming fluids for mummification. When Alexander the Great died, he was preserved and immersed in a golden coffin filled with honey. The honey in Tutankhamen's tomb was still edible when it was rediscovered several thousand years after he was buried.

In ancient civilisations, such as Samaria, Assyria and Babylon, honey was offered to the gods in religious ceremonies, and honey and wine were poured over bolts and other fastenings to be used in the construction of sacred buildings. It is likely that the ancient Greeks took honey from wild bees, for writers, such as Homer, refer only to wild honey being collected from nests in rock crevices and hollow tree trunks. Followers of the Greek mathematician Pythagoras ate only bread and honey. Greek and Roman athletes thought that eating honey improved their performance, and it was considered to be important for a long life.

Bees were taken very seriously by the Romans; honey was a major harvest and an important cash crop. They sweetened their wine with honey. There are many written references to bees, including an entire tome on the subject by Virgil, who was struck by the insects' apparent intelligence. He even hid his valuables in beehives to protect them from thieves.

The Romans also found another use for bees. They discovered that angry bees made good allies. Using giant catapults, they lobbed beehives filled with bees into enemy camps and fortifications, and let the infuriated bees do their work – an early example of biological warfare. It was a technique employed by many armies afterwards, including that of Richard the Lionheart who used catapult-launched beehives against the Saracens during the third Crusade in the twelfth century CE.

This was not the first time that bees – or in this case, their honey – had been used in warfare, though. In the first century BCE a thousand of Pompeii the Great's troops were marching through a narrow mountain pass on their way to a battle against the Heptakometes in what is now Turkey, when they came across a cache of honey. The column stopped and ate the honey, but to a man they all suffered delirium and vomiting. The Heptakomete defenders had left the honey deliberately and their Roman attackers' illness enabled the Heptakometes to overrun them. They had taken advantage of a natural occurrence. At certain times of the year, the nectar from local species of rhododendrons and azaleas, such as *Rhododendron ponticum* and *Azalea pontica*, is toxic to humans yet harmless to bees, so any honey produced by bees is not wholesome. Even to this day it is routinely removed so that the entire crop is not ruined, and then fed back to the bees during the winter.

In other cultures honeybees have always been revered. In Indian folklore the gods Vishnu, Indra and Krishna are called *Madhava*, meaning 'nectar-born'. Vishnu, known also as the 'preserver', is often depicted as a blue bee resting on a lotus flower. Indra's first meal was said to be of honey, and Krishna is sometimes shown with a blue bee on his forehead. Kama, the Indian god of love, has a bow made of sugar cane with its string made of bees.

Bees are also trusted messengers that carry messages to the gods. It has been the custom in many countries, even in recent years, to tell the bees when somebody in the house has died.

Almost everywhere, cultured peoples considered bees to be symbols of purity, order, thrift, community, a good work ethic and godliness. Purity was important to the Catholic Church. The wax for its candles was once made exclusively of beeswax because it is produced by 'virgins', i.e. female worker bees that do not usually mate. The increased use of beeswax candles in Christian times meant that monks, nuns and the clergy became enthusiastic beekeepers. On occasions their bees became good defenders. There is a story from Beyenburg (meaning 'Beetown') in northern Germany that tells of a gang of thieves who tried to plunder a local convent. The nuns turned loose their bees, whipped them up into a frenzy, and then retired to shelter while the bees drove off the intruders.

The notion of 'community' comes from the way in which each bee works together with the other bees for the good of the entire colony; therefore in the Mormon sect bees are used to represent the perfect society. Shakespeare reflected this in *King Henry V:* 'For so work the honey bees, creatures that by a rule in nature teach the act of order to a peopled kingdom' (*King Henry V*, I.ii).

'Busy as a bee' is appropriate idiom, as bees are undoubtedly industrious. During the course of a day, for instance, a foraging worker bee can make about ten excursions between flowers and hive to collect pollen and nectar, each a round trip of up to 3.5km (2 miles). It is estimated that to make just one pound of honey, bees from a hive must travel 88,000 km (55,000 miles) and visit more than two million flowers – now that's industrious!

HORNET

Another social insect with a reputation for ferocity is the hornet (Family: Vespidae) – *tzir'ah* in Hebrew. Its identity is not questioned and it appears in the Bible as an instrument to punish and exclude the Canaanites: 'And I will send hornets before thee, which shall drive out the Hivite, the Canaanite, and the Hittite, from before thee' (Exodus 23:28).

Tristram writes that hornets were abundant in the Holy Land. He and his party found four species living there in the nineteenth century, all very common. He cites place names, such as Zoreah, meaning 'place of hornets', as evidence of their occurrence. He also writes that they could be more than just a nuisance, large and angry swarms causing livestock to panic. In fact, when any of their horses disturbed a nest, it was necessary, according to Tristram, to 'retreat with all speed, for the attack of the enraged insects at once caused a stampede throughout the camp'.

SCORPION AND SPIDER

Another venomous creature to watch out for is the scorpion (Subclass: Scorpiones) – *akrab* in Hebrew. Scorpions are not insects but arachnids, and therefore more closely related to spiders. They are recognised by the large and menacing pincer-like pedipalps and the narrow tail ending in a sting that arches over the back. They are mentioned several times in both the Old and New Testaments, usually in passages relating to desolation and danger: 'Who led thee through the great and terrible wilderness, wherein were fiery serpents, and scorpions, and drought' (Deuteronomy 8:15); 'be not afraid of them, neither be afraid of their words, though briers and thorns be with thee, and thou dost dwell among scorpions' (Ezekiel 2:6); 'Behold, I give unto you power to tread on serpents and scorpions, and over all the power of the enemy: and nothing shall by any means hurt you' (Luke 10:19).

The sting of the scorpion was feared more than that of the hornet. Tristram's muleteers were stung several times, and the good canon writes how scorpions were so numerous that one could be found under every third rock. He also notes that they are found in cracks and crannies just about anywhere, both in the wilderness and in the home. In the main, a scorpion sting is not especially dangerous. Most people who are stung have swelling and pain, but live. Tristram, however, tells how one man leaning against a wall was stung in the neck and died. It is a fear that found its way into the Bible: 'and their torment was as the torment of a scorpion, when he striketh a man'; 'And they had tails like unto scorpions, and there were stings in their tails: and their power was to hurt men five months' (Revelation 9:5 and 10). The apostles in the New Testament were promised immunity from such a fate.

Scorpions, of course, are not interested in people. Their sting is a defensive reaction to being disturbed. In reality, they are night hunters that catch beetles and grasshoppers. The females are diligent mothers, carrying their young on their back until they are big enough to fend for themselves.

Hebrew legend also has it that the wicked suffer after death by being placed with scorpions. It is significant, perhaps, that Joseph's brothers placed him in a pit with scorpions – perhaps the worst possible thing to do to someone. Significantly, scorpions appear in the works of authors writing at the same time as the AV translators. Topsell was forthcoming about who and what would be stung:

> It is thought hares are never molested by scorpions because if a man or beast be anointed with the rennet of a hare, there is no scorpions or spider that will hurt him. Wild goats are also said to live without fear of scorpions. The seed of nose wort burnt or scorched doth drive away serpents and resist scorpions and so doth the seed of violets and of wild parsnip. The smell of garlic or wild mints set on fire or strewed on the ground and dittany have the same operations: and above all other one of

those scorpions burned doth drive away all his fellows that are within the smell thereof.

He thought that a person's spittle could kill a scorpion. Lupton, on the other hand, thought that the sniffing or eating of herbs could have the opposite effect:

> An Italian, through the oft smelling of an herb called Basil, had a Scorpion bred in his brain, which did not only a long time grieve him, but also at the last killed him. Jacobus Hollerius, a learned physician, affirms it for truth. Take heed, therefore, ye smellers of Basil.

'Take heed of Jacobus Hollerius' might have been a better instruction. I wonder what he would have made of spiders. Like scorpions, some species of spiders are venomous, and it was widely believed in AV times that they were virtually all dangerous. Bartholomew relates the extremes to which people will go to tend a spider bite: 'Against all biting of spiders, the remedy is the brain of a capon drunk in sweet wine with a little pepper: also flies stamped and laid to the biting draweth out the venom and abateth the ache and sore. And the same doth the ashes of a ram's claw in honey.'

Spiders are in the same group as scorpions (Class: Arachnida, Subclass: Araneae). In the Bible two Hebrew words have been translated as spider. The first is *accabish*, and is used in passages that relate the flimsy schemes of the sinful to the seemingly fragile texture of the spider's web: 'Whose hope shall be cut off, and whose trust shall be a spider's web' (Job 8:14); 'They hatch cockatrice' eggs, and weave the spider's web' (Isaiah 59:5).

In reality, the spider's web is an incredible structure. Both the architecture and the construction materials are remarkable. Comparing like with like, a strand of spider's silk is actually more flexible and stronger than steel.

In Hebrew folklore David was saved by a spider's web.

Previously David had questioned why God had created such a useless creature but when he was holed up in a cave while pursued by Saul, the value of the spider was made only too clear. A spider weaved its web across the cave entrance. Saul's men saw the intact web and knew that nobody could have passed through. Saul called his men away, for he considered it would be pointless to search the cave. David's life was protected by the very creature he had ridiculed.

The second word is *setnatninth*, which is rendered 'spider' in the AV but is thought to refer to the gecko: 'The spider taketh hold with her hands, and is in kings' palaces' (Proverbs 30:28). But it might also refer to the way the spider runs over its web with such ease, and weaves its web just about anywhere in the world – including royal palaces!

POSTSCRIPT

O ne of the more striking aspects of our journey through the pages of the Bible has been the wealth of wildlife that once lived in the Bible lands. Today many of those animals are either thin on the ground, like the gazelles and the antelope, or have disappeared from the region altogether, such as the lion, and their demise started long ago. Destruction began in Solomon's time with the felling of the Lebanon's cedar trees; with them went the Persian deer – today no more than a very small population surviving in Iran. Since then domestic livestock has caused increased and irreversible desertification, and hunters have made a progressively bigger impact as new hunting techniques have developed.

In fact, hunting of wild game has featured strongly in the Middle East, just as it has elsewhere in the world, and there are many references in the Bible to wildlife being used for food – not only the species being killed and consumed, but also the method of capture. Some birds, for example, were caught in snares: 'Our soul is escaped as a bird out of the snare of the fowlers: the snare is broken, and we are escaped' (Psalms 124:7); 'As a bird hasteth to the snare, and knoweth not that it is for his life' (Proverbs 7:23). There is also mention of nets and gin traps: 'The proud have hid a snare for me and cords; they have spread a net by the wayside; they have set gins for me' (Psalms 140:5); 'He is cast into a net by his own feet, and he walketh upon a snare. The gin shall take him by the heal . . . a trap is laid for him in the way' (Job 18:8–10); 'Man knoweth not his time: as the fishes that are taken in an evil net, and as the birds that are caught in the snare'. (Ecclesiastes 9:12); 'Can a bird fall in a snare upon the earth, where no gin is set for him? Shall one take up a snare from the earth, and have taken nothing at all?' (Amos 3:5).

Another technique was for twenty or thirty men with cloaks at the ready to surround a flock of birds, especially birds such as quails that touch down, exhausted, during their migration and rush at them, throwing their cloaks over the birds before they have time to escape. It is alluded to in the Bible: 'My net also will I spread upon him, and he shall be taken in my snare' Ezekiel 12:13). There is also mention of decoys: '. . . they set a trap, they catch men. As a cage is full of birds, so are their houses full of deceit' (Jeremiah 5:26–27); 'Like as a partridge taken and kept in a cage, so is the heart of the proud; and like as a spy, watcheth he for thy fall' (Ecclesiasticus 11:30).

But the most primitive weapon in the region is the throw-stick, which can still be seen in use today. It consists of a thin branch, about 45cm (18in) long, which is hurled so that it revolves in the air and, on contact with the target it entangles the victim's legs and feet. It is used to catch birds, such as partridge and bustards that tend to first run then fly when being pursued on open ground. Today, however, the throw-stick is for boys . . . men use guns.

Even before Canon Tristram arrived in the region there were guns available during the eighteenth century, but they were inefficient muzzle-loaded, flintlock rifles and pistols. At the same time traps, nets, spears and bows and arrows were still in use just as they were in ancient times but come the nineteenth century things changed. The founding of the German 'Templer' colonies in 1868 was considered a turning point in the fortunes of wildlife in the Holy Land. The settlers brought with them modern guns and they liked hunting; they also consumed vast quantities of game. Then followed an arms proliferation and by the First World War everyone in the Middle East possessed modern rifles. This marked the beginning of the end for wildlife.

But there were some people in the community who wouldn't accept this and General Joffe was one such fighter. He was director of the Society for the Protection of Nature in Israel and a leading figure in the Hai-Bar (meaning 'wildlife' in Hebrew) Project, which has conserved a 35 sq km (14 sq miles) piece of alluvial plain bordered by mountains that has become known as the Yotvata Hai-Bar Reserve. It is located in the Arava Plain in southern Israel, sandwiched between Yotvata Kibbutz and Samar Kibbutz, about 35km (22 miles) north of Eilat, near the border with Jordan. Its role has been to conserve, breed and release back into the wild native desert animals such as the four Mesopotamian roe deer – a breed on the edge of extinction – saved from western Iran. The reserve also has herds of onager (wild ass), African wild ass, addax, Arabian and scimitar oryx, and ostrich in open pens featuring three desert habitats: acacia forest, salt marsh and sand dunes. Predators such as wolves, foxes, sand cats, leopards, striped hyena and caracals are confined to a caged area. Day and night a Desert Night Life Exhibition Area reverses to allow visitors to see active nocturnal wildlife, such as gerbils, jirds, dormice, spiny tail mice and fat sand rats, during the day. The project has been so successful that a second northern reserve focusing on woodland and its associated animals such as bears, deer and some of the other animals found in the ancient cedar forests has been opened.

So, in these two small corners of Israel some of the endangered animals of the Bible have been given a second chance. With the successful release of rare onagers back into the wild in the Mackhtesh Ramon Crater (neither a volcanic nor a meteorite crater but a broad valley surrounded by steep-sided walls) in the Negev, it seems the passage from Job 39:5–8 rings true:

> Who hath sent out the wild ass free? Or who hath loosed the bands of the wild ass? Whose house I have made the wilderness, and the barren land his dwelling . . . The range of the mountains is his pasture, and he searcheth after every green thing.

SOURCES

Aldrovandi, Ulisse (1640) *Serpentum et Draconum Historiae*, Bononiae apud CI. Ferronium.

—— (1642) *Historia Monstrorom*, Bononiae, Typis N. Tebaldini.

Allen, G. M. (1916). 'The whalebone whales of New England', *Memoirs of the Boston Society of Natural History*, 8: pp. 107–322.

Alon, Azaria (1968) *The Natural History of the Land of the Bible* (Doubleday, New York).

Ambrose, J. T. (1973) 'Bees and Warfare' in *Gleanings in Bee Culture* (A. I. Root Company, Medina, Ohio, pp. 343–46).

Anonymous (*c.* 4th century) 'Physiologus', trans. James Carhill (1924) in *The Epic of the Beast* (George Routledge & Sons, London).

—— (1490–1517). *Hortus Sanitatis* – quoted in Seager (1896).

—— (1856) 'Hailstorm in Guildford County, N.C.' *American Journal of Science*, 2:22: p. 298.

—— (1930) 'Red Rain Falls Over 20,000 Square Miles.' *Nature*, 125: pp. 256.

—— (1930) 'Remarkable Hailstorm in Iraq', *Meteorological Magazine*, 65: pp.143–4.

—— (1936) 'Destructive Hailstorm in the Transvaal', *Nature*, 137: pp. 219–20.

—— (1975) 'Animals That Broke the Law', *Reader's Digest Book of Strange Stories, Amazing Facts*, Reader's Digest Association, London.

—— (2000) 'Seasonal Changes in the Swan River Estuary'; last accessed 06.01.05 at http://www.wa.gov.au/srt/publications/pdf/resource_sheet5.pdf

—— (2005) 'The Most Incredible Insects', Smithsonian Institution; last accessed 06.01.05 at http://www.si.edu/resource/fqq/nmnk/buginfo/incredbugs.htm

Anonymous and Kotwall, B. J. (1994–96) 'An exchange of views on the Jonah Debate', *Investigator*, March 1994–January 1996.

Antoniadi, Eugene Michel (1934) *L'Astronomie Egyptienne Depuis les Temps le Plus Reculs* (Gauthiers-Villars, Paris).

Aquinas, Thomas (*c.* 13th century) *The Literal Exposition on Job: A Scriptural Commentary Concerning Providence* – Anthony Damico (ed.) and Martin D. Yaffe (Interpretive Essays and Notes, Classics in Religious Studies 7, (Scholars Press, Atlanta, 1988).

Archer, G. E. and Godman, E. M. (1937) *The Birds of British Somaliland and the Gulf of Aden* (Gurney and Jackson, London and Edinburgh).

Aristophanes (*c.* 4th century) 'four-winged fowl' cited in O. Keller (1913) *Die Antike Tierwelt*Yol. II, p. 455 (W. Engelman, Leipzig).

Aristotle (trans. A. L. Peck, 1965). *Historia Animalium* (Loeb Classical Library, Heinemann, London).

Asimov, Isaac (1968) *Azimov's Guide to the Bible: Volume 1 – the Old Testament* (Avon, New York).

Bahn, Paul (1990) 'Bible-plague lice preserved in combs' *Sunday Correspondent* (18 March 1990).

Bannikov, A. G. (1945) 'Data on the biology and distribution of the wild camel' *Zoolgicheskiy Zhurnal* 24: pp. 190–9.

Bartholomew (1535, trans. by J Trevisa) *Bartholomeus de Proprietatibus Rerum* – as quoted in Seager (1896).

Beebe, W. (1938) *Zaca Venture*, Harcourt Brace & Co., New York.

The Bible: Authorized King James Version with Apocrypha, Oxford World Classics, ed. Robert Carroll and Stephen Prickett (Oxford University Press, Oxford 1998).

The Bible: King James Version – online; last accessed on 16.05.05 at:
http://wvvw.hti.umich.edu/k/kjv/
http://etext.lib.virginia.edu/kjv.browse.html
http://www.lib.uchicago.edu/efts/ARTFL/public/bibles/kjv.search.html
http://www.bartleby.com/108/
http://www.bibles.net/
http://www.bibleontheweb.com/Bible.asp
http://www.biblegateway.com/
http://www.ibs.org/
http://www.christiananswers.net/bible/home.html

Blegvad, H. and Loppenthin, B. (1944) *Fishes of the Iranian Gulf* (Einar Munksgaard, Copenhagen).

Bochart, Samuel (1663) *Hierozoïcon, sive bipertitum opus de animalibus sacrae scripturae* (Tho. Roycroft, London).

Bodenheimer, F. S. (1960) *Animal and Man in Bible Lands* (E. J. Brill, Leiden).

Brander, A. A. Dunbar (1927) *Wild Animals in Central India* (Edward Arnold & Co, London).

Bright, Michael (1999) *The Private Life of Sharks* (Robson Books, London).

—— (2000). *Man-eaters* (Robson Books, London).

Brown, Thomas (1905) *Interesting Anecdotes of the Animal Kingdom*, Simpkin, Marshall, Hamilton, Kent & Co., London.

Brown W. G. (1912) 'Explosive Hail', *Nature*, 88: p. 850.

Browne, Sir Thomas (1646) *Pseudodoxia Epidemica or Enquiries into Very Many Received Tenets and Commonly Presumed Truths*, T.H. for Edward Dod, London; and last accessed 04.01.05 at http://penelope.uchicago.edu/pseudodoxia/pseudo323.html

Brunt, D (1928) 'Remarkable Hailstorm', *Meteorological Magazine*, 63: pp. 14–15.

Bulfinch, Thomas (1855) *The Age of Fable or Beauties of Mythology*, last accessed 04.01.05 at http://bulfinch.org/fables/bull36.html

Bullen, Frank T., First Mate (1899) *The Cruise of the "Cachelot" Round the World After Sperm Whales* (Smith, Elder & Co., London).

Burgess, Robert (1970) *The Sharks* (Doubleday, New York).

Burkholder, J.M. *et al.* (1992) 'New "phantom" dinoflagellate is the causative agent of major estuarine fish kills'. *Nature* 358: pp. 407–10.

Butler, Charles (1609) *Feminine Monarchie* (Joseph Barnes, Oxford).

Butler, Samuel (1662/63/78) *Hudibras*; last accessed 08.01.05 at http://www.exclassics.com/hudibras/hbcnts.htm

Calvert, D. (1962) 'Hail Five Inches in Diameter', *Marine Observer*, 32: pp. 112–13

Camtimpré, Thomas de (*c*. 13th century) *Libera de Natura Rerum* (Helmet Boese ed. 1973, Walter de Guyter, Berlin/New York).

Canaan Dog Club of America 'What is a Canaan dog?'; last accessed on 26.03.05 at http://cdca.org/what.html

Cansdale, George (1970) *Animals of Bible Lands* (Paternoster Press, Exeter).

Carroll, Lewis (1872) *Through the Looking Glass*; last accessed on 12.05.05 at http://www.sabian.org/Alice/lgchap07.htm

Clair, Colin (1967) *Unnatural History: An Illustrated Bestiary* (Abelard-Schuman, New York).

Clark, Ann (1975) *Beasts and Bawdy* (Taplinger, New York).

Clark, Raymond (1978) *Catabasis: Vergil and the Wisdom Tradition* (B. R. Grüner, Amsterdam).

Clarke, R. (1955) 'A giant squid swallowed by a sperm whale', *Norsk-Hvalfangsttidende* 44: pp. 589–93.

Coleridge, Samuel Taylor (1771–1834) *The Complete Poems of Samuel Taylor Coleridge*. Introduction by William Keach.

Penguin Classic. (Penguin Books, London 1997).

Collodi, C. (1883) *The Adventures of Pinocchio:* trans. from the Italian by Carol Delia Chiesa; last accessed 06.01.05 at Project Guttenberg http://www.gutenberg.org/etext/500

Cook, Harriet N. (1842) *The Scripture Alphabet of Animals* (American Tract Society, New York.)

Corbet, Jim (1948) *Man-eating Leopard ofRudraprayag,* (Oxford University Press, London).

Corliss, William R. (1977) *Handbook of Unusual Natural Phenomena,* Sourcebook Project (Glen Arm, Maryland).

Cousteau J. and Paccalet Y. (1986) *La Planète des Baleines* (Editions Robert Laffout, South Africa).

Cramp, S. *et al.* (1977) *Handbook of the Birds of Europe, the Middle East and North Africa,* (Oxford University Press, Oxford).

Darton, Mike and Clark, John O. E. (1994) *The Dent Dictionary of Measurement* (J. M. Dent, London).

Davis, Edgerton Y. (1947) 'Man in Whale', *Natural History,* New York, 56: p. 241.

Davis, Edward B. (1991) 'A Whale of a Tale: Fundamentalist Fish Stories', *Perspectives on Science and Christian Faith,* 43: pp. 224–37.

Day, Alfred Ely *The International Standard Bible Encyclopaedia,* last accessed on 26:03.05 at http://www.studylight.org/enc/isb/

Dent, Anthony (1972) *Donkey: The Story of the Ass from East to West* (George G. Harrap & Co, London).

Dog Society, The (2005) 'About the Canaan Dog'; last accessed 26.03.05 at http://www.thedogscene.co.uk/breedinfo/c-f/canaan/

Dove, W. Franklin (1935) 'Artificial Production of the Fabulous Unicorn', *Scientific Monthly,* 42: pp. 431–36.

Dupris, Malcolm (2004) 'Canaan Dog Breed History'; last accessed on 26.03.05 at http://www.barkbytes.com/history/canaan.htm

Earl of Tankerville (1956) 'The Wild White Cattle of Chillingham', *Agriculture,* 63: pp. 176–9.

Eastern's Bible Dictionary; last accessed on 26:03.05 at http://bible.crosswalk.com/Dictionaries/EastonBibleDictionary/

El-Aref, Nevine (1999) 'A different kind of stable' *Al-Ahram Weekly* (23–29 December 1999).

Elliman, Wendy and Ortal Reuven (2001) 'Fauna and Flora in Israel'; last accessed on 23.03.05 at http://www.mfa.gov.il/MFA/MFAArchive/2000_2009/2001/9/Flora%20and%20Fauna%20in%20Israel

Encyclopaedia Britannica (1997). s.v. Unicorn, 12:129.

Fabri, Felix (1483) *The Book of Wanderings of Felix Fabri*, trans. Aubrey Stuart (1896), Palestine Pilgrims Text Society, London; last accessed on 04.01.05 at http://chass.colostate-pueblo.edu/history/seminar/fabri.html

Feldman, Asher (1924) *The Parables and Similes of the Rabbis* (Cambridge University Press, Cambridge).

Feliks, Jehuda (1962) *The Animal World of the Bible* (Sinai, Tel Aviv).

Fergusson, Ian K. (1998) 'Review of the great white shark *Carcharodon carcharias*', on the Mediterranean Shark Site, last accessed on 25.03.05 at http://www.zoo.co.uk/~z9015043/gws_conserv.html

—— (1998) 'Adriatic Encounter Provides First Footage of Free-Swimming Mediterranean White Shark,' from Shark Trust Press Release ST-6/98, Plymouth.

Ferrero, Jean-Paul (1977) 'Animals of the Bible in Israel's Hai-Bar Reserve', *Wildlife* (December 1977).

France, Peter (1986) *An Encyclopedia of Bible Animals* (Croom Helm, London).

Franck, Pierre *et al.* (1998) 'The origin of west European subspecies of honeybees: new insights from microsatellites and mitochondrial data'. *Evolution: International Journal of Organic Evolution* 52:4 pp. 1119–34.

Gaius Julius Caesar (50 BCE) *Bellum Gallicum*, trans. W. A. McDevitte and W. S. Bohn (1869) and published as Caesar's War

Commentaries, Harper & Brothers, New York; last accessed on 04.01.05 at http://classics.mit.edu/Caesar/gallic.html

Ginsberg, Louis (1909–38) *The Legends of the Jews* – 7 vols. (Jewish Publication Society of America, Philadelphia).

Goffman, Oz (1996) 'Sperm whale sighting in Eastern Mediterranean', http://whale.wheelock.edu/archives/whalenet96/0156

—— *et al.* (2000) 'Cetaceans from the Israeli coast of the Mediterranean', *Israel Journal of Zoology*, 46: pp. 143–47.

Good News Bible: Scriptures and additional materials quoted are from the Good News Bible © 1994, 2004 published by the Bible Societies/HarperCollins Publishers Ltd., UK Good News Bible © American Bible Society 1966, 1971, 1976, 1992. Used with permission, http://www.biblesociety.org.uk

Gorion, Joseph Bin (1976) *Mimekor Ysrael: Classical Jewish Folktales* (Indiana University Press).

Green, Lawrence G. (1958) *South African Beachcomber* (Howard Timmins, Cape Town).

Grimmelt *et al.* (1990). 'Relationship between demoic acid levels in the blue mussel and toxicity in mice', *Toxicon*. 28 (5): pp. 501–8.

Guggisberg, C. A. W. (1975) *Wild Cats of the World* (David and Charles, London).

Gunkel, Herman (1984) 'The Influence of Babylonian Mythology upon the Creation Story'. In *Creation in the Old Testament*, ed. Berhard W Anderson. (Fortress, Philadelphia).

Gzimek, Bernhard (1972) *Gzimek's Animal Life Encyclopedia* (VanNostrand Reinhold, New York).

—— (1990) *Gzimek's Encyclopedia of Mammals* (McGraw-Hill, New York).

Hall, Stephen (1989) 'The White Herd of Chillingham', *Journal of the Royal Agricultural Society of England*, 150: pp. 112–119.

Handcock, Percy S. P. (1912) *Mesopotamian Archaeology* (Putnam, New York).

Hartlib, Samuel (1655) *Reformed Commonwealth of Bees Presented in Severall Letters and Oberservations* (G. Calvert, London).

Hedin, Sven (1910) *Overland to India* (Macmillan, London).

Henry, Michael (1989) 'About Red Tide', Mote Marine Laboratory; last accessed 06.01.05 http://mote.org/~mhenry/WREDTIDE.phtml

Heuss, Michael R. 'About Mark Twain', Great Literature Online. 1997–2005; last accessed on 12.05.05 at http://www.mostweb.cc/Classics/Twain/tramp/

Highfield, A. C. (1992) 'Observations of Testudo (graeca) ibera in Lycia, Turkey'. *Tortuga Gazette* 28 (9): pp. 1–3.

Hoffmann, Roald (1990) 'Blue as the Sea'. *American Scientist* 78: pp. 308–9.

Hort, Greta (1957, 1958) 'The Plagues of Europe', *Zeitschrift fur die Alttestamentliche Wissenschaft*, 69: pp. 84–103, 70: pp. 48–59.

Hunter, Luke and Yamaguchi, Noboyulin (2000) 'Resurrected King of Myth: The Barbary Lion'. *Africa – Environment and Wildlife* (April 2000).

Jewish Encyclopedia (1901–06); last accessed on 28.03.05 at http://www.jewishencyclopedia.com/index.jsp

Jones, R. (2001) 'Honey and Healing through the ages', in *Honey and Healing*, ed. P. Munn and R. Jones (International Bee Research Association, Cardiff).

Jonson, Ben (1610) *The Alchemist*; last accessed on 12.05.05 at http://www.hti.umich.edu/cgi/p/pd-modeng/pd-modeng-idx?type=HTML&rgn=TEI.2&byte=43605716

Josephus, Flavius (*c.* CE 93/94) *Antiquities of the Jews*, Books VI and XX; accessed last on 08.01.05 at http://reluctant-messenger.com/josephus.htm

Khalaf, Norman Ali (2004) Gazelle: Palestinian Biological Bulletin; last accessed on 26.03.05 at http://www.gazelle.8m.net/

Kircher, Athanasius (1664/78) *Mundus Subterraneus* (Amsterdam).

Klimley, A. P. and D. G. Ainley (eds.) (1996) *Great White*

Sharks: The Biology of Carcharodon carcharias. (Academic Press, San Diego).

Lachman, Esther (1983) 'Birdwatching in Israel'. *The Israel Economist.*

Leeman, Sue (1999) 'Rebirth of Barbary Lions', *The Associated Press.*

Lindemann, W. (1950) 'Beobachtungen an wilden und gezaehmten Luchsen.' *Zeitschr. F. Tierpsychologie*, bd. 7, heft 2.

Lucan (Marcus Annaeus Lucanus) (c. 61/5 CE) *Pharsalia*, Book IX, line 968, English trans. Sir Edward Ridley, 1896 (Longmans, Green & Co, London).

Lupton (1627) 'A Thousand Notable Things of Sundry Sorts, Whereof Some Are Wonderful, Some Strange, Diverse . . . etc' – quoted in Seager (1896).

Macloskie, G (1942) 'How to test the Story of Jonah', *Bibliotheca Sacra*, 72: p. 336.

McCormick, Harold W, Tom Allen and Captain William Young (1958) *Shadows in the Sea* (Weathervane Books, New York).

Megenberger, Konrad von (1475) *Buch der Natur* (Johann Bämler, Augsburg); published as *Das Buch der Natur*, Robert Luff and Georg Steer, eds. 2003 (M. Niemeyer, Tübingen).

Mendelssohn, H. (1982) 'Wolves in Israel', in *Wolves of the World*, ed. Fred H. Harrington and Paul C. Paquet (Noyes Publications, New Jersey).

Menzel, R. & R. (1948) 'Observations on the Pariah Dog' in *The Book of the Dog*, ed. Brian Vesey-Fitzgerald (Nicholas & Watson, London).

Milton, John (1667) *Paradise Lost* (Samuel Simmons, Golden Cockerel Press, London).

—— *The Major Works*, ed. Stephen Orgel and Jonathan Goldberg (Oxford University Press, Oxford 2003).

Morse, R. A. (1955) 'Bees Go to War'. In *Gleanings of Bee Culture* (ed. A. I. Root), pp. 585–7.

Nave, Orville J. (1841–1917) *Nave's Topical Bible;* last accessed on

26.03.05 at http://bible.crosswalk.com/Concordances/NavesTopicalBible/

Nelson, Bryan (1973) *Azraq, Desert Oasis* (Allen Lane, London).

—— (1980) *Seabirds: their Biology and Ecology* (Hamlyn, London).

Norman, J. R. and Fraser, F. C. (1938) *Giant Fishes, Whales and Dolphins* (Norton, New York).

Ovid (trans. Sir James George Frazer, 1931) *Fasti* (William Heinemann, London).

Owen, Denis (1985) *What's in a Name* (BBC, London).

Parmalee, Alice (1959) *All the Birds of the Bible* (Harper and Row, San Francisco).

Patterson, Col. J. H. (1907) *The Man-eaters of Tsavo* (reprinted 1986, St Martins Press, New York).

Payne, J. Barton (1969) *Wycliffe Bible Commentary* (ed. Charles Pfeiffer and Everett Harrison) (Oliphants, London).

Pease, Sir Alfred E. (1913) *The Book of the Lion* (Murray, London).

Pfeiffer, C. F., Vos, H. F., and Rea J., (eds) (1975) *Wycliffe Bible Encyclopedia* (The Moody Bible Institute of Chicago).

Phelps, Tony (1989) *Poisonous Snakes* (Blandford Press, London).

Philippe de Thaun (1119) Les Livres des Creatures, included in *Popular Treatises on Science written during the Middle Ages, in Anglo-Saxon, Anglo-Norman and English*, ed. Thomas Wright (1841) (Historical Society of Science, London).

Pinney, R. (1964) *The Animals of the Bible* (Chilton Books, Philadelphia).

Pliny the Elder. Historia Naturalis, Book 8:31 in *The Historie of the World*, trans, into English by Philemon Holland (1601), last accessed on 04.01.05 at http://penelope.uchicago.edu/holland/pliny8.html

Polo, Marco and Rustichello of Pisa, *et al.* (c.1298), *The Travels of Marco Polo*, Vol. 2, ed. Henry Yule and Henri Cordier (1903 and 1920), last accessed on 22.03.05 at http://library.beau.Org/gutenberg/1/2/4/1/12410/12410–8.txt

Porta, John Baptista (Giambattista della Porta) (1658) 'Bees are generated out of an Ox', in *Natural Magick*, Book II 'Of the Generation of Animals'; transcribed by Scott Lincoln Davis from the English Edition (printed for Thomas Young and Samuel Speed, London) as accessed last 10.01.05 at http://homepages. tscnet. com/omardi/jporta2. htmal

Pusey, E. B. (1886) *The Minor Prophets* (Baker, Grand Rapids 1974).

Raban, D. and P. (1983) 'Victim of a Glandular Disorder', *New England Journal of Medicine* 309 (16) p. 992.

Raspe, R. E. (1785) *Baron Munchhausen's Narrative of His Marvellous Travels and Campaigns in Russia;* last accessed 06.01.05 as The Surprising Adventures of Baron Munchausen at Project Guttenberg http://onlinebooks.library.upenn.edu/webbin/gutbook/lookup?num=3154

Root, Waverley (1981) 'St John, the Carob and Locusts' *International Herald Tribune*, (24 June 1981).

Ryan, W. B. and Pitman, W. C. (1998) *Noah's Flood: the New Scientific Discoveries About the Event That Changed History* (Simon and Schuster, New York).

Scheffer, Victor (1969) *The Year of the Whale* (Charles Scribner's Sons, New York).

Schweinfurth, G. (1878) *The Heart of Africa* (London).

Seager, H. W. (1896) *Natural History in Shakespeare's Time: being extracts illustrative of the Subject as he knew it* (Elliot Stock, London).

Shakespeare, William *Complete Works of William Shakespeare*, introduced by Germaine Greer and Anthony Burgess (Collins, London 1951/2003).

—— *The Complete Works of William Shakespeare;* last accessed on 12.05.05 at http://www-tech.mit.edu/shakespeare/

—— *Shakespeare's Tragedies*, Everyman's Library 155 Poetry and Drama, (J. M. Dent & Sons Ltd., London 1906).

—— *The Tragedy of Hamlet, Prince of Denmark*, The Penguin Shakespeare edited from the original text by G. B. Harrison

(Penguin Books, London 1937).

Shelley, Percy Bysshe *Shelly: Poems,* selected by Isabel Quigly (Penguin Poetry Library, New York 1954).

Shulov, Aharon (1961) 'The Biblical Zoo in Jerusalem'. *New Scientist* 12: pp. 431–33.

Smith, William (1884) *Smith's Bible Dictionary* (Christian Classics Ethereal Library, Grand Rapids, MI).

Solinus, Gaius Julius (*c.* 280 AD) *Collectanea Rerum Memoralbilium* (Polyhistor), published as *The excellent and Pleasant Worke of lulus Solinus Polyhistor. Contayning the noble actions of humaine creatures, the secretes & prouidence of nature, the description of Countries, the maners of the people: with many maruailous things and strange antiquities, seruing for the benefit and recreation of all sort of persons.* Translated out of Latin into English by Arthur Golding, Gent. I. Charlewood, printer (Quarto, London, 1587).

Stead, D. G. (1963) *Sharks and Rays of Australian Seas* (Angus & Robertson, London).

Steel, Rodney (1989) *Crocodiles* (Christopher Helm, London).

Stephens, Dianne (2004) 'Unicorns: the complete story of unicorns through the ages'; last accessed on 26.03.05 at http://www.unicorncollector.com/legends.htm

Strong's Concordance with Hebrew and Greek Lexicon; last accessed on 26:03.05 at http://www.eliyah.com/lexicon.html

Tegart, Brian 'Mythology and Mysterious Creatures in the KJV, http://www.tegart.com/brian/bible/kjvonly/satyr

Thompson Bert (2000) 'Unicorns, Satyrs and the Bible', *Reason and Revelation*, 20 (4) pp. 29–30, (Apologetics Press, Montgomery, Alabama).

Tomlinson, David (1978) 'Every Winged Fowl After His Kind', *Country Life,* 30 November 1978.

Topsell, Edward (1607) *The History of Four-footed Beasts and Serpents Describing at Large Their True and Lively Figure, their Several names, Conditions, Kinds, Virtues (Both Natural and Medicinal)* . . . quoted in Seager (1896).

Tristram, Henry B. (1868), *The Natural History of the Bible* (Society for Promoting Christian Knowledge, London).

Trompf, G. W. (1989) 'Mythology, Religion, Art, and Literature', pp. 156–71, *Crocodiles and Alligators*, eds. C. A. Ross and S. Garnett, *Crocodiles and Alligators* (Facts On File, Inc., New York).

Tschernezky, W. (1959) 'Age of *Carcharodon megalodon?*' *Nature* 184: pp. 1331–32.

Ullman, M. (1978) *Islamic Medicine* (University Press, Edinburgh).

Velikovsky, I. (1950) *Worlds in Collision* (Doubleday, New York).

– (1973) *Ages in Chaos* (Sphere Books, London).

Virgil (trans. J. W. Mackhail, 1910) *The Eclogues and Georgics of Virgil* (Longmans, Green & Co., London).

Vitaliano, Dorothy B. (1973) *Legends of the Earth: Their Geological Origins* (Indiana University Press, Bloomington).

Wilford, John Noble (1994) 'First Settlers Domesticated Pigs Before Crops', *New York Times* (31 May 1994).

Winston, Mark L. (1987) *The Biology of the Honey Bee* (Harvard University Press, Cambridge).

Wood, Gerald L. (1982) *The Guinness Book of Animal Facts and Feats* (Guinness Superlatives Ltd, Enfield, Middlesex).

Wood, J. G. (1869) *Bible Animals*. Longman, Green & Co., London.

Xenophon (*c.* 401–399 BCE) *Anabasis*, trans. H. G. Dakyns (1998); last accessed 08.01.05 at http://www.fordham.edu/halsall/ancient/xenophon-anabasis.htm#Project%20Gutenberg

ACKNOWLEDGEMENTS

I would like to thank: Liz Cooper and Mary Bergin-Cartwright at Oxford University Press, Linda Nicol at Cambridge University Press, Rachel Atkinson of the Penguin Group and Teresa Heskins of the British and Foreign Bible Society for their help with permissions; the Bible Society for permission to quote passages from the *Good News Bible*; Peter France for permission to quote extracts from *An Encyclopedia of Bible Animals*; Jeremy Robson, for encouraging the idea in the first place; Jane Donovan, Rob Dimery and Libby Willis for recovering meaningful parts of the English language from my original draft; Rob Collis at the BBC's Bristol Research Centre and the staff of the British Library for acquiring obscure and ancient tomes; and finally to Family Bright, who waited patiently at mealtimes for 'just one more sentence' to be completed.

INDEX